VIOLENCE AND CIVILIZATION

VIOLENCE AND CIVILIZATION

STUDIES OF SOCIAL VIOLENCE
IN HISTORY AND PREHISTORY

edited by

Roderick Campbell

Oxbow Books
Oxford and Oakville

Joukowsky Institute Publication 4

General series editor: Prof. John F. Cherry
Joukowsky Institute for Archaeology and the Ancient World
Brown University, Box 1837/60 George Street, Providence, RI 02912, USA

ISBN 978-1-78297-620-2

A catalogue record for this book is available from the British Library

Library of Congress Cataloguing-in-Publication Data

Violence and civilization : studies of social violence in history and prehistory / edited by
Roderick Campbell.
    pages cm
(Joukowsky Institute publication ; 4)
Includes bibliographical references and index.
ISBN 978-1-78297-620-2
1. Violence--Social aspects--History. 2. Violence--Social aspects--History--To 1500. 3.
Political violence--History. 4. Political violence--History--To 1500. 5. Social change--
History. 6. Civilization--History. 7. Civilization, Ancient. I. Campbell, Roderick (Roderick
B.)
   HM1116.V523 2013
   303.6--dc23
                                    2013042423

This book is available direct from
Oxbow Books, Oxford, UK
(Phone: 01865-241249; Fax: 01865-794449)
and
The David Brown Book Company
PO Box 511, Oakville, CT 06779, USA
(Phone: 860-945-9329; Fax: 860-945-9468)

www.oxbowbooks.com

*Front cover: Detail from the Narmer palette (Egypt, ca. 31st century B.C.), showing the inspection
of decapitated captives.*
*Back cover: Detail of a fine line ceramic painting of the Moche Presentation Theme or Sacrifice
Ceremony.*

Printed by
Berforts Information Press, Eynsham, Oxfordshire

Contents

List of Figures

Notes on Contributors

Philippe Bonditti is a lecturer in International Relations at the Institute of International Relations of the Political University of Rio de Janeiro and associate researcher at the Ceri-Sciences Po, Paris. Bonditti's research focuses on political violence and counter-terrorism, the transformations of war and security, as well as critical perspectives on international relations.

Ari Bryen is Assistant Professor of History at West Virginia University. His interests are in the law, culture, and society of Rome's eastern provinces. His book *Violence in Roman Egypt: A Study in Legal Interpretation (Empire and After)* was published by the University of Pennsylvania Press in 2013.

Roderick Campbell is Assistant Professor of East Asian Archaeology and History at the Institute for the Study of the Ancient World, New York University. His research interests focus on deep-time anthropological phenomenologies of violence, social organization, and world. Recent publications include theoretical work on early complex polities, the archaeology of ancestors, and sacrifice and Shang history. He is currently co-directing work on a gigantic Shang bone artifact production site and recently completed *The Archaeology of the Chinese Bronze Age* to be published by the Cotsen Institute of Archaeology in 2014.

Severin Fowles is Assistant Professor of Anthropology at Barnard College, Columbia University. His interests revolve around the role of ritual practice in the development of Pueblo societies and he has studied theocratic organization as well as broader questions related to taboo, iconography, the archaeological study of immateriality, and the relationship between landscape and cosmology. He is the author of *An Archaeology of Doings: Secularism and the Study of Pueblo Religion,* published by the School for Advanced Research Press in 2013.

Catherine Lutz is the Thomas J. Watson Family Chair in Anthropology and International Studies at Brown University. She is the author of *Homefront: A Military City and the American Twentieth Century* (Beacon Press, 2001), *The Bases of Empire: The Global Struggle against US Military Posts* (New York University Press, 2009), and *Breaking Ranks: Iraq Veterans Speak Out Against the War* (University of California Press, 2010, with Matthew Gutmann).

Ellen Morris teaches in the Department of Classics and Ancient Studies at Barnard College, Columbia University. She has published extensively on issues pertinent to ancient Egyptian imperialism. Her first book is entitled *The Architecture of Imperialism: Military Bases and the Evolution of Foreign Policy in Egypt's New Kingdom* (Brill, 2005), and she is currently in the process of finishing a book that provides an explicitly anthropological investigation of pharaonic imperialism, entitled *Ancient Egyptian Imperialism*. Her ongoing research interests and other publications focus on the dynamics of political fragmentation, state formation, sexuality and sacred performance, retainer sacrifice, and divine kingship. She has excavated in the Nile Valley at Abydos and Mendes, and at the site of Amheida in the Dakhleh Oasis.

Edward Swenson is Assistant Professor of Anthropology at the University of Toronto. He is currently directing large-scale survey and excavations at the prehistoric urban complex of Cañoncillo in Northern Peru. Swenson's theoretical interests include the pre-industrial city, violence and the institutionalization of social inequalities, the archaeology of ritual and ideology, and the politics of social memory as mediated by the production and experience of architectural space. He has written technical reports on his research, as well as numerous published articles in books and academic journals.

Contributor Addresses

Ellen F. Morris
Department of Classics and Ancient Studies
Barnard College
219b Milbank Hall
New York, NY 10027
emorris@barnard.edu

Roderick Campbell
Institute for the Study of the Ancient World
New York University
15 East 84th Street
New York, NY 10028
Rbc2@nyu.edu

Edward Swenson
Department of Anthropology
University of Toronto
19 Russell Street
Toronto, Ontario M5S 2S2
Canada
edward.swenson@utoronto.edu

Catherine Lutz
Department of Anthropology
Brown University
Providence, RI 02912
Catherine_Lutz@brown.edu

Severin Fowles
Department of Anthropology
Barnard College
3009 Broadway Avenue
New York, NY 10027
sfowles@barnard.edu

Ari Z. Bryen
Departments of Classics and Rhetoric
University of California, Berkeley
7327 Dwinelle Hall
Berkeley, CA 94720
azbryen@berkeley.edu

Philippe Bonditti
Instituto de Relações Internacionais
Rua Marqués de São Vicente, 225
Vila dos Diretórios, Casa 20
Gávea-Rio de Janeiro
Brazil
Philippe-bonditti@puc-rio.br

Acknowledgements

The idea for this book arose out of my dissertation work on Chinese Bronze Age sacrifice and war. The challenge of understanding what seemed monstrous acts of violence as something somehow intelligible forced a critical reconsideration of contemporary constructions of worth, expediency, and justification. The feeling that these issues were not being addressed in archaeology led to the organization of a session on Violence and Civilization at the 2007 Society of American Archaeology conference in Austin, Texas. The participants in that session included Jonathan Haas, Severin Fowles, Ellen Morris, Ed Swenson and Liz Arkush, with David Carrasco as discussant. Wanting to expand the discussion beyond archaeology and ancient societies, a faculty reading group was established in the Fall of 2008 at Brown University and a second symposium on violence and civilization was held in the spring of 2009, sponsored by the Joukowsky Institute for Archaeology and the Ancient World and the Cogut Center for the Humanities. In addition to Fowles and Swenson from the 2007 symposium, the participants included Bruce Lincoln, Ari Bryen, Rebecca Molholt, Susan Alcock, Ömür Harmansah, Kerry Smith, Laurel Bestock, Philippe Bonditti, and Catherine Lutz as presenters and/or discussants. The reading group also benefitted from the frequent insights of Carl Jacoby and Ian Straughn. The disciplines represented included archaeology, cultural anthropology, history, art history, and history of religions, while the symposium papers ranged from ancient Peru to early 20th-century Japan, and from human sacrifice to vigilante violence. This volume is a direct and indirect product of those papers and the many discussions held during, between, before and after the symposium and reading group sessions. My thinking on violence and order was also immeasurably enriched through discussions with the brilliant students of my ARCH 1780 seminar at Brown University.

In addition to the generosity of the Joukowsky Institute for Archaeology and the Ancient World [JIAAW] and the Cogut Center for the Humanities in supporting the reading group and second symposium, I would personally like to express my gratitude to the Graduate School of the Arts and Sciences, Harvard University for the support provided by a dissertation completion grant during the 2007 symposium; the Institute for the Study of the Ancient World, NYU, for a one year post-doc between 2007 and 2008; and JIAAW for its postdoctoral support in 2008–2009 and Spring 2010, as well as the opportunity to teach a course on Violence and Civilization at Brown in the Spring of 2009.

Among the many people who helped and supported me in this project I would like especially to single out my advisors Rowan Flad and Michael Puett whose enthusiasm gave me the initial courage to undertake what might seem to some a quixotic or even megalomaniacal project. At Brown I benefitted from the warmth and encouragement of many people. Cathy Lutz's support and participation encouraged me to believe that there was a conversation to be had across disciplines and time periods on this topic. Sarah Sharp and Diana Richards provided instrumental logistical support for the workshop at Brown, while John Cherry's editorial expertise and mentorship have been hugely helpful. I would also like to thank Tom Leppard for his help in the initial formatting and editing of most of the individual chapters. Special mention goes to Sue Alcock whose advice and mentoring have sustained me not only in this project, but in what has turned out to be an extended postdoctoral career. Final thanks must go out to my long-suffering family whose love keeps me sane.

Introduction:
Toward a Deep History of Violence and Civilization

Roderick Campbell

… It should be this evening that we use three hundred *qiang*-captives (in sacrifice) to (Ancestor) Ding. Use.

> (Heji 293, Late Shang oracle-bone divinatory inscription [ca. 1200 B.C.])

Fan Chi asked about benevolence. The Master said, "loving humanity." He asked about knowledge. The Master said, "knowing humanity."

> (Attributed to Confucius [6th century B.C.], *The Analects* XII. 22)

The current amazement that the things we are experiencing are "still" possible in the twentieth century is *not* philosophical. This amazement is not the beginning of knowledge – unless it is the knowledge that the view of history which gives rise to it is untenable.

> ("Theses on the Philosophy of History," Walter Benjamin, 1940)

The above three quotations, spanning 3000 years, frame the enduring issue of violence and civilization. On first sight, the moral and cultural distance between the large-scale use of human beings as offerings to the gods and ancestors, interchangeable with cattle or sheep – hacked, burned, drowned, or buried alive, and the moral philosophy of Confucius a mere 600 years later, seems an impassable chasm. Yet to shrug off Shang practices of collective violence as mere reflections of Bronze Age savagery is to hold that view of history that Benjamin claims is untenable. It is, moreover, to forget that in the time of Confucius the practice of retainer sacrifice was still going strong (Huang 2004), even as inter-polity violence reached hitherto unprecedented scale and destructiveness. Even more troubling, the hierarchy of being and caring fundamental to Confucius's moral philosophy and foundational to major currents in later Chinese constructions of authority, bears more than a family resemblance to the hierarchy of being that structured the Late Shang moral economy of war and sacrifice (Campbell 2007).

Nor, in this current era of genocide, war, and terror can we claim the high ground of history. Rather, we must recognize that violence is a human problem (Scheper-Hughes and Bourgois 2004: 3) and when broadened to include symbolic (Bourdieu 1990, 1998, 2000), structural (Galtung 1969; Farmer 1997) and everyday violences (Kleinman 2000) – in short, all the various mechanisms by which social suffering comes about – violence, broadly construed, becomes one of the most central social-historical issues. Violence and Civilization, moreover, have been topics long intertwined in the social sciences. While Marx and scholars inspired by him have seen human history in terms of the dialectics of class struggle, and social complexity as attended by relations of dominance and inequality, Weber (1966 [1915]) famously defined the state in terms of a monopoly over the use of force. In archaeology however, despite being the discipline most directly involved in the study of the origins or early stages of civilizations and states, and despite the recent shift from evolutionary typologies to a focus on how ancient polities actually worked (Marcus and Feinman 1998; Van Buren and Richards 2000; Trigger 2003; Yoffee 2005), where violence has been considered at all in relation to socio-political change attention has generally been focused on functionalist, adaptationist treatments of only the most extreme forms of physical violence. As I will argue below, to study only the most obvious and spectacular is to see only the tip of the phenomenological iceberg (Das and Kleinman 2000; Žižek 2008; Schinkel 2010).

At the same time, while a number of disciplines have recently contributed to the study of violence in human societies and the anthropology of violence has become a burgeoning sub-field, relatively little attention has been given to the deep historical dimensions of social violence, both in the sense of studies of ancient societies and in the sense of long-term diachronic changes in practices of violence (Wieviorka 2009). If it is true, as the war, oppression, terrorism, and genocide of the last hundred years tragically suggests, that violence in its many forms is still very much with us, then it is also true that some forms of violence, such as human sacrifice or slavery, appear to be more features of past societies than present ones. If practices and institutions of violence are fundamentally social/cultural (*contra* Hobbes) and intertwined with political and economic regimes in the modern world, then changes in those cultural, political, and economic regimes over time ought to affect the forms (structural, symbolic, or physical) and roles (direct or indirect) of violence. An exploration of the relationships between changing socio-cultural orders and violence broadly conceived would then be a productive, if under-explored, avenue of research. Indeed, if violence, broadly construed, is a potential aspect of power on the one hand, and of inequality on the other, then studies of inequality and social complexity can scarcely afford to ignore it.

As controversial and multivalent as "violence" is the concept of "civilization." Whether seen as part of the conceptual baggage of European colonialism (e.g., Patterson 1997), the unfinished work of the Enlightenment (e.g., Elias 1994) or simply the larger cultural sphere in which polities are discursively and practically embedded (e.g., Yoffee 2005; Trigger 2003; Marcus and Feinman 1998), "civilization" is always seen in some relationship to violence (whether overt or structural, whether taming it or promoting it). While it might be argued that this ambiguity is reason enough to abandon the concept of "civilization," I would instead claim that this very ambivalence points to the significance of the nexus of normativity, order, identity, distinction, and power that all the above conceptions of civilization hold in common – a nexus about which we are still unsure what to think. If the violence of the 20th century shattered much of the 19th-century optimism concerning the inevitable progress of "civilization" (seen in terms of a reified Western tradition) and undermined its justifications for imperialism and colonialism, the continued relevance of "civilization" is nevertheless on display in its strategic deployment by former US defense secretary Donald Rumsfeld's renaming of the "war on terror" as the "struggle against the enemies of freedom and civilization." If Western constructions of civilization have had an ambivalent relationship to violence and domination, including and excluding, hierarchically ordering and structuring both agency and power, it is also true, as some archaeologists (e.g., Baines and Yoffee 1998; Van Buren and Richards 2000) have shown in their studies of early civilizations, that the creation of discursive as well as political dominions and world orders is not a phenomenon limited to the modern West.

Violence

The *Oxford English Dictionary* defines violence as follows,

> Violence, *n.*
> 1. a. The exercise of physical force so as to inflict injury on, or cause damage to, persons or property; action or conduct characterized by this; treatment or usage tending to cause bodily injury or forcibly interfering with personal freedom.

The conventional understanding of the English noun "violence" and its many extensions revolve around three root elements: harm (especially physical), transgression, and intention. While probably every language in the world has a term in its lexicon that might be translated as "violence," this particular placement of damage, transgression, and intention within an idiom of individual rights is historically specific. The example of the corresponding Chinese term is instructive. The Maoist-inflected PRC-published *Xiandai Hanyu cidian* defines *"baoli,"* the usual translation for the English "violence," as follows,

> 1) Coercive force: military force. 2) Especially concerning coercive power of the state: military, police and courts' [actions] against enemy classes are a kind of violence. (Author's translation).

The Taiwan-published and more traditional, Confucian-oriented *Guoyu huoyong cidian*, on the other hand, explicitly links *"baoli"* with both force and transgression, "using barbarous methods without resort to reason, conducting illegal activities, generally referring to force of arms." Interestingly, the PRC dictionary places *baoli* with the state and implies its operation as a pragmatic course of political practice. Given Mao's famous dictum that "power comes from the barrel of a gun," this definition would be unremarkable, if it were not for the negative connotations that almost always adhere to *"bao,"* the first morpheme of the binome *"baoli."* The moral approbation surrounding the term is clearly seen in the Taiwanese dictionary definition. Indeed the normative judgment of the second definition, defining "illegal activities" as *"baoli,"* goes even further than the English "violence" in being defined in opposition to the established order. What divides the two Chinese definitions of *"baoli"* are political philosophies that place opposing values on transgression and coercive force (the one revolutionary, the other counter-revolutionary). What unites them is a focus on order/institution and modes of action as opposed to the concern with individual rights seen in the *Oxford English Dictionary* definition of "violence." Differences in legal traditions and political philosophies aside, what is apparent with both "violence" and *"baoli"* is their inescapable political, ethical, and legal entanglements. While the causing of harm and its moral valence is not a set of issues unique to any human culture, what the contrasting Chinese and English cases do show is that the "intentionality" and individual rights so important to Modern Western legal traditions are not necessarily the terms in which force and legitimacy are contested in other times or places.

That violence is by its nature discursively contested is one of the central insights of scholarship on violence of the last thirty years. Riches (1986: 8) for instance, defines violence as "an act of physical hurt deemed legitimate by the performer and illegitimate by (some) witnesses." Whitehead (2004: 11), on the other hand, refuses to define violence claiming that this refusal,

... serves to underline the fact that part of what has hampered attempts to understand violence is the presumption that all acts that might be termed "violent" share some typological characteristic, whereas often the contested nature of what should count as "violent" (with the connotations of illegitimacy the term carries) is at the heart of the very conflicts that gave rise to those violent behaviors.

While Riches' focus on physical harm and his claim that the "performer" views his/her actions as legitimate is unnecessarily predicated on mind/body dualisms and rational actor agency, and while Whitehead's insistence on violence's undefinability is overstated and ultimately unproductive (see also Schinkel 2010), the point remains that what constitutes transgression or harm can be and usually is contested on a number of levels. This fact is a crucial one, contributing to the peculiar "slipperiness" of violence (Schinkel 2010; Whitehead 2004; Scheper-Hughes and Bourgois 2004; Schmidt and Schroder 2001; Bauman 1995), demonstrating with particular force the impossibility of the etic perspective, even while the moral entanglements of violence prod most, if not all of us, to demand absolute positions, especially where it matters to us directly.

A concomitant observation is that violence is culturally patterned behavior, and that rather than being seen as the absence of order, both harmful practices and their contested legitimacy have their roots in cultural logics and socially inculcated dispositions. While this is in some sense an anthropological truism, it is crucial in the case of violence, since it is often defined in terms of its anti-sociality, its opposition to order. The paradox of claiming violence's sociality might be summed up thus: "if violence is by definition transgressive, then how can it also be of the social order?" There are two complimentary solutions to this question. The first, in Agamben's (1998) paradoxical usage, is that violence is "included by its exclusion": the creation of the rule defines the possibilities for transgression. The second solution lies in pointing out the problem of envisioning societies statically or normatively in terms of a social contract. Social fields and institutions constantly change in response to actors bending, breaking, or re-writing the rules of play on a variety of scales. Moreover, if violence can be ambiguous, power is less so: struggle over the definition of an act or modes of action as transgressive and harmful generally favors the strategically located. Transgression then, is both an assumption of the social game and an element of its processual development, even while naming violence is integral to claiming the spoils. This being so, violence is not only an intensely moral problematic, but also in intensely political one.

Violences

As I have been arguing, "violence," in trans-cultural or trans-historical study, need not be centered on the intentional infliction of bodily harm. Coercion through the confiscation of land or livelihood, imprisonment, hostage-taking, ostracization, excommunication, stripping of rank or honors, public humiliation, etc. can all be seen as forms of non-physical violence. Indeed, the idea of a sharp dividing line between direct, instrumentally delivered physical trauma and the suffering caused by non-physical or indirect means (such as being forced to witness a loved one's torture, or being set adrift on the open ocean) is dependent on philosophies of self that separate mind from body and privilege the instrumental rationality of individual actors. Not only are there other possible ontologies of the self available in the ethnographic literature (e.g., de Castro 1992), there are good theoretical and empirical reasons for deploying an inter-subjectively constituted, socially-distributed self for a comparative study of transgressive harm. While this is again something of an anthropological truism, the fact that the body-self experiences and is shaped by its social environment through webs of inter-personal interaction, as opposed to being a self-contained, free-willed, social billiard ball, is a matter of crucial importance for the study of violence. That is because it is those inter-subjective spaces and webs of social meaning that are the location of violence. Physically identical acts distinguished as sport or crime by social context may, for instance, result in similar bodily injuries but radically different psychological traumas. Physical violence even at its most instrumental is never directed at bodies alone, but at individuals or categories of person (or non-person), nor is its effect ever limited to the body of the victim. Just as Levinas (2000) notes that death is experienced through relationships to others, so too non-fatal harm is experienced not only by the victim but also indirectly by those around them. This of course, is the larger point of physical acts of terror or instrumental coercive violence.

If the usual understanding of "violence" in terms of physical damage is problematic for downplaying the inter-subjective location of both harm and legitimation, framing violence in terms of the intentional action of individuals is problematic for another reason as well. In understanding violence in these terms, entire regimes of destructive practices can be made invisible through their exclusion. Indeed, given that the deflection of personal responsibility through bureaucratic structures was part of what made the holocaust possible (Bauman 1989) and that one of the most constant themes of violence is the strategic play over the assignment or avoidance of blame, we would be better served to shift focus from intentions to effects. Discussing the relationship between genocide and modernity, Hinton (2002), for instance, states that, "with the rise of the nation-state and its imperialist and modernizing ambitions, tens of millions of 'backward' or 'savage' indigenous peoples perished from disease, starvation, slave labor, and outright murder." With this we see that there is another sense of violence potentially intertwined with civilization – that is, the non-intentional, or non-instrumental structures or processes of destruction and suffering. This type, or these types, of violence include what Galtung (1969) and Farmer (1997, 2004) refer to as structural violence, and what Bourdieu (1990, 1998, 2000) terms symbolic violence. An overarching term for these violences might be systemic violence (Žižek 2008), in so far as they are the destructive indirect, material, or discursive effects of social orders and institutions. Violence in this sense is generally directly related to social hierarchies and inequalities. Historical examples might include retainer sacrifice in Ancient Egypt (Morris, this volume) or the Chinese Bronze Age (Campbell, this volume), or the Malthusian logic of the English response to the Irish potato famine (Kearns 2007). Modern-day examples might include the translation of domestic economic hierarchies into inequalities of access to medical care, or the sacrificial logic of live organ donor transplants (Scheper-Hughes 2006). As Bauman (2006: 100) argues, "the distinction between a killing by an intentional individual act and killing as a result of 'the egotistic citizens of rich countries focusing their concerns on their own well-being while the others die of hunger' is becoming less and less tenable".

Although a key aspect of "violence" and related concepts in other languages is that its local definition is always a strategic site of contest, it does not follow that there can and should never be an analytical definition. In fact, the disinterested position that violence can never be defined without imposing violence oneself smells not only of scholastic impotence, but disingenuousness. Perhaps more clearly than any other phenomena, violence brings home the poverty of objectivity and the perspectiveless observer. Instead, with recent thinkers, I would argue that the phenomenological kernel of violence is the reduction of being (Schinkel 2010; Žižek 2008). While the variance of which reductions of being count or do not count as transgressive will define local understandings of violence, on the level of trans-local analysis all reductions of being must be seen as violent. To the objection that this definition would dilute violence beyond usefulness, I would invoke Scheper-Hughes and Bourgois' (2004) concept of "the broad spectrum of violence." The importance of defining violence in this way is that it lifts the cloak of invisibility with which local constellations of power endeavor to cover up their violent practices and harmful structures and allows us to see the ways that, for instance, defaming, discrediting, and dehumanizing are linked with physical acts of destruction (see, e.g., Gourevitch 1998). More ambivalently, this understanding of violence allows us to see it as productive of social orders such as that of Confucius's famous normative hierarchical ranking of the "five relations": the agency and status of the inferior must be limited so as to increase that of the superior. While different ethical systems take opposing views on the primacy and desirability of equality vs. hierarchy, the fact remains that hierarchy involves sometimes extreme reductions of being and society would be impossible without violence in this sense.

Moral Economies of Violence

The broad notion of violence that I propose here moves away from its usual understanding in terms of intention to a focus on effects, such as the causes of "social suffering" (Kleinman et al. 1997). For, as Bauman (2006: 100) argues, "intent" is "totally inadequate to cope with the present challenge of a planet-wide interdependence …" where the proximate causes of suffering frequently have their ultimate origins in larger structures and logics of inequality. A focus on social suffering would also open a conceptual space for the grounding of violence in terms of its local moral experience. If we follow Kleinman (1999) in seeing moral experience in terms of local, inter-subjective claims about "what matters," then violence can be seen as an overturning or ignoring of those claims. Moreover, as this inter-subjective space is always culturally constructed as well as performatively brought into being, and, in so far as not everyone's suffering counts equally, it is constructed in a moral economy structured with hierarchies of being and caring. That is to say, the context of social violence must include its "moral economy."

In another line of reasoning productive to the study of social violence, Kleinman (1999) contrasts moral experience with ethical discourse stating that while "the latter is an abstract articulation and debate over codified values" is "conducted by elites, both global and local" (1999: 363), "moral experience is always about practical engagements in a particular local world, a social space that carries cultural, political, and economic specificity. It is about positioned views and practices: a view from somewhere and an action that becomes partisan" (1999: 365). What is productive about this distinction from the point of view of studying regimes of violence over time is the potential for disjuncture:

> … to be sure, what is at stake in a local world may involve a moral economy of systematic injustice, bad faith, and even horror. Yes; from an ethnographic perspective what is at stake, what morally defines a local world, may be, when viewed in comparative perspective, corrupt, grotesque, even downright inhuman. That is to say, the moral may be unethical, just as the ethical may be irrelevant to moral experience [Kleinman 1999: 366].

For understanding of social violence, this distinction and possible disjuncture between ethical and moral action suggests at least two levels of analysis. It opens up the question of the relationships or tensions between local moral economies of violence and their larger (ethical) institutional and discursive contexts.

Moreover, since both the moral and the ethical are grounded in local and trans-local economies, institutions, and practices, analysis must proceed both diachronically and over a number of scales:

> … to specify a local world and its transformations, it is crucial to understand how moral experience changes under the interactions between cultural representations, collective processes, and subjectivity, interactions that are in turn shaped by large-scale changes in political economy, politics, and culture. Moral experience then, possesses a genealogy just as it does a locality [Kleinman 1999: 373].

A historical study of social violence then, as implicated in moral experience and ethical discourse, must be grounded in the contexts and histories of local and trans-local worlds. This in turn suggests the study of the *longue durée* of social violence, in addition to the scales of institutional and individual time. What are the changing bases of ethical discourse and moral experience over time and space? What social economies of violence do they construct or resist in their collusion or disjuncture?

Another, perhaps more troubling, use of Kleinman's notion of moral-experience as inter-subjective claims about "what matters" is its inversion in a dialectics of inter-personal violence. This involves not so much misunderstandings or lack of care about what matters for others, as the vampiric dialectic of inter-subjective power discussed by such diverse authors as Hegel, Scarry, Patterson, Girard, and Bourdieu, across topics ranging from slavery to symbolic violence. In ways subtle or visceral, from adolescent put-downs (or academic "bloodsport") to the radical subjugation of "enemies" (whether through the spectacle of sacrifice or the ritual of political trial), the inter-subjective basis for moral claims can also be the site of a dialectical struggle for relationally-constituted being. As Scarry (1985: 60) writes of torture, "what by the one is experienced as a continual contraction, is for the other a continual expansion, for the torturer's growing sense of self is carried outward on the prisoner's swelling pain." If Bourdieu (2000) is correct in his claim that symbolic capital (honor, regard, status, recognition, etc.) grants people a "theodicy of their existence" yet can only be "won from others competing for the same power," then forms of this agonistic dialectic of being underlie some of the most basic social relations. Nevertheless, the social opportunities for, and moral economies of, expanding one's being at the expense of another vary widely in time and space (from taking heads in battle, to competition for promotion), and are the results of local and trans-local historical processes which ought to figure prominently in any diachronic study of violence and civilization.

Violence and Order

Implied in a dialectics of relational being and caring is the potential for more or less permanent hierarchies to form. Orlando Patterson (1982), for instance, argued that a commonality of institutions of slavery cross-culturally is the production of the "socially dead," and, conversely, through the ownership of slaves, the socially exalted. Hierarchy then, normally thought of in terms of economic, political, or symbolic status, can be seen in more immanent, existential terms, while violence, in both overt and covert forms, becomes intertwined with the social order. Nevertheless, violence (physical or symbolic) can serve the interests of more or less egalitarian social orders as well (Clastres 1994; Fowles, this volume). In these cases, it is not that the suffering of some individuals is deemed unimportant or even the natural order of things, but that through their actions some groups or individuals are perceived to have placed themselves beyond the community – in effect, as Agamben (1998) would have it, under the ban. These transgressors are thus constructed as situationally less than human: dangerous, monstrous, witches or sorcerers – aggressors against the social order (Douglas 1966), against whom society is forced to take action. With this we can see the inter-relationship of violence and cultural orders in general (whether egalitarian or hierarchical) in local constitutions of being and trans-local politics of identity and worth. Moreover, if genocide is the limit case of violence against the Other (or insider made Other), constructed as life not worth living, then it is also true that similar (if less extreme) cultural or "civilizational" logics of relative worth shape practices of social violence as widely varied as human sacrifice, slavery, colonial domination, and the bombing of foreign civilians justified as "collateral damage" (Chomsky 2004).

Civilization

The word "civilization" in both academic and common use has three related senses. In its broadest meaning it is synonymous with culture as in Tylor's (1924 [1871]: 1) definition:

> Culture, or civilization, taken in its broad, ethnographic sense, is that complex whole which includes knowledge, belief, art, morals, law, custom, and any other capabilities and habits acquired by man as a member of society.

In a narrower but more usual sense, "civilization" refers to a certain level of socio-political development, often associated with cities, writing, craft specialization, and hierarchy, however difficult this stage might be to define precisely in practice. The third sense is the normative one, set up in opposition to "barbarism" or "savagery," the sense of right action and proper order that is also the interior view of the first sense and the hidden historical assumption of the second. Indeed, if the first sense is predicated on a nature/culture divide, the second sets that divide into a historical trajectory of increasing distance, while the third provides a moral valency to that trajectory. What makes "civilization" so ambivalent are the different values that can be assigned to nature/artifice, history's alternative readings, and the ironic potential of disjuncture between "civilization's" positive moral connotation and its contested meaning.

Moreover, although many of the world's languages have words like "civilization," the differences can be instructive. Ibn Kaldun's "*umran*" for instance, though usually translated "civilization" and sometimes "society" or "culture," literally means "to fill, to make prosper, to build" (Mitchell 1988). For Ibn Kaldun civilization was a process of growth and decay based on interaction between nomads and cities. Cities were seen as the seats of arts, sciences, crafts, and culture, but they also corrupted and softened their inhabitants, robbing them of vigor and martial potency. Nomads of the desert on the other hand were morally pure, cohesive, vigorous, and desirous of the wealth of cities. In this historical vision, nature and artifice cyclically renew one another, the wild violence of the desert re-energizing the decaying vigor of the corrupting city. For Ibn Kaldun history was cyclical and morality on the side of nature, not culture.

The modern Chinese word for "civilization" is "*wenming*" and like many sociological words in Chinese it is a modern, Western import. Its local characteristics, however, make for an interesting case. In some of its early 20th-century uses, anti-traditionalism was manifested in the conflation of Western and "civilized" in such terms as "*wenming xi*" for Western-style drama. In the contemporary PRC, *wenming*'s strong normative and progressive sense is deployed everywhere in civil society campaigns, while the central government maintains a Chinese Civilization website, (http://www.wenming.cn/), dedicated to "spreading civilization and steering customs" under "the great flag of socialism with Chinese characteristics."

Nevertheless, despite "*wenming*'s" Western pedigree and introduction at time of anti-Confucianism, the first morpheme of "*wenming*," "*wen*," is of crucial importance to Confucian philosophy. From the earliest Chinese writing, "*wen*" (literally patterns), contrasted with "*wu*" (martial, pertaining to war), the two terms encompassing the dual prerogatives of ancient

Chinese elites. In one famous episode, when Confucius found himself in danger in Kuang, he purportedly said, "with King Wen's death, does not *wen* reside here with me? If Heaven wishes this *wen* to be lost, then those who die after will not be able to participate in this *wen*. If Heaven does not yet wish this *wen* to be lost, what can the men of Kuang do to me?" (*The Analects* IX.5, author's translation). Though 6th-century B.C. China had no word that exactly corresponds to "civilization," Confucius's use of *wen* here is close. His claim was to be carrying on the traditions and arts of the Zhou dynastic founders, traditions passed down from the sages of antiquity and modeled on the patterns of Heaven itself. These patterns, encapsulated in proper ritual, dress, comportment, action, and relations between people was what set the Huaxia states apart from the Yi and Di barbarians and allowed Confucius to make statements such as, "the Yi and Di having a ruler are not the equal of the Xia states without one" (*The Analects*, III.5, author's translation). For Confucius, even with their attenuated practice of the way of the former kings, the people of the Xia states were superior to those who had never known the proper order of things. This Confucian version of "civilization" then was singular, highly normative, and tied to a tragic-heroic vision of history.

As the examples of Ibn Kaldun and Confucius show, understandings of normativity, hierarchy, social order, human artifice, and history can be variable and differently inter-related. The significance of these inter-relations for the study of violence will be shown below, but for now it is sufficient to point out that the modern, Western concept of "civilization" is merely one possible understanding (or rather a cluster of related versions or interpretations) of history, nature/culture, and ethics. Moreover, as a concept with a built-in origin point and progressive narrative, the perspectives of pre/proto-historians on the nature of "early civilization" is particularly germane. Probably the most influential attempt to codify the "rise of civilization" in the Anglo-American archaeological tradition is that of Gordon Childe (1950) whose 10 criteria are paraphrased as follows: 1) cities; 2) specialization of livelihood; 3) surplus paid to religious leaders; 4) monumental architecture; 5) non-producing ruling class; 6) recording systems; 7) development of sciences; 8) monumental art; 9) importation of raw materials; and 10) specialist craftsmen under the control of elites. While trait lists have fallen out of favor and the specifics of Childe's formulation have been contested, his Marxist focus on historical epochs defined by political-economic revolutions, the redistribution of resources, the alienation of labor, and elite ideology misrecognized as religion are still very much a part of the archaeological genealogies of "early civilization" and "state formation." While much of the neo-evolutionary work on states in the 1970s to 1990s was focused on defining social evolutionary stages based on criteria of specialization, monopolization, and control (chiefly economic and political), the shift to more contextual understandings of ancient polities at the end of the 1990s was accompanied by a renewed interest in "ideology" and with it the concept of "civilization." The touchstone work in this shift was that by Baines and Yoffee (1998), who used "'civilization' to denote the overarching social order in which state governance exists and is legitimized" (1998: 254). Moreover, in keeping with the Western historical development of the term, they stressed the importance of elite practices in the definition of civilization:

> We take high culture to be characteristic of civilizations rather than simply of states, and we see the boundary between one form of high culture subscribed to by local elites and another as the boundary between one civilization and another [1998: 235].

In this definition, then, high culture is the central element of civilization which may be shared among polities, but which articulates with the hierarchical power structures of the state in giving the inner elite, who represented themselves as the carriers of "civilization," "a central legitimation that overrode the 'moral economies' of smaller organizations" (Baines and Yoffee 1998: 206). This approach thus forefronts the role of legitimation, the centrality of hierarchy to "civilization" and its link with "the state." Nevertheless, although this latter connection is latent in most Modern Western understandings of both "civilization" and "state" (e.g., Elias 1994), it is at best a historically specific construct. Thus, if the control-systems approaches of the neo-evolutionary archaeologists sought for the analogues of the Weberian state in ancient polities (Campbell 2009), Baines and Yoffee (1998) reproduce the Enlightenment terms of "civilization". This includes a positive valuation of "artifice" over "nature," an understanding of ideologies and religions as elite tools, and "the good life" as the sole cultural product of high elites. As with "violence," however, "civilization" is a strategic term, and, as such, the site of discursive struggle. As seen with the example of Ibn Kaldun's *umran*, the relationship between civilization and its opposite could alternatively be seen as a mutually complementary dialectic, leaving no real outside to the civilizing process, even while the high cultural artifice and wealth of urban elites can be seen as corrosive rather than conducive to the development of power and right. For Confucius, *wen* and *li* were embodied patterns of performance imbued with moral-numinous significance – patterns, moreover, with which he believed the high elites of his time were out of touch. While a notion of "civilization" as a component of Early Chinese elite political legitimation could be formulated and connected to patterns of "high" material culture, in so far as normativity, cultivation, wealth, and legitimacy are all largely discursive constructs, the specifics of how they were thought is a central issue. In other words, "civilization," like "violence," has its local genealogies and moral economies. Instead of a single nomothetic concept for "civilization" such as proposed in the recent archaeological literature, what I am arguing for here is an inter-emic approach (Campbell 2007) shuttling between local and trans-local scales, one that while concerned with things like community, hierarchy, normativity, history, nature/artifice, and their relationships to political organization, nevertheless does not assume *a priori* how they relate to one another or over-determine the contents of those categories.

Naturally, "inter-emic," like inter-subjective, requires a location and a starting point. To be sure "civilization" has a Western genealogy, but that does not detract from the fact that it points to a cluster of issues that, while perhaps framed differently in different times and places, have common ground. A soft definitional starting point for "civilization," then, at its broadest must include that it is a world ordering. This ordering is based on local ontologies of being and power, but need not be hierarchical (or rather the degree of stratification is variable). The inclusiveness and scale of the community bounded by this order is also variable. While I have intentionally kept the broader, more inclusive, sense of "civilization," where there is marked hierarchy, "civilization" itself is often one of the sources of capital through which status is negotiated.

Violence and History: Civilizing Processes?

… [V]iolence and its arbitrariness were taken for granted and therefore neglected; no one questions or examines what is obvious to all. Those who saw nothing but violence in human affairs, convinced that they were "always haphazard, not serious, not precise" (Renan) or that God was always with the bigger battalions had nothing more to say on either violence or history. Anybody looking for some kind of sense in the records of the past was almost bound to see violence as a marginal phenomenon [Arendt 1970: 8].

Although few would agree today with Arendt's claim that violence has received little serious study, it nevertheless remains the case that there have been few who have looked carefully at the relationship between violence and history. Norbert Elias was a notable exception. Elias (1994) famously proposed that civilizing processes in Europe since Medieval times led to a reduction and a removal of violence behind the scenes. Complexly linking historical social-psychology to political economy, Elias argued that the decentralized, warrior-society of feudal Europe made the capacity for physical violence a valued form of cultural capital and created a knightly *habitus* oriented toward immediate gratification, emotional extremes, and aggressive behavior.

> The life of the warriors themselves, but also that of all others living in a society with a warrior upper class, is threatened continually and directly by acts of physical violence; thus measured against life in more pacified zones, it oscillates between extremes [Elias 1994: 449].

Societies with warrior elites, then, suffer from what Giddens (1981) terms a lack of "ontological security" – they are high-risk societies, and this is reflected in the "attitude structures" of their social subjects.

Over time, however, and through a long process of pacification, violence becomes the monopoly of the state. And:

> ... [W]ith this monopolization, the physical threat to the individual is slowly depersonalized. It no longer depends quite so directly on momentary affects; it is gradually subjected to increasingly strict rules and laws; and finally, within certain limits and with certain fluctuations, the physical threat when laws are infringed is itself made less severe [Elias 1994: 449].

Attending this "civilizing process," "physical clashes, wars and feuds diminish, and anything recalling them, even the cutting up of dead animals and the use of the knife at table, is banished from view or at least subjected to more and more precise social rules" (Elias 1994: 452–453). A crucial part of this story is the "courtierization" of warrior elites: the simultaneous increase in the cost of private physical violence, along with the increased value placed on courtly etiquette attendant on the shift of political power from feudal lords to a central court. While Elias makes a persuasive argument for the elite social conditions that placed a premium on self-control and increasingly complex codes of interaction, as well as their eventual spread to a rising middle class, it does not follow that historical conditions of pacification necessarily give rise to increased self-repression or restriction of behaviors. While it might be the case that Europe has seen a long-term reduction in private, physical violence, mores over emotional restraint, bodily expression and social interaction seem to have a much less clear trajectory. Thus, while it is probably true that a university student would have less chance of dying in a knife fight in contemporary France than in the 15th century, it is no less true that 19th-century Frenchmen would undoubtedly be shocked by the lack of modesty shown on the beaches of southern France today.

Moreover, even as Elias describes it, this "civilizing process" can also be seen as ambiguous, and if violence is widened to include non-physical and non-instrumental forms, it can no longer be said to be the antithesis of even Elias's sense of "civilization."

> Forms of non-physical violence that always existed, but hitherto had always been mingled or fused with physical force, are now separated from the latter; they persist in a changed form internally within the more pacified societies. They are most visible so far as the standard thinking of our time is concerned as types of economic violence. In reality, however, there is a whole set of means whose monopolization can enable men as groups or as individuals to enforce their will upon others [Elias 1994: 447].

Thus, a re-reading of Elias might argue for a *transformation* of *violences* attendant on "increasing webs of interdependence," "advancing division of functions," and growing social spaces over which social networks extend and into which they integrate (Elias 1994: 448), rather than a reduction and a removal of violence behind the scenes. Indeed, from an anthropological point of view, Elias's Hobbsian understanding of pre-civilization as nearly unfettered war of man against man seems potentially naïve and culturo-centric, buying into, as one critic puts it, "the etiological myth of the West" (Bauman 1989: 107).

Elias' narrative of the "civilizing process" has also been explicitly critiqued by authors such as Bauman (1989) who, in his work on the Holocaust, writes of the "moral invisibility" created by the very lengthening webs of interdependence celebrated by Elias. "With most of the socially significant actions mediated by a long chain of complex causal and functional dependencies, moral dilemmas recede from sight, while the occasions for more scrutiny and conscious moral choice become increasingly rare" (Bauman 1989: 25). Societal conditions that lead to the reduction of one form of violence, then, may create the potential for others.

More radical theorists of violence and politics such as Foucault (1995) and Agamben (1998) have argued that what Elias sees as the reduction of violence attending the civilizing process is actually the much more sinister transformation of overt and unsystematic violence into soft, covert, and omnipresent regimes of power (Foucault 1995). Indeed, in Agamben's teleological reading, Western political history amounts to the growth and intensification of the "biopolitical" basis of political power, a power that has always been grounded in violence. For Agamben (following Carl Schmitt) sovereign power is based on the exceptions which, intersecting with life and law, resolve themselves in the ban, or the ability to remove members of the polity from its protective circle figuratively or literally, essentially making them available for violence (Hansen and Stepputat 2006).

While "civilization" as a kind of normative "we-image" (Fletcher 1997) can take many forms and need not follow the trajectories of Western history, there are some useful insights to be gleaned from Elias, Foucault, and Agamben in a comparative context. From Elias comes the notion of changing moral economies of violence embodied in different historical *habitus* and the role that political-economic processes have to play in them. If the fuzzy definition of "civilization" proposed here departs from Baines and Yoffee's (1998) assertion of the linkage between civilization and states, it still retains a sense in which political forms are related to normative orders, their associated practices, and the embodied dispositions they produce. Foucault, likewise, foregrounds the production of social subjectivities and couples it with an expanded understanding of power that shares a family resemblance to the sense of violence used here. That is to say, while not all power is violence, all violence involves power, and for that matter, truth. Thus "regimes of violence" are shaped by local epistemes of power and truth: what does and does not counts as transgressive, in what circumstances, with respect to whom. This last aspect is also where Agamben is most insightful: the relationship between power, community and violence. The creation of political communities and normative orders also creates boundaries beyond which outsiders live and outcasts can be exiled and the very creation of these ontological boundaries, these hierarchies of being, is an act of discursive violence that is productive of other forms of violence. It is at the boundaries of community or of civilization, in states of exception, that some of the most spectacular instances of physical violence have occurred. The space of contact or translation can easily become the space of death (Taussig 1987). At the same time, the gradations of being, contingent or permanent, are implicated in the production of social orders and their regimes of violence. Violence is not only to be found at the edges of civilization, but also in its very foundations.

Bruno Latour wrote that we are not separated from the past by radical epistemological breaks, but in fact, now as then, live in "collectives" that are neither entirely social nor entirely natural:

> No one has ever heard of a collective that did not mobilize heaven and earth in its composition, along with bodies and souls, property and law, gods and ancestors, powers and beliefs, beasts and fictional beings. … Such is the ancient anthropological matrix, the one that we have never abandoned [Latour 1993: 107].

If Latour is correct, then the human sacrifice, warfare, and slavery of early civilizations, as part of that "anthropological matrix" cannot be ignored or dismissed as an embarrassing residue of "primitive" social organization or mentality, nor as an artifact of pre-civilization. They are as much a part of their world orders as genocide, nuclear weapons, and terrorism are a part of ours. Our civilization too has its hierarchies of relative worth implicit in the global and domestic distributions of poverty, sickness, and risk, our theodicies of privilege deployed by its winners and moral condemnation for its losers.

If history for Hegel entered its final phase with the peace of Westphalia (Hegel 1956), for most archaeologists it seems to end with the rise of "states" (Campbell 2009). Political theorists focusing on Modernity, for their part, frequently begin history around the fifteenth century, consigning everything before to a changeless "traditional society." From the point of view of diachronic political anthropology, violence and civilization offer a bridge between archaeological theorizing about ancient polities and modern political theory, making the study of ancient societies of more than antiquarian interest, while at the same time providing a deep historical framework for issues of truly anthropological scope. If, as Willey and Phillips (1958) once wrote, "archaeology is anthropology or it is nothing," then archaeologists should not stop at the traditional boundaries of their discipline in embracing issues worthy of a "science of humanity." Indeed, if I am correct in my assertion that moral economies of violence construct hierarchies of being, then the topic of violence and civilization challenges the very heart of Western Humanism, and by extension anthropology, by pointing to the locally and historically constituted nature of the category of "human" itself. Moreover, if hierarchies of care, honor, and worth were intimately connected to both world orders and structuring practices of violence in ancient societies such as that of the Shang (Campbell, this volume) or Moche (Swenson, this volume), and if, no matter how transformed or disguised, our civilization, our world order is still predicated on hierarchies of being, suffering, and worth, on hidden structural and overt sanctioned practices of violence, then the comparative study of the constitutive, if ambivalent, roles of violence in civilization is surely a topic whose time has come.

References

Arendt, Hannah
    1970 *On Violence.* Harcourt, Brace, Jovanovich, New York.
Agamben, Giorgio
    1998 *Homo Sacer: Sovereign Power and Bare Life.* Translated by Daniel Heller-Roazen. Stanford University Press, Stanford.
Baines, John, and Norman Yoffee
    1998 Order, Legitimacy, and Wealth in Ancient Egypt and Mesopotamia. In *Archaic States,* edited by Gary M. Feinman and Joyce Marcus, pp. 199–260. School of American Research, Santa Fe.

Bauman, Zigmunt

  1989 *Modernity and the Holocaust*. Polity Press, Cambridge.

  1995 *Life in Fragments: Essays on Post-Modernity*. Blackwell, Oxford.

  2006 *Liquid Fear*. Polity Press, Cambridge.

Bourdieu, Pierre

  1990 *The Logic of Practice*. Translated by Richard Nice. Stanford University Press, Stanford.

  1998 *Practical Reason: On the Theory of Action*. Translated by Richard Nice. Stanford University Press, Stanford.

  2000 *Pascalian Meditations*. Translated by Richard Nice. Stanford University Press, Stanford.

Bourdieu, Pierre, and Loïc Wacquant

  1992 *Invitation to Reflective Sociology*. Chicago University Press, Chicago.

Campbell, Roderick

  2007 Blood, Flesh and Bones: Kinship and Violence in the Social Economy of the Late Shang. Unpublished Ph.D. dissertation, Departments of Anthropology and East Asian Languages and Civilizations, Harvard University, Cambridge, MA.

  2009 Toward a Networks and Boundaries Approach to Early Complex Polities: The Late Shang Case. *Current Anthropology* 50(6): 821–848.

Childe, Gordon V.

  1950 The Urban Revolution. *Urban Planning Review* 21: 3–17.

Chomsky, Noam

  2004 The New War Against Terror: Responding to 9/11. In *Violence in War and Peace: An Anthology*, edited by Nancy Scheper-Hughes and Philippe Bourgois, pp. 217–223. Blackwell, Malden, MA.

Clastres, Pierre

  1994 *Archeology of Violence*. Semiotext(e), New York.

Das, Veena, and Arthur Kleinman

  2000 Introduction. In *Violence and Subjectivity*, edited by Veena Das, Arthur Kleinman, Mamphela Ramphele, and Pamela Reynolds, pp. 1–18. University of California Press, Berkeley.

de Castro, Eduardo Viveiros

  1992 *From the Enemy's Point of View: Humanity and Divinity in an Amazonian Society*. Translated by Catherine Howard. University of Chicago Press, Chicago.

Douglas, Mary

  1966 *Purity and Danger: An Analysis of Concepts of Pollution and Taboo*. Routledge, New York and London.

Elias, Norbert

  1994 *The Civilizing Process: Vol. 1, The History of Manners, and Vol. 2, State Formation and Civilization*. Translation by Edmund Jephcott. Blackwell Publishers, Oxford.

Farmer, Paul

  1997 On Suffering and Structural Violence: A View From Below. In *Social Suffering*, edited by Arthur Kleinman, Veena Das and Margaret Lock, pp. 261–283. University of California Press, Berkeley.

2004 An Anthropology of Structural Violence. *Current Anthropology* 45(3): 305–325.

Feinman, Gary M., and Joyce Marcus (editors)
1998 *Archaic States*. School of American Research Press, Santa Fe.

Fletcher, Jonathan
1997 *Violence and Civilization: An Introduction to the Work of Norbert Elias*. Polity Press, Malden, MA.

Foucault, Michel
1995 *Discipline and Punish: The Birth of the Prison*. Vintage Books, New York.

Galtung, Johan
1969 Violence, Peace and Peace Research. *Journal of Peace Research* 6(3): 167–191.

Giddens, Anthony
1981 *A Contemporary Critique of Historical Materialism*. Macmillan Press, London.

Gourevitch, Philip
1998 *We Wish to Inform You That Tomorrow We Will be Killed With Our Families: Stories from Rwanda*. Farrar, Strauss & Giroux, New York.

Guo Moruo (editor)
1978 *Jiaguwen heji* (Collected Oracle-bone Inscriptions). Zhonghua shuju, Beijing.

Hansen, Thomas, and Finn Stepputat
2006 Sovereignty Revisited. *Annual Review of Anthropology* 35: 295–315.

Hegel, Georg Wilhem Friedrich
1956 [1899] *The Philosophy of History*. Dover, New York.

Hinton, Alexander (editor)
2002 *Annihilating Difference: The Anthropology of Genocide*. University of California Press, Berkeley.

Huang Zhanyue
2004 Gudai rensheng renxun tonglun (On Ancient Human Sacrifice). Wenwu chubanshe, Beijing.

Kerns, Gerry
2007 Bare Life, Political Violence, and the Territorial Structure of Britain and Ireland. In *Violent Geographies: Fear, Terror, and Political Violence*, edited by Derek Gregory and Allan Pred, pp. 7–36. Routledge, London.

Kleinman, Arthur
1999 Experience and its Moral Modes: Culture, Human Conditions, and Disorder. In *Tanner Lectures on Human Values* 20, edited by Grethe Peterson, pp. 355–420. University of Utah Press, Salt Lake City.
2000 The Violences of Everyday Life: The Multiple Forms and Dynamics of Social Violence. In *Violence and Subjectivity*, edited by Veena Das, Arthur Kleinman, Mamphela Ramphele, and Pamela Reynolds, pp. 226–241. University of California Press, Berkeley.

Kleinman, Arthur, Veena Das, and Margaret Lock (editors)
1997 *Social Suffering*. University of California Press, Berkeley.

Latour, Bruno
   1993   *We Have Never Been Modern.* Harvard University Press, Cambridge, Mass.
Levinas, Emmanuel
   2000   *God, Death and Time.* Translated by Bettina Bergo. Stanford University Press, Stanford.
Mitchell, Michael
   1988   *Colonizing Egypt.* University of California Press, Berkeley.
Patterson, Orlando
   1982   *Slavery and Social Death: A Comparative Study.* Harvard University Press, Cambridge, MA.
Patterson, Thomas.
   1997   *Inventing Western Civilization.* Monthly Review Press, New York.
Riches, David.
   1986   The Phenomenon of Violence. In *The Anthropology of Violence,* edited by David Riches, pp. 1–27. Basil Blackwell, Oxford.
Scheper-Hughes, Nancy
   2006   The Tyranny of the Gift: Sacrificial Violence in Living Donor Transplants. *American Journal of Transplantation* 7(3): 507–511.
Scheper-Hughes, Nancy, and Phillipe Bourgois
   2004   *Violence in War and Peace: An Anthology.* Blackwell, Malden, MA.
Schinkel, Willem
   2010   *Aspects of Violence: A Critical Theory.* Palgrave Macmillan, New York.
Schmitt, Bettina, and Ingo Schröder
   2001   *Anthropology of Violence and Conflict.* Routledge, London.
Taussig, Michael
   1987   *Shamanism, Colonialism and the Wild Man: A Study in Terror and Healing.* University of Chicago Press, Chicago.
Trigger, Bruce
   2003   *Understanding Early Civilizations.* Cambridge University Press, Cambridge.
Tylor, Edward B.
   1924 [1871]   *Religion in Primitive Culture: Researches into the Development of Mythology, Philosophy, Religion, Language, Art and Custom.* Brentano's, New York.
Van Buren, Mary, and Janet Richards
   2000   Introduction: Ideology, Wealth, and the Comparative Study of 'Civilizations'. In *Order, Legitimacy, and Wealth in Ancient States,* edited by Mary Van Buren and Janet Richards, pp. 3–12. Cambridge University Press, Cambridge.
Yoffee, Norman
   2005   *Myths of the Archaic State.* Cambridge University Press, Cambridge.
Weber, Max
   1966   *The Theory of Social and Economic Organization.* Translated by Talcott Parsons. Free Press, New York.

Whitehead, Neil

    2004 Introduction: Cultures, Conflicts, and the Poetics of Violent Practice. In *Violence,* edited by Neil Whitehead, pp. 3–24. School of American Research Press, Santa Fe.

Wieviorka, Michel

    2009 *Violence: A New Approach.* Sage Publications, London.

Willey, Gordon, and Philip Phillips

    1958 *Method and Theory in American Archeology.* University of Chicago Press, Chicago.

Žižek, Slavoj

    2008 *Violence.* Picador, New York.

— Part I —

Sacrifice

There is probably no more indexical act of pre-modern violence than human sacrifice. As Swenson notes in his contribution on violent ritual spectacle in early polities, sacrifice has been seen as a point of origin for everything from theatre to the state. There is perhaps some justification, then, in beginning this collection of essays on violence and civilization with three papers on sacrifice, following at once a more or less chronological order, and yet attempting to account for long-term trends in violent practices without falling into Western civilization's teleological myths of rationality and progress.

Beginning with the recurrent issue of history and the visibility/invisibility of violence, Swenson writes about spectacular blood ritual and its association with early polities in several prominent cases. Contrasted with the invisibility of violence associated by many theorists with Modernity, Swenson examines the opposite case – orchestrated violence that is both associated with political power and extremely, intentionally, visible. In the course of his exploration, Swenson makes several interesting contributions: the first is to a comparative study of human sacrifice and perhaps to religious violence in general. Combining Herrenschmidt's (1979) symbolic vs. effective sacrifice with Handelman's (1990) typology of public spectacles, Swenson arrives at an effective framework for understanding the underlying factors of violent religious-political spectacle and motivates them with illustrative examples. In doing so, several useful generative insights arise, including the importance of local cosmologies/ontologies in structuring the logic of sacrifice and potentially hiding its violence in plain sight under a cloak of legitimacy, even necessity. A second point, and one that relates to the wider implications of Swenson's paper, is the potentially transformative nature of both sacrifice and violence in general. This insight allows for the linkage of "effective sacrifice," "re-presenting events" and human immolation in public, politically inflected ritual. That is to say, Swenson draws provocative connections between the charged spectacle of human transformation into inert object or divine being through death and events that aim actively to transform the world, participants, and/or audience. These insights help to explain why in cosmologies based on sacrificial renewal, or during periods of instability (states of exception), or the initial consolidation of new inequalities, spectacular, ritualized violence has apparently been good to think with in disparate historical and cultural contexts.

The connections between transformatively oriented ritual and transformative historical moments, moreover, hinge on the crucial insight that violence enacts a dialectic that is also its phenomenological kernel: the reduction of one for the expansion of another. In stressing the transformative aspect of the dialectic, however, Swenson makes the key observation that from at least some perspectives, the transformation enacted by the dialectic of sacrifice need not be negative: ritual destruction might be figured as apotheosis rather than reification in some contexts. In either case, however, local hierarchies of being are re-structured and subjectivities shaped in dramatic enactments of violence. This, in turn, points to a crucial issue suggested in Swenson's paper and taken up more fully in Morris's and Campbell's contributions. What accounts for the "vastly different forms" that "biopolitics" took "in ancient and modern societies" (Swenson, this volume)? In part, this problematic may be a product of the myopia created by our own normalized categories: terrorism is a modern form of violence that very much relies on the power of spectacle in shaping social subjectivities, with suicide bombing in particular a kind of transforming religious-political action, even while gang initiations, lynchings, and certain paramilitary violence can all unfold the dialectic drama of violence, enacting world views and their attendant hierarchies of worth. And yet, as Swenson notes, there are limits to the analogies that can be drawn between ancient state-sponsored blood sacrifice and modern phenomena. I would here like to propose that there are other reasons for the rise and demise of human sacrifice than the disenchantment of the world or the progress of Civilization. While different historical and geographical localities will have their own regimes of violence and moral economies, a generalizable and related cluster of theses is that physical violence is protean and often ambiguous (whatever dominant discourses may do to legitimize it), hierarchies of being are never monolithic or uncontested, and spectacular violence is generally a relatively costly and unpredictable site of subject formation (Foucault 1995). Moreover, without revisiting the culture vs. practical reason debates of 1990's cultural anthropology (Sahlins 1996; Obesekere 1992), it is nonetheless a truism that legitimating ideologies work best when they work with perceived interest. Dramatic physical violence is affectively powerful and a high-risk strategy, especially in so far as it is open to subversive or contested readings (Arendt 1970; Morris, this volume). A related observation militating against the efficiency of spectacular displays of physical violence to mold social subjectivities is the way in which violence's dialectic gains (and potential condemnations) tend to adhere to the sacrificer/executioner, whatever the ideology of acting on behalf of the group or cosmic order. This aspect motivates elite monopolization of sacrificial practices, frequently making the sovereign "sacrificer-in-chief." From the perspective of large-scale societies, however, this dialectic aspect of physical violence presents two problems for the systematization and normalization of institutional power: the first is the necessity of separating the dialectic gains of sovereign power's exercise from its delegates; and the second is to disperse and disembody responsibility for the violent act such that no moral stain arising from violence's ambiguity adheres to the sovereign. These factors, at least under conditions of stability and growth, tend to militate against the use of spectacular violence over time.

As mentioned above, the innately inter-subjective moral space of violence's dialectic (instrumental or systemic) presents a potentially treacherous ground for the permanent or contingent stratification of being. A crucial reason for this resides in the duality of local constructions of humanity: on the one hand a site of moral claims, on the other a category or set of categories shaped by power and community. The first aspect makes all persons potentially recognizable as such, the second constructs their being permanently or contingently in hierarchies of honor or worth. This duality, diffracted through socialized dispositions, can make a ruler at once more than human and at the same time "just a man," or, on the other side of the spectrum, make a fellow human being no more than vermin to be exterminated. This potential for aspect shift (Schinkel 2010) is what makes violence so ambiguous. The paradox is that the symbolic capital or discursive status gained in shaming a rival, sacrificing a victim, or exerting force over a slave is two-edged: the source of the power and its inversion are the same and only an aspect shift apart. Thus the more direct the association with violent dialectics, the more individual power/status can be accrued – but only at the cost of its constantly present potential for reversal.

In her contribution, instead of focusing on the spectacle of ritual violence, Morris considers the practice of retainer sacrifice in Egypt and elsewhere. Like Swenson, she seeks to understand the relationship between early polities and human sacrifice, noting with Childe that they tend to co-occur with "quantum leaps of power" and perhaps the surplus of expendable bodies made available by recent conquest or pacification. The argument might thus run that new orders, in themselves transgressive of previous norms, require legitimating ritual and the human lives expended mark the seriousness of the occasion. Could the French Revolution, for instance, and the subsequent executions be seen as solemn ritual, as much performing the new social order in blood in the name of Fraternity, Liberty and Equality, as expedient acts of consolidation? Perhaps marrying Elias with Geertz, we could say that historical *habitus* with higher thresholds of tolerance for risk, harm and antagonism, perhaps inculcated by the war and turmoil that sometimes precede new orders, are more amenable to violent poetics and aesthetics of power.

Along with Campbell, Morris makes a connection between the underlying conditions that structure both retainer and captive sacrifice cross-culturally, despite their apparent differences. Perhaps the greatest commonality is the dialectical performance of hierarchies of being and social order. Thus, both royal advisor and slave might share a fate in common with their attached dependent statuses with respect to the ruler, while the captive soldier is ritually executed – all enacting civilization's proper order as performed by the sovereign.

Despite the focus thus far on physical violence, a crucial issue made clear in Morris's more recent examples of retainer sacrifice, such as Indian suttee, was the dual operation of symbolic and structural violence in setting the stage for physical destruction. Symbolic violence on the one hand, operating as mystification, promoted the widow burning as self-sacrificing loyalty, while structural violence on the other, combined the relatively low (expendable) status of women, traditional expectations, the pornography of violence (vicarious enjoyment of another's death and, thus, one's own survival), and the material and social interests of relatives.

Nevertheless, as Morris argues and the empirical data appear to bear out, there generally seems to be an inverse relationship between invisible, systemic violence and more visible forms of physical or instrumental violence. Over the long-run, and despite some lingering or re-occurring incidences (such as Middle Imperial Chinese widow suicides), the use of other human beings as grave goods is the product of particular historical conditions and world views that seem to have more or less disappeared. This trend toward less visible forms of violence in my re-reading of Elias can be seen in Morris's West African examples, where "compensation" is offered to encourage prospective death attendants. In this we can see an amelioration of the dialectic of spectacular violence and efforts to re-shape the moral ground of the killing as consent.

In Campbell's contribution, the issue of human sacrifice and its disappearance is also taken up, but in the context of a single traditional/ cultural locus over the span of 1,000 years. The central problematic for this paper was how certain forms of violence became unthinkable even as new, and arguably more lethal forms emerged. From the perspective of Swenson's paper, Campbell attempts to understand the historical specifics of a sea-change in "biopolitics" that does not correspond to a Modern/Premodern split.

Viewing the three papers together, in addition to the trend toward the rise of systemic violence at the expense of instrumental violence corresponding to internal pacification and ever-larger polities, there also seems to be a movement of visible, instrumental violence from the center to the spatial or temporal periphery of civilization (Todorov 1992). Thus, if the low-risk, pacified *habitus* has a low threshold for physical violence, and the routinization of power requires a naturalization or anonymization of the dialectic, then civilization as the proper order of things must exile visible, instrumental violence to its borders or to reserves of exceptional circumstance. Thus if captive sacrifice and retainer sacrifice can be seen as the internal and external embodiments of Bronze Age Chinese hierarchies of being and moral economies of violence, by Early Imperial times spectacular legitimatizing violence had all but been removed to the courts, the fortified frontier, and the exceptional circumstances of rebellion and civil war.

References

Foucault, Michel
  1995 *Discipline and Punish: The Birth of the Prison.* Vintage Books, New York.
Handleman, Don
  1990 *Models and Mirrors: Towards an Anthropology of Public Events.* Cambridge University Press, Cambridge.
Herrenschmidt, Olivier
  1979 Sacrifice: Symbolic or Effective? In *Between Belief and Transgression: Structuralist Essays in Religion, History, and Myth*, edited by Michel Izard and Pierre Smith. Translated by John Leavitt. Chicago University Press, Chicago.
Obeyesekere, Ganath
  1992 *The Apotheosis of Captain Cook: European Mythmaking in the Pacific.* Princeton University Press, Princeton, New Jersey.
Sahlins, Marshall
  1996 *How Natives Think: About Captain Cook, for Example.* Chicago University Press, Chicago.
Schinkel, Willem
  2010 *Aspects of Violence: A Critical Theory.* Palgrave Macmillan, New York.
Todorov, Tzvetan
  1992 *The Conquest of America: The Question of the Other.* Translated by Richard Howard. Harper Perennial, New York.

Dramas of the Dialectic:
Sacrifice and Power in Ancient Polities

EDWARD SWENSON

Introduction

This chapter focuses on highly visible traditions of spectacular violence in pre-modern polities, as opposed to the professed invisibility of structural and symbolic violence endemic in the contemporary world. The latter constitutes structures of economic and cultural domination which propagate physical forms of political repression or domestic abuse (see Bourdieu and Wacquant 1992; Bourgois 2001, 2004; Scheper-Hughes and Bourgois 2004; see also Lutz and Bonditti, this volume). Spectacular bloodshed that was moralized, aestheticized, and sanctified would seem far removed from the regularly "misrecognized" (invisible) matrices of economic and symbolic violence which condition structures of poverty, international warfare, sexism, ethnic conflict, and political coercion common in the present era of global capitalism (Farmer 1996). Indeed, the sacrificial construction of authority is commonly held to index the "pre-modern," which contrasts with the institutionalization of "rational" and juridically sanctioned violence characterizing so-called modern "civilizations" (Elias 1994; Weber 1966). Violent spectacles of a religious nature also diverge from blood sport, military campaigns, and genocide, although theorists have sought to draw links between these disparate genres of carnage (Futrell 1997; Marvin and Ingels 1999). Certainly, violence invites generalization, and scholars are often reluctant to foreground the culturally specific structures of bloodshed and brutal exploitation in their interpretations of hierarchical political formations.

The following paper examines the performative framework of religious sacrifice in ancient polities in order to demonstrate that ritual violence was no less complicit than "modern" systems of violence (economic, juridical, etc.) in legitimating authority structures, creating political subjectivities, and constructing relations of inequality. In fact, focusing on the theatrical aspects of ritual homicide brings into sharp relief how domination is effectively and perhaps even universally "somaticized" through violence. Physical harm viscerally objectifies ontological and sociopolitical categories of personhood, identity, status differences, and alterity by directly re-inscribing bodies. "Hierarchies of being" (see Campbell, this volume) are thus naturalized (reified) or contested through the somatic power of violence, whether spectacular, religious, structural, military, or delinquent.

Despite the force of this generalization, comparing Aztec ritual homicide with the profound structural violence of the Apartheid regime has its obvious limitations, beyond recognizing the generalized "somatic" reach of state oppression. To be sure, the political effects and cosmological significance of ritual violence also varied considerably in early polities. Nevertheless, I argue that spectacles of authoritative sacrifice were commonly predicated on a dialectical metaphysic that effectively depersonalized and dehumanized subjects. Such "dramas of the dialectic" contributed to the legitimization of stratified sociopolitical systems; political subjects were reified and reconstituted in gory spectacles showcasing the metamorphic power of ritually encapsulated destruction. However, the meaning and political ramifications of the religiously transformative effects of violence varied cross-culturally: violent subject reformulation (whether involving dehumanization, ancestralization, super-humanization, etc.) could entail either degrading vicitimization or martyrdom, and even apotheosis itself. The following analysis of the performative power of ritual violence serves to highlight both intriguing commonalities and important cultural differences in the religiously violent construction of political authority in ancient complex societies.

Theoretical Problem and Objectives of the Paper

Foucault (1977) famously argued that institutionalized power in the pre-modern era was largely predicated on ostentatious public displays, which he contrasted with the technologies of surveillance, correction, and discipline that would come to characterize social control in post-Enlightenment Europe. In a similar vein, Geertz (1980) contended that the "poetics and aesthetics of power" are as relevant to interpreting the complexities of political hierarchy as Weberian mechanics of institutional order (see Inomata and Coben 2006: 28; Lewis 1990). Bloch (1989) also theorized that traditional forms of authority are concretized and reproduced primarily through an investment in ritual theater. Ritual molds political dispositions through aesthetically powerful drama which conflates the emotional and sensual with the traditional and authoritative (Bloch 1989; Dietler 1999: 137; Inomata and Coben 2006:

21–24; Schechner 1985; Tambiah 1979). Therefore, it is not surprising that emotionally charged ritual performances have frequently been interpreted either as formidable forces of oppression in processes of subject formation, or as critical mediums of liberation that enable the creative appropriation and even ludic challenge of normative sociopolitical orders (Butler 1999; Turner 1974, 1982).

Of all genres of religious ceremony, blood sacrifice has secured center-stage in theories proposed to explain the special power of theatrical performance to construct authority and reify political boundaries. Staged killing (or even just its symbolic evocation) has commonly been viewed as the ultimate form of both ritual and spectacle, and scholars of varying theoretical persuasions have proposed that the origins of theater, political inequalities, and society itself are to be found in sacrificial rites (Bataille 1990: 20–22; Carter 2003; Detienne and Vernant 1989: 2; Freud 1950 [1905]; Girard 1977; Hamerton-Kelly 1987; Nietzsche 1966: 158–159, 270). In fact, a brief survey of theories on the political significance of ritual violence reveals a rather striking penchant among social scientists to directly link sacrificial acts with the development of power asymmetries and gender inequalities (Hamerton-Kelly 1987; McWilliam 1996: 129). From Freud's civilizing patricide to Girard's scapegoat theory to Nancy Jay's contention that blood sacrifice appropriated the procreative power of women in patrilineal societies, ritual violence has been interpreted as laying the foundations for social controls, judicial norms, and hierarchy (Beers 1992; Brumfiel 2001; Combs-Schilling 1989: 256–257, 270; Daly 1990; Jay 1992; Marcuse 1955; Nietzsche 1966 [1886]; Sered 2002). Of course, Frazer's (1890) famous theory directly links kingship and royalty with the institution of sacrifice (see also Gordon 1990; Ray 1991).

Although grand sweeping theories on the origins of the state and organized religion are in most instances reductive, the widespread recognition that sacrifice is intimately related to power in a metaphysical, religious, and political sense is highly relevant to the archaeological analysis of early complex society. Indeed, the strong association between the formation of centralized polities in antiquity and the intensification of religious ideologies based on sacrificial tenets warrants theoretical scrutiny (Swenson 2003). It might seem logical that ceremonies of ritual homicide would accompany political hierarchization; few would deny that the authority to take an individual life represents tyranny and conspicuous consumption in their purest form (Bourdillon 1980: 13; Law 1985: 74). However, the central role played by religious sacrifice in many early stratified societies demonstrates a complexity and diversity of meaning that defy reduction to cynical arguments of this kind.

I argue that dialectical principles underlying the sacrificial process constitute a general pattern worthy of consideration in the cross-cultural analysis of ritual violence in past political systems. Sacrifice in many cultures, despite important differences in religious meaning and sociopolitical effects, was generally implicated in native philosophies of difference, process, and order – elementary principles commonly manifest in cosmological beliefs relating to creation, fertility, empowerment, and being. Sacrifice, as the ritually controlled mediation of the ultimate dialectical dyad of life and death, not only materialized in sensational bodily form the abstraction of dialectic thinking, but also performatively dramatized "power" as transformative efficacy, reproductive force, and instrument of social differentiation. Therefore, the spectacle of sacrifice animated culturally-specific categories of power on both a metaphysical and political plain (De Heusch 1985; Lewis 1989; Valeri 1985). Central to my argument is that elites in many early state systems ideologically constructed authority by "performing the dialectic" of reproductive empowerment through dramatic rituals of sacrificial destruction (creation). The theatrical enactment of dialectical processes (as opposed to their precise theological-philosophical articulation) appears to have played an important role in the exercise of power in many centralized societies in the past. By foregrounding the "dialectics" of performance, I do not imply that diverse sacrificial systems were actually understood in these terms. Instead, I stress the irrefutable transformative "power" of violence consummated in spectacular ritual acts of bodily negation. Indeed, this dialectical metaphysic was not founded necessarily on unconscious cognitive structures or explicit ideological programs; rather it was engendered by a phenomenology of violence that inhered in affective dramas of ritual killing. In fact, a "performative consciousness" induced in the experience or anticipation of the dialectical moment of ritually staged death contributed directly to the construction of authority and the sensual embodiment of social inequalities in ancient societies. In adopting this position, I am not arguing that ritual violence served simply as pageantry, propping up ideologically dependent "theater states" where real economic and coercive force was underdeveloped (Geertz 1980). Rather, by identifying the sacrificial-dialectical principles animating political theater in ancient polities, I suggest that the elaboration of "performed ideologies" of this kind facilitated the rise of hierarchical political economies in certain societies, especially in the ancient Americas, where sacrifice was deemed as "effective" (and not simply symbolic) in maintaining interdependent cosmological, social, and natural orders (Herrenschmidt 1982). Indeed, the development of early complex societies in many regions of Mesoamerica and the Andes was often accompanied by an intensification of the aesthetics and theatrical demarcation of ritual violence, culminating in the great political theaters of sacrifice defining Aztec and Moche "stagecraft."

Nevertheless, in this paper I also stress that an archaeological examination of the *performative effects* of ritual violence can reveal the culturally particular meanings that variably informed the conflation of blood sacrifice and authority in ancient societies. Certainly, the ritual dispatching of human life within grand public amphitheaters, such as in the Aztec tradition, contrasts significantly (in its social, ritual, and symbolic aspects) from the more private, intimate, and less sanguinary sacrifices suffered by *capa cocha* victims on high mountain peaks of the Inka empire (Ceruti 2004; Schobinger 1991; Zuidema 1977). In truth, the act of killing itself may constitute the least theatrical, visible, or even ritualized aspect of complex celebrations centered on sacrifice in specific cultures – a fact that would seem relevant to understanding the varied political ramifications of sacrificial ideologies (Bowen 1992: 661–664; Humphrey and Laidlaw 2007). Therefore, the political implications and ideological valence of these dialectical dramas were highly varied. A brief comparison of Mesoamerican political theologies with the traditions of authoritative sacrifice defining statecraft in Sumer, Rome, and elsewhere will highlight some of these important historical variations. Finally, a more detailed analysis of Moche political theology will serve to demonstrate how archaeologists can interpret the performative and political context of "dialectical dramas" of sacrifice from an examination of iconographic and architectural data.

Sacrifice as Catalyst of Signification, Transformation, and Process

Scholarly endeavors to distill the great variety of sacrificial institutions into a single explanatory model run the risk of reduction and dehistoricization. With this caveat in mind, social scientists have nonetheless recognized that diverse religious complexes predicated on violent ceremony share an underlying processual logic. In many cultures, this sacrificial ontology articulates native social theories of difference, signification, and change. The power of sacrifice rests in its catalyzing capacity to bring about transformation and distinction, often through a release, negation, or transfer of "vitality," realized by the act of killing and the extinction of life (Beattie 1980: 32; Bloch 1992). Sacrifice physically activates the creation or conversion of distinctive states of being; it thus commonly functions as a vehicle of process and an engine of categorical and experiential differentiation (or its antithesis – unification; Bataille 1988). Sacrificial "process," then, is predicated on notions of dynamic negation which conform at a rudimentary level to Hegel's dialectic, a processual framework that finds parallels in earlier Greek philosophy and world religious theologies including Hinduism, Taoism, and Buddhism (Bataille 1990; Desmond 1992; Kojève 1980).[1] Of course, sacrifice, commonly defined as the ritual "immolation" of an animate essence to achieve elevated religious goals, conforms closely to dialectical thinking (Nancy 1991). What precise dimension of sacrificially mediated (negated) transformation is actually valorized (sacralization or desacralization, prophylaxis or empowerment, etc.; see De Heusch 1985; Evans-Pritchard 1954; Hubert and Mauss 1964) is largely contingent on the society in question. Therefore, even though the manifest meaning of sacrifice can differ considerably in varied cultural and historical contexts, this underlying processual pattern holds remarkably firm. Whether understood as a gift to surrender, as conspicuous waste, or as an empowering act enabling intervention in the flow of life/vitality, the force of sacrifice ultimately lies in materially creating new becomings and states of being (relationally, materially, spiritually). What is significant, then, is that culturally specific regimes of value are corporeally materialized through sacrificial ritual (Lewis 1990: 3; see also Ruel 1990).

The meaning of the Latin-derived word "sacrifice" (to make holy, sacred) itself intimates a processual movement of sacralization and by extension empowerment, effectively realized through dramatic destruction. The Nahuatl (Aztec) word for sacrifice is *uemmana* or *tlamana*, meaning to "spread out" or "set into motion," terms that similarly underscore the dialectical and transformative power of sacrifice (Read 1998: 144–147). Of course, it seems undeniable that sacrifice commonly serves to empower in some capacity, and the prevalence of such "no pain, no gain" social philosophies (or more subtle *do ut des* theologies) is remarkable in light of notable cultural diversity in the meaning and social context of ritual violence. From the Pauline kenotic ethic in Christianity to Hindu asceticism and Marx's materialization of Hegel's dialectics as class struggle, violence – in consummating a dialectical movement of negation – is perceived as a prerequisite to transformation and reproduction, however conceived.

In fact, blood sacrifice has been variably interpreted as the ritual act *par excellence* which effectively mediates entities (from the physical to the symbolic), given that such actions are defined and propelled by destructive sublation indispensable for processual continuance or regeneration (Bloch 1986; Carter 2003; Chilton 1992; Hubert and Mauss 1990; Smith 1987). The widely recognized mediating power of sacrifice can be explained in part by its intimate relationship to problems of life and death – constructs that express the most salient processual poles of human existence. What could be more fundamental to an understanding of process, creation, metamorphosis, even the passage of time, than the movement from life to death (and subsequently to rebirth – where life and death can be perceived as the ultimate form of reciprocated gifting – Bataille 1989, 1990: 19; Bloch and Perry 1982; De Heusch 1985; Derrida 1995)? The sacrificer's attempt to manipulate the temporal, experiential, and metaphysical domain of death in order to control life itself is a demonstration of power with manifest political consequences (Bourdillon 1980: 19–21; Eilberg-Schwartz 1990: 178–194; Futrell 1997: 177; Rosaldo and Atkinson 1975). In many societies, killing a victim (whether human, animal, or thing) represents the decisive and irrevocable instant of transformation, creation, or perhaps erasure of distinction (Bataille 1988, 1989; Bloch and Perry 1982; Turner 1977). The moment of ritual slaughter is unquestionably imbued with – and expressive of – "power" on multiple planes of metaphor and experience. Similarly, theorists have argued that as the ultimate indexical act, sacrifice reifies gender differences as well as other distinctions structuring particular social orders (Jay 1992; Valeri 1985). This explains in part why periods of crisis and social chaos have often called for sacrifice, for it palpably and sensually recreates the distinctions needed to restore an ideologically accepted "order" (Burkert 1983; Carter 2003; Girard 1977; Heinsohn 1992; Herrenschmidt 1982; Jay 1992; Maccoby 1982).

Elsewhere, I have designated this general processual scheme a "consumptive-reproductive dialectic" (Swenson 2003). In many different cultures, sacrifice is dialectically and inextricably intertwined with sexuality, commensality, and political power (Combs-Schilling 1989; Detienne and Vernant 1989; Lewis 1990; Lincoln 1991; Robertson-Smith 1894; Smith 1987). Of course, eating, sex, and childbirth, among the most fundamental of biological and social acts, often presuppose generative destruction (or painful creation). Therefore, it is unsurprising that fertility, power, and commensalism are recurring tropes underpinning religious sacrifice cross-culturally.[2] Importantly, consumption of vitality, as a prerequisite to production and regeneration, is transposable to the structuring of hierarchical and unequal political relations; control over consumption (as a direct means of empowerment) defined status and authority in past societies (see below) (Bloch 1992; Lewis 1990; Veblen 1953). Indeed, in many centralized polities, grand spectacles of violent consumption, intimating a generative or reproductive power, formed (in truth, *per-formed/ trans-formed*) the basis of institutionalized political power.

Performing the Dialectic

For Valerio Valeri, the symbolic content of life is made real through its sacrificial performance; violent rituals are powerful in their physical dramatization (and hence embodied realization) of symbolic and existential categories pivoting on polarities of life and death. As Valeri (1985: 52–55) argues, sacrifice animates and substantiates words, thoughts, and actions.

The signifying force of sacrificial spectacles was also expressed much earlier by Sallustius, the neo-platonic defender of pagan religions, in the fourth century AD. He claimed that ritual slaughter makes real otherwise abstract forces of power and process: "prayers divorced from sacrifice are only words, prayers with sacrifices are animated words, the word giving power to the life and the life animation to the word" (cited in Lewis 1980: 3). Janet Hoskins (1993) demonstrates that public mass sacrifice of bulls among the Kodi of Sumba (Indonesia) dramatically showcases the hierarchical social relations and antagonisms of the society (mainly economic and reproductive dependencies of juniors toward elder men). This awareness is achieved by representing social relationships in metonymic and metaphoric symbols that are viscerally "experienced" in the changing corporeal condition of the bull as it passes through sequential stages of veneration, brutal humiliation, violent death, and somber ritual re-consecration. Hoskins writes (1993: 175): "The body is not simply the vessel left behind, emptied of the soul and quickly devoured, but part of a dynamic movement between polarities, from beast to man, from conquered to conqueror, from death to new life." Evidently, the signifying and "socializing" power of the sacrificial process among the Kodi is dramatically dialectical, and it is the sequencing of public spectacle that secures its effectiveness. In a similar vein, Nancy Jay (1992: 37) notes that "when sacrifice works in this performative way it is what Thomas Aquinas called an effective sign, one that causes what is signified." Action that can cause what it signifies intimates a propensity to "power" at its most fundamental.

As the above analysis suggests, the staged pornography of ritual killing constitutes among the most powerful genres of theatrical performance which radically showcases (indeed creates) distinctions in efficacy, social status, and symbolism more generally. Scarry (1985: 121–131) observes, for instance, that dramas pivoting on dying bodies confer a "compelling realism that imbues unanchored reality claims as authentic and uncontestable." To be sure, controlled spectacles of dying entail a sacrificial "interpellation" for all participants concerned, because they constitute performative acts that do more than simply declare or metaphorically represent. Rather, ritual killing interpellates subjects directly and incontrovertibly into bodily existence, whether involving a Brechtian social distancing or a unifying communion as differently theorized by Robertson-Smith or Bataille (Austin 1962; Bourdieu 1991: 42; Butler 1999: 125; Fischer-Lichte 2005; Pizzato 2005).

Significantly, a common cross-cultural theme underlying sacrificial rites is the desired physical and spiritual perfection of victims (or their inverse – polluting and marginal scapegoats). Thus in China, only flawless specimens of animals were considered worthy of sacrifice, while the god-impersonators of the Aztec tradition were honored for their attractiveness and purity (Carrasco 1999; Lewis 1990: 20; Read 1998). The Inka *capa cocha* (cf. p. 32) sacrifices were also restricted to nobles distinguished by unblemished beauty, virginity, and physical perfection (Ceruti 2004; Zuidema 1977). Evidently, sacrifice relates to either the categorically definitive or ambivalent, which is understandable given its signifying, valorizing, and transformative powers in enhancing or negating structural oppositions (see De Heusch 1985). The anticipated or realized violence directed at the intended victims of impeccable beauty heightened the imagery, spectacle, and power of the dialectical transformation that the sacrificial rite ultimately encapsulated, thus forcefully inculcating a distinctive performative consciousness among participants. Beauty could be variably conceived as either the antithesis or symbolic portent (synthesis?) of death, and the effects of the sacrifice would be all the more emotionally evocative and aesthetically charged through such a performed interpenetration of opposites. The practice of *molech* (child sacrifice) in Carthage also appears to have been reserved for high-status families (accentuating the purity and status of the victims; Futrell 1997: 176; Stager 1992). The deification of sacrificial slaves in the Aztec tradition served a similar role, and the repeated comingling and negation of statuses (passage from slave to god to mutilated corpse), made visible through carefully orchestrated rites, unequivocally *performed* sacrificial powers of transformation. Ritual violence represented the ultimate and irreversible instrument of subject formation, explaining in part why slaves, war captives, children, women, and kings – figures occupying the extreme ends of culturally variable social spectrums – were common candidates of sacrificial death.

Dramas of the Dialectic and the Comparative Analysis of Ancient "Stagecraft"

If the performed killing and thus theatrically choreographed negation (transformation) of vitality effectively dramatizes power in its polyvalent meanings (thus rendering power decidedly real and less abstract – indeed, wedding the metaphysical and political strains of power in a symbolically charged climactic action), then the frequent association of ritual slaughter and elite authority in ancient society becomes readily comprehensible (Lincoln 1991: 174). Authority was realized in part by monopolizing politically encapsulated spectacles of sanctioned violence conceived to push through dialectical processes of life (i.e., revitalization, reproduction, purification, reciprocal distributions, etc. in their varied guises). Lewis argues (1990: 20–21) that in ancient China (specifically during the Eastern Zhou period):

"Not only was sacrifice seen as a form of killing, but the link between taking life and authority was emphasized by the fact that the king and the feudal lords acted as their own sacrificers; they personally performed the sacrifice in their own state." In a similar manner, whenever the emperor is depicted in imperial Roman art (coin series, reliefs), he is shown engaged in ritual sacrifice (Gordon 1990; Heyman 2007). As Heyman (2007: 90) observes, "As chief officiant, he is depicted both as a negotiator with the gods, and implicitly as the benefactor who distributes the largess of sacrificial rituals." Gordon (1990: 202) contends that the *princeps* as sacrificer of animals and thus benefactor of his subjects provided a model for elite authority in both Rome and the provinces (see also Price 1989). By presiding over emotionally-charged spectacles of sacrifice, one secured the ability to concretize, subvert, or convert embodied distinctions in status, socio-cosmic dependencies, mortality, and time itself. In a sense, power became vested in "sacred dialecticians" whose authority was expressed through a performed aesthetic of violent process. This largely explains why discourses on elite political legitimacy are commonly tied to cosmogonic ritual (Lincoln 1991: 170). As Lambek notes (2007: 30–33), sacrificial death, in conflating the transitive with the intransitive, provides a sharper sense of "beginning" than does even birth: "a birth can be undone through death... but a death cannot be undone." Sacrifice is thus foundational, "a definitive and irreversible political act," an execution of a person that effects the "execution of a course of action."

Exercising power through the spectacular control of the processual (dialectical) unfolding of time, space, and sociopolitical order, usually within specially built theaters of high sacrificial drama, was remarkably widespread in the ancient world (Herskovtiz 1967; Green 2001; Lewis 1990; Ray 1991; Smith 2006; Swenson 2003). It is not difficult to appreciate how those who sacrifice and were sacrificed in turn were often perceived to be closest to the divine in stature, power, and efficacy. Elites who presided over charged spectacles of ritual violence would have been in a stronger position to exercise the right to "consume" their subjects politically and economically for ideologically stated material, spiritual, or reproductive boons (Bloch 1992); such consumptive practices (taxation, corporeal punishment, labor-service, demanded deference to elites, etc.) intimating superordinate-subordinate social relations simulated the reciprocal and consumptive channels structuring human-divine dependencies. Individuals who were charged as sacred dialecticians in overseeing ritual process and temporal-spatial transformation were obvious candidates for privileged status.

In light of this argument, we can better interpret why the formation of early centralized polities was often marked by the elaboration of political theologies predicated on spectacular performances of violent ritual. A striking sacrificial aesthetic accompanied the development of early stratified polities in many parts of the world. For instance, an aesthetic redolent with violent imagery marked the emergence of centralized monumental complexes in core regions of Mesoamerica and the Andes (for a full discussion of these "formative" sites, see Arnold and Hastorf 2008; Benson and Cook 2001; Burger 1992; Cordy-Collins 2001; Flannery and Marcus 1983; Joyce 2000; Samaniego et al. 1982; Schele and Friedel 1990; Schele and Miller 1986; Swenson 2003). The iconographic traditions associated with these ceremonial complexes commonly celebrated predatory animals, sacrificial imagery, fertility, and the transformative power of violent death.

Although the sacrificial performance of power was remarkably prevalent in early complex polities, the nature of these performances, and the religious and civic authority that they structured, differed considerably in space and time. In other words, underlying cultural values and cosmological principles largely determined the political implications of such dialectical dramas. On first inspection, there may be little justification to compare animal sacrifices orchestrated in the royal courts of ancient Rome or Mesopotamia with spectacles of ritual homicide staged at Tenochtitlan. However, in both instances, the control of violent ritual was constitutive of political authority defined according to varied cultural expectations and theological tenets. In fact, comparing the differing "theatrical contexts" of elite sacrificial rituals sheds light on their specific religious meanings and overarching political significance.

In early Sumerian cities, the act of killing animals in royal temples was not publically dramatized (it occurred behind the scenes) and was downplayed ceremonially, in comparison to the highly ritualized feeding of the god (Abusch 2002). The power of the divinity was sustained by sacrificial food provided by the people, and the god in his or her temple was seen as analogous to the king feasting in his palace. One expressed allegiance to a city and royal authority by feeding and caring for its god and royal representative (which justified taxation and corvée labor in turn). Significantly, in early Mesopotamian cosmogonies, the human race was created not by the death of a god or the infusion of divine blood to enliven mortals, but from the molding of clay by disgruntled divinities who wished to be free of the onus of everyday labor (Abusch 2002; Oppenheim 1977). In other words, celebrating "blood" ties with kin and deity was not highly valued in urban Sumer (Abusch 2002). Therefore, these Sumerian rites of sacrificial consumption to engineer the reproductive continuity of the polity (and not necessarily the cosmos in this instance) would obviously have had little need for rituals and symbols of human sacrifice. Moreover, in such a cosmological framework, one could assume that ostentatious spectacles foregrounding the public slaughter of animals, orchestrated directly by elites or their proxies, would not demand special elaboration.

Alimentary symbolism undergirding conceptions of sacrificial reciprocity also characterized societies in the ancient Americas. However, in the instance of Maya and Aztec theology, such symbolism was much more literal and predicated on re-enacting divine events of cosmogonic creation. Hamann (2002) has defended the ascription of "Mesoamerica" to a single "spatio-temporal generalization" on the basis of a Braudelian "*mentalité*" defined by pervasive cosmologies of "original debt" or destruction. Cosmologies based on original debt assert that the current world order was created by the violent autosacrifice of divinities whose resurrection as life-giving providers could only be sustained by the *direct* "return" of human offerings to the newly created earth and sky. In the Aztec creation story, the god Nanahuatzin hurled himself into a blazing fire at Teotihuacan, and this paradigmatic act of self-destruction led to the first sunrise and his re-apotheosis as the sun. The re-created world was thus a product of destructive performance, and violent exchanges would forever define civilized human-divine relations. Consumption of agricultural products among the Aztec and in many other Mesoamerican polities was understood as tantamount to consuming the flesh and blood of deities (Carrasco 1990, 1999; Clendinnen 1991; Read 1998). Read has argued that the Aztec adhered to a "sacrificially transformative cosmos" (a theory of sacrifice she calls "alimentary" and "metabolic"); reciprocated actions of production, sacrifice, and eating propelled the ordered movement of space-time. Agriculture and fertility were dialectically synonymous with violence in Mesoamerican worldviews (Hamann 2002: 361; Read 1998: 132), and the earth's bounty could only be replenished by the divine consumption of human flesh and blood. "Covenant narratives" of this kind detailing the consubstantial union linking the human and the divine characterized many other Mesoamerican civilizations, as indicated by detailed studies of archaeological remains, iconography, and surviving pre-Columbian codices (Hamann 2002; Joyce 2000; Monaghan 1990, 1995; Schele and Freidel 1990).

Significantly, the ordering of the social realm in Mesoamerica was largely shaped by these cosmological understandings and the ritual re-enactments of mythical archetypes. The status of Aztec elites was defined by their role as sacrificers; they were called *teuitzio,* one's spine, and *teauaio,* one's thorn, metaphorical references to the paraphernalia of bloodletting. As Hamann notes (2002: 357): "From nobles to priests to the *tlatoani* himself, Aztec ideology justified elite privilege by claiming that elites were specially skilled in their ability to repay the original debts established at Teotihuacan, debts which all humans, elite or commoner, owed to the gods." The commoner class was called the *macehualtin* in Mexica society, which means to merit, to perform worthy deeds, and to do penance (Hamann 2002: 357). The *macehualtin* therefore sacrificed to the lords as the elite sacrificed to gods, and a hierarchy of sacrifice – ranging from the mundane and everyday, to the great pageants of elite-orchestrated human sacrifice – shaped the contours of Aztec social, political, and religious life (Clendinnen 1991; Read 1998). In the Aztec world, subject formation pivoted on a sacrificial metaphysic.

The downplayed slaughter and convivial consumption of an animal sacrifice in Sumer was integral to the construction of community identity and social hierarchy, but it was far removed from Aztec principles of "original debt" grounded in lavish spectacles of human sacrifice. Clearly, different cultural values and cosmological schemes shaped the political and economic effects of dialectical dramas of sacrifice. Herrenschmidt's (1982) dichotomy between symbolic and effective sacrifice proves useful in interpreting the salient distinctions in the political and performative characteristics of Aztec and Sumerian traditions of authoritative sacrifice. The symbolic type prevails in religious traditions where an omnipotent creator deity (for instance, the Judeo-Christian god) stands apart from creation and is not dependent on "material benefits" from sacrificing humans to maintain the order of the cosmos. In contrast, sacrifice is deemed "effective" in religious systems including Vedic Brahmanism, where a direct homology holds between the mortal, cosmic, and supernatural – and where both humans and the gods are subject to cosmic laws and even cosmic energy transfers, regulated ultimately by the eminent position occupied by priests as sacrificers. Therefore, Brahmanic ritual immolation of animals differed fundamentally from Abraham's sacrifice of a ram in place of Isaac. The sacrifice of Abraham establishes a new covenant with the Old Testament god symbolizing his obedience; the dialectical process underscoring the killing of the ram is thus decisively and powerfully *symbolic*, for the ram is otherwise useless to the divinity and does not affect a direct cosmic alteration (the alteration lies instead in a changed relationship between God and people). Although in most instances sacrifices likely assumed both forms, the earlier Sumerian royal festivals correspond more closely to the symbolic type, while sacrifice documented in Mesoamerica was construed as decidedly effective. Along with the aforementioned cultural variables, this particular dichotomy can partly explain the variant emphases placed on the public performance and iconographic celebration of violent death distinguishing ancient political formations such as the Sumerian or Mesoamerican. Much more was at stake in the traditions of lordly sacrifice among the Maya or Aztec; the direct ordering power and efficacy of elite-directed human sacrifice would need to be forcefully communicated in highly dramatic public performances and aesthetically charged images of violent process.

Handelman's (1990) typology of the sociopolitical functions of public spectacles – "events that present," "events that model," and "events that re-present" – also serves as a useful heuristic for comparing the political effects of sacrificial ritual in ancient polities, and it complements Herrenshmidt's broader distinction between symbolic and effective sacrifice. By "events that present," Handelman means public spectacles that directly mirror and reinforce social orders in Durkheimian fashion, even if just idealized, through the design and internal orderliness of the event itself. Events that model, on the other hand, are intended to directly transform ritual participants, often via the efficacious display of contradictory forces and their eventual synthesis through the ordering power of rite. The initiation of adolescents into adulthood epitomizes ritual events that directly model the social world. Finally, events that re-represent designate spectacles that do not so much transform social members or legitimize society by performatively replicating it; rather, they are replete with ambivalence and ambiguity and often provide a context for the critical reinterpretation or playful inversion of the presiding social order. Although I do not discuss them here, Hoskins (1993) and Hammoudi (1988) provide fascinating examples of the "re-presentational" and even subversive qualities of sacrificial theater. In truth, Handelman recognizes that these kinds of spectacles are ideal types (or effects), and that ritualized performances can implicate all three forms.

The presentation of food in ancient Mesopotamian temples and covenantal sacrifices among the ancient Israelites certainly enhanced the binding and affective power of contracts with divinities and their representatives (and established a sense of identity and alterity). In the end, however, they conform more closely to the "presentational" characteristics of Handelman's typology as exemplified by the subdued symbolism and de-emphasis of the physical act of ritual slaughter (which was symbolically only a step or two removed from everyday butchery). Similarly, in the ancient Roman Empire, sacrificing to the *princeps* was symbolic of a community's obedience to the apotheosized ruler, and at least from the perspective of the Roman elite, an acknowledgement of the emperor's piety and benevolence in providing for his subjects and maintaining peace. As Gordon notes:

> … [T]he fusion of the euergetic system with the sacrificial system in [the imperial] civic priesthood evokes both the divine necessity and the social responsibility of the existing social order. The relationships proposed by the sacrificial system between god and man (inferiority; reciprocity between unequals; providential beneficence; changelessness) is implicitly offered as a model of the relationship between the elite and the rest of the community [1989: 229].

Of course, social scientists have long accepted Lienhardt's observation that "the people are put together as the bull is put together," wherein the coded distribution of particular body parts of a sacrificed bull indexes ("presents") social distinctions (Lienhardt 1961: 23). In like manner, offerings of sacrifice to apotheosized emperors directly symbolized similar political relationships, hierarchies, and dependencies.

Finally, events that "model" obviously conform closely to Herrenschmidt's "Brahamanic" type of sacrifice and best describe the sacrificial spectacles prominent in New World polities as well. Participating in the prodigious acts of human sacrifice at Tenochtitlan that accompanied the oppressive festival round of the Aztec calendar was likely all the more powerful in affect and symbol given the desired metamorphic and biological (metabolic) outcomes of such rites (Read 1998). In the political realm, at least, the mass sacrifice of war captives did in fact physically "re-model" the social world, a point that highlights the enormous conceptual and political chasm separating rites of human and animal sacrifice (Maccoby 1982).[3]

Archaeological Analysis of Spectacles of Sacrificial Power Among the Moche

In the absence of ethnographic or ethnohistorical documentation, an analysis of the theatrical orchestration of ritual violence, as can be inferred from architectural and iconographic data, can provide an effective means to interpret the cosmological structure and political effects of past sacrificial complexes. A brief examination of the iconographic and architectural corpus of the Moche of ancient Peru reveals not only that the spectacular control of dialectical process underscored their sacrificial politics, but that elite-encapsulated performances of ritual violence were public events that intended to effectively "model" the social, natural, and cosmic worlds, in a manner similar to sacrificial programs that have been documented in ancient Mesoamerica.

Moche refers to an ideological and religious complex variably propagated throughout the North Coast of Peru, from the Huarmey Valley in the South to the La Leche region in the north, and covering nearly 500 km of coastline. Moche civilization thrived from approximately A.D. 100–800 and is marked by the emergence of powerful ruling elites, far removed from the mass of commoners and distinguished by semi-divine roles and the consumption of magnificent sumptuary goods. This unprecedented social stratification was accompanied by the development of some of the largest urban complexes, irrigation-based political economies, and state political systems in the Andes (Bawden 1996; Chapdelaine 2001, 2002; Shimada 1994; Uceda 2001a; Uceda and Mujica 1994, 2003).

Figure 2.1.   Fineline ceramic painting of the Moche Presentation Theme or Sacrifice
Ceremony. (Adapted from Alva and Donnan 1993: fig. 143.)

Although we will never be able fully to reconstruct the complex cosmological symbolism of Moche art and iconography, the data nevertheless suggest that formal dramas of ritualized warfare and human sacrifice underwrote Moche statecraft. The rich iconographic and mortuary records demonstrate that elite control of ritual warfare, prisoner capture, and ceremonies of human sacrifice defined elite status and political relations among the Moche (Alva and Donnan 1993; Bawden 1996; Donnan 2001; Swenson 2003). The primary religious event depicted in Moche iconography is the "Sacrifice Ceremony" (Presentation Theme), in which the fanged deity (*Ai Apaec)* or his priestly avatar is being presented a goblet of human blood by a supporting troupe of three subsidiary deities (Donnan 1978; Quilter 1997) (Figure 2.1). Naked warriors are shown in the margins of such depictions having their throats cut by zoomorphic figures (who are collecting blood in goblets), and the Presentation Theme is commonly associated with scenes of warfare (Alva and Donnan 1993; Verano 2001). Recently, ceramic goblets originating from the Moche Valley were tested by immunological analysis (Bourget 2001: 95). The examined residues exhibited a strong reaction to human antiserum, supporting the iconographic record that blood was collected from sacrificed victims and consumed by high priests. The consumption of human blood in goblets provides a parallel to the alimentary and metabolic connotations of Aztec sacrifice (Read 1998).

Correlations made between excavated lordly burials and divine figures depicted in the famous "Sacrifice Ceremony" iconographic complex indicate that Moche rulers legitimated their status by performing the cosmogonic and sacrificial roles of powerful creator-destroyer deities (Alva and Donnan 1993; de Bock 2005; Donnan 1978; Donnan and Castillo 1994). The iconographic record further demonstrates that elites were both the instigators and victims of ritual warfare (Donnan 2001). Thus the performance of sacrificial roles – as either sacrificer or victim in the dialectical spectacle of violent death – was constitutive of power and elite status.

The architectural layout and iconography of Moche monumental complexes support the argument that Moche political authority was founded on sacrificially mediated performances of cosmological ordering and consubstantial union with supernatural forces (de Bock 2005; Swenson 2003). Moche ceremonial centers such as Huaca de la Luna (Moche Valley) were veritable theme parks of violent spectacle; the built aesthetics of the Moche city were grounded in cosmological principles of generative and productive violence – principles which distinguish the Moche center from comparable arenas of violent sport such as the Coliseum of imperial Rome (Franco et al. 1994; Uceda 2001a, 2001b). At Huaca de la Luna and Cao Viejo (Chicama Valley), for instance, graphic representations on large polychrome wall murals of warfare, decapitation, dismemberment, and consumption of blood are juxtaposed with images of cosmological creation, earthly bounty, and fertility (Franco et al. 1994; Uceda 2001a, 2001b) (Figures 2.2 and 2.3). Significantly, these temple complexes are comprised of massive northern plazas that could have contained audiences of well over a thousand people. Spectators would have been confronted by a highly developed aesthetic presentation of predatory violence as reproductive power. The tiered platforms of the southern temple, upon which many of these visually-arresting murals are displayed, likely served as the stage for the public sacrificial rites as illustrated in Moche fineline ceramics. The archaeological discovery of numerous sacrificial victims (young male warriors with slit throats) at the principal Moche temples, many of which are associated with symbols of rebirth, further corroborates the likely generative, "modeling," and reproductive connotations of Moche dramas of the dialectic (Bourget 1997, 2001, 2006; Verano 2001). In the end, the architectural and iconographic data reveal that Moche spectacles of religious authority conform closely to Herrenschmidt's "effective sacrifice" and Handelman's "public event that model."

"Civilized" Violence and the Sacrificial Foundations of the State

To conclude, violent religious spectacles should be understood not simply as epiphenomenal pageantry, tactics of terror or intimidation, which shored up coalescing hierarchical polities; instead, sacrificial performances seem to have played a key role in the actual institutionalization and embodied realization of power asymmetries characteristic of variably structured states in

Figure 2.2. (A) Monumental Complex of Huaca Cao Viejo, Chicama Valley (Adapted from Franco et al. 1994: fig. 4.12); (B) Painted Adobe Frieze Depicting Sacrificial Violence.

Figure 2.3 (A) Painted Adobe Frieze from Huaco Cao Viejo, Chicama Valley, Showing
          Sacrificial Violence; (B) Huaca de La Luna, Moche valley, Showing Cosmic
          Creation and Earthly Bounty.

different regions of the world. This argument applies particularly to the cases
of Mesoamerica and the Andes, where notions of effective sacrifice as public
"events that model" in mediating reciprocal energy transfers were especially
well developed. Although the search for origins is outmoded in archaeology,
our lasting interest in process (history) and social transformation must take

stock of the "processual" connotations of sacrificial dialectics. It does not require a great leap of the imagination to link the creative, transformative, and differentiating functions of ritual violence as dialectical process to actual processes of stratification. In other words, sacrificial rites designed to create, distinguish, and empower through consumptive violence (and effectively realized through the medium of performance) were likely instrumental in engineering the institutionalization of asymmetrical power relations expressed in varied strategies of domination. It is particularly intriguing that we can theoretically subsume popular gift theories of sacrifice within this broader scheme of sacrificial dialectics ("consumptive-reproductive dialectics"). That gifting (enveloping relations of production and consumption at the moment of exchange) is central to structuring relations of power, debt, dependency, and religious communion has long captured the attention of anthropologists (Godelier 1999; Hubert and Mauss 1990). Commenting on the homology between reciprocal gift-giving and sacrificial acts, Godelier (1999: 29–30) notes that "in certain social and mental worlds, men who give more than they have been given or who give so much that they can never be repaid, raise themselves above other men and are something like gods, or at least they strive to be." Therefore, it becomes less problematic to theorize how power differentials in socially stratifying societies might have become anchored materially through the elaboration of ideologies of sacrificial production. Moche lords who expressed their authority by sacrificing (and being worthy of eventual sacrifice themselves) could more convincingly legitimize economic appropriation as "sacred dialecticians" (semi-divine providers and agents of socio-cosmic process). Non-elite participation in such systems (offering goods, energy, and time to their lordly intermediaries) could have been effectively naturalized in turn. Commenting on the centrality of sacrifice and militarism as signifiers of lordly power in early China, for instance, Lewis (1990: 17, 19) remarks:

> The actions that set the rulers apart from the masses were the 'great services' of those altars, and these services were ritually directed violence in the form of sacrifices, warfare, and hunting... Indeed, the two major forms of taxation in the Warring States and early empires were simply transformations of the 'feudal' levies for sacrifices and warfare.

Bloch's (1992) notion of "rebounding violence" recognizes, at least implicitly, that the dialectical properties of religious performance can have direct consequences for social transformation, including the intensification of political inequalities. By "rebounding violence," Bloch refers to the secondary and outward projection of violence which follows the initial, consumptive act framing liminal ritual experience cross-culturally. This ricocheting violence is unleashed in order to incorporate lost vitality discarded in the initial consumptive concession or simply to demonstrate a tapped supernatural power harnessed by performing the preliminary violent rite. Bloch thus identifies a two-fold process of violence in liminal experiences. The initial violent act or its metaphor consummates the critical consumptive (concessionary) moment necessary for the dialectic of productive empowerment (and often required to set in motion systems of reciprocal, though asymmetrical, exchange). That is to say, the essential function of sacrificial ritual is to empower and entitle, a process made tangible and physically real through the projection of an absorbed supernatural force to capture and augment "vitality" residing in the material, temporal realm.

An example drawn from the election of an Aztec king, or *tlatoani*, illustrates the effects of ritualized "rebounding violence" in Mexica political dramas. After his appointment, the *tlatoani*-elect had to endure four days of fasting, bloodletting, and atonement within the precincts of Huitzilopochtli's pyramid temple (Clendinnen 1991: 77–79). This phase represents the initial consumptive violence associated with the liminal stage of transcendent contact and spiritual/physical renewal. Only after completion of this liminal rite was the king considered purified and worthy to enter the palace. Significantly, however, following the royal seclusion, the king launched a raid to capture sacrificial victims for his installation ceremony. This militaristic finale with ensuing human sacrifices constituted the rebounding violence of the ritual sequence and palpably demonstrated the newfound ritual and political empowerment of the Aztec king. Of course, a symbolic rebounding violence underlay this rite and Aztec sacrifice more generally: the extraction of tribute and the right of the *tlatoani* to subjugate others economically and politically.

Bloch argues that the rebounding violence characterizing diverse ritual systems is a source of considerable political power in many societies (Bloch 1992). He shows in his comparative study that expansionist violence against neighbors or even the domination of one group by another are manifestations of ritually-generated rebounding violence. However, the above analysis focusing on the diverse performative frameworks of authoritative sacrifice suggests that Bloch's rebounding violence cannot be accepted as the "irreducible core" of ritual. The dialectical unfolding engineered by violent spectacles (often an experiential or sensual, as opposed to an intellectual, problem for participants) can take varied forms as determined by cultural traditions, historical conditions, and cosmological tenets. Neither a symbolic nor experientially manifest (performed) rebounding violence accompanied the sacrifice of animals in ancient Sumer, for instance, even though authority rested on the direction of commensal sacrificial rites. Although Bloch ignores the New World in his comparative analysis, his notion of rebounding violence can account compellingly for the political effects of Aztec and Moche "stagecraft." The symbolic emphasis placed on consumption, metabolic transfers, and alimentary exchanges, as well as the ultimate fertilizing power of sacrifice, are manifestations of rebounding violence at the level of both cosmic process and mechanism of political control.

Despite the comparative focus of my argument, no single determining factor (including Bloch's rebounding violence) can account for the sacrificial foundations of many early states. Certainly, the dialectical logic undergirding sacrificial violence possibly points to commonalities in cognitive structures. However, historical, economic, and especially cultural forces shaped the institutionalization of dialectical dramas that differently "somaticized" social hierarchies in ancient polities. Although such spectacles were far from epiphenomenal in constituting political power, identifying the historical variables structuring the permutations of authoritative sacrifice remains an important challenge of archaeological research (a critical subject not fully addressed here).

Nevertheless, this chapter stresses the importance of comparatively investigating bloodshed as an agent of sociopolitical change. Indeed, the "historically dynamic relevance" of violence, as exemplified in this instance by the dialectical and transformative power of authoritative sacrifice, demands nuanced and comparative analysis by anthropologists (Campbell, this volume). Obviously, then, spectacular, structural, or political forms of brutality do not represent fleeting aberrations of more determinative economic and social processes leading to the development of "civilization" (i.e., complex command economies and hierarchical political formations). Rather, civilization is born of, and begets, violence (*contra* Elias 1994).

This truism, however, begs another fundamental question of how best to interpret violence as universal to "civilization" in general. Although civilization is an ideological category lacking heuristic value, an obvious corollary can be drawn between the somatic power of violence and "sovereignty" in stratified states, both past and present. The sacrificial construction of authority proves that biopolitics are not simply a condition of modernity or of a specifically western political history (*contra* Foucault 1978; see Agamben 1995). Of course, biopolitics assumed vastly different forms in ancient and modern societies, and, in this instance, I define the term broadly as political power founded on the violent classification of bodies, life, and death (a "thanatology" as much as a political ontology) . If Agamben contends that the concentration camp represents the paradigm of late modern biopolitics, can the sacrificial altar symbolize an analogous prototype for ancient "civilizations" in the Americas and possibly elsewhere? The analogy is thought-provoking but admittedly problematic. As he argues (Agamben 1995: 114), the elimination of non-persons (Agamben's bare life of *homo sacer*) in modern biopolitics constitutes neither sacrifice nor homicide. In contrast, the highly moralized, visible, and aesthetically charged public displays of human sacrifice were deemed generative of life and divinity itself; depersonalization and subject formation entailed a creative apotheosis that differed remarkably from the anonymous violence of technocratic biopolitics defining the contemporary era. This is not to espouse a romanticized view of religious sacrifice in the spirit of Bataille; nor am I claiming that religiously-inspired sacrifice represents a more "civilized violence." Instead, I conclude by stressing the shared exploitative qualities of dialectical dramas with other modalities of "state" violence. Sacrificial death facilitated economic and political dominance through the embodied creation of political subjects that articulated historically specific structures of inequality. Certainly, the sovereign control over life and death (whether divinely exalted or "bare") characterizes civilizations defined as traditional and theocratic as well as those described as efficient, bureaucratic, and thus "modern" (Bauman 1989). As Agamben argues, in one form or another, life has been the "definitive object of civilized politics" (Norris 2000: 39).

Notes

1. The anthropologist Edmund Leach observed that "there is a strongly Hegelian strain in the way even the simplest peoples organize and utilize categories for the purposes of religious expression… the facts of reality are classified in essentially the same way, and ritual again serves as an operation of 'changing time' for 'changing potency' from one side of the equation to the other" (emphasis added) (Leach 1968: 2).

2. Commenting on the sacrificial foundations of the Moroccan monarchy, Combs-Schilling (1989: 11, 255) argues: "The most basic physical templates that the monarchy uses to reinforce itself are sexual intercourse and human birth – the thrust of the phallic-shaped object into white tissue to make lifeblood flow and bring the hope for creation into being." Similarly, she adds: "Sacrifice builds a form of death that is convincing as a pathway to eternal life by modeling itself on the actions that bring life in this world. In mimicking the processes that set life in motion, the knife sacrifice evokes the potency of sexual intercourse and childbirth and engenders a profound physical response in the ritual's participants, a subliminal recognition of the momentousness of the actions involved".

3. In deploying Handelman's typology, I am not arguing that state-sanctioned spectacles of sacrifice can be neatly pigeon-holed into one of the three performative types; rather, it aids in interpreting the political context of culturally specific "dialectical dramas." In fact, events that model through means of ritual violence were not always public affairs. The exclusivity of elaborate sacrificial events may even have heightened the power and privileged status of the officiant, and effective sacrifices could also be staged out of sight or behind the scenes (a secrecy which might have even accentuated their ultimate effectiveness and mystery). Rites that modeled (such as an initiation ceremony) often also involve the complex interplay between sequentially linked spaces and times of exclusion and inclusion.

References

Abusch, Tzvi
    2002 Sacrifice in Mesopotamia. In *Sacrifice in Religious Experience*, edited by Albert I. Baumgarten, pp. 39–48. Brill, Leiden.

Agamben, Giorgio
    1995 *Homo Sacer: Sovereign Power and the Bare Life*. Translated by Daniel Heller-Roazen. Stanford University Press, Stanford.

Alva, Walter, and Christopher B. Donnan
    1993 *Royal Tombs of Sipán*. Fowler Museum of Cultural History, University of California, Los Angeles.

Arnold, Denise Y., and Christine A. Hastorf
    2008 *Heads of State: Icons, Power, and Politics in the Ancient and Modern Andes*. Left Coast Press, Walnut Creek, CA.

Austin, John
    1962 *How To Do Things with Words*. Clarendon, New York.

Bauman, Zygmunt
    1989 *Modernity and the Holocaust*. Polity Press, Cambridge.

Bataille, George
    1988 *The Accursed Share: An Essay on General Economy. Volume I: Consumption*. Zone Books, New York.
    1989 *Theory of Religion*. Zone Books, New York.
    1990 Hegel, Death, and Sacrifice. In *On Bataille*, edited by Allan Stoekl, pp. 9–28. Yale French Studies 78. Yale University Press, New Haven.

Bawden, George
    1996 *The Moche*. Blackwell, Oxford.

Beattie, John H.M.
    1980 On Understanding Sacrifice. In *Sacrifice*, edited by Michael F.C. Bourdillon and Meyer Fortes, pp. 29–44. Academic, New York.

Beers, William
    1992 *Women and Sacrifice: Male Narcissism and the Psychology of Religion*. Wayne State University Press, Detroit.

Benson, Elizabeth P., and Anita G. Cook (editors)
    2001 *Ritual Sacrifice in Ancient Peru*. University of Texas Press, Austin.

Bloch, Maurice.
    1986 *From Blessing to Violence: History and Ideology in the Circumcision Ritual of the Merina of Madagascar*. Cambridge University Press, New York.
    1989 *Ritual, History and Power: Selected Papers in Anthropology*. London School of Economics Monographs on Social Anthropology 58. Athlone Press, London
    1992 *Prey into Hunter: The Politics of Religious Experience*. Cambridge University Press, Cambridge.

Bloch, Maurice, and Jonathan P. Parry (editors)
    1982 *Death and the Regeneration of Life*. Cambridge University Press, Cambridge.

Bourdieu, Pierre
    1991   *Language and Symbolic Action*. Harvard University Press, Cambridge.
Bourdieu, Pierre, and Loïc Wacquant
    1992   Symbolic Violence. In *An Invitation to Reflective Sociology*, edited by Pierre Bourdieu
            and Loïc Wacquant, pp. 167–173. Chicago University Press, Chicago.
Bourdillon, Michael F.C.
    1980   Introduction. In *Sacrifice*, edited by Michael F.C. Bourdillon and Meyer Fortes, pp.
            1–28. Academic Press, New York.
Bourget, Steve
    1997   Las excavaciones en la Plaza 3A de La Huaca de la Luna. In *Investigaciones en la
            Huaca de la Luna 1995*, edited by Santiago Uceada, Elias Mujica, and Ricardo
            Morales, pp. 51–59. Facultad de Ciencias Sociales, Universidad Nacional de la
            Libertad, Trujillo, Peru.
    2001   Rituals of Sacrifice: Its Practice at Huaca de La Luna and its Representation in
            Moche Iconography. In *Moche Art and Archaeology in Ancient Peru*, edited by Joanne
            Pillsbury, pp. 89–110. Studies in the History of Art 63; Center for Advanced Studies
            in the Visual Arts, National of Gallery of Art, Washington D.C., Symposium Papers
            40. Yale University Press, New Haven.
    2006   *Sex, Death, and Sacrifice in Moche Religion and Visual Culture*. University of Texas
            Press, Austin.
Bourgois, Philippe
    2001   The Power of Violence in War and Peace: Post-Cold War Lessons from El Salvador.
            Ethnography 21(1): 5–34.
Bowen, John R.
    1992   On Scriptural Essentialism and Ritual Variation: Muslim Sacrifice in Sumatra and
            Morocco. *American Ethnologist* 19(4): 656–671.
Brumfiel, Elizabeth
    2001   Aztec Hearts and Minds: Religion and the State in the Aztec Empire. In *Empires*.
            Edited by Susan Alcock, Terence D'Altroy, Kathleen Morrison, and Carla Sinopoli,
            pp. 283–310. Cambridge University Press, Cambridge.
Burger, Richard L.
    1992   *Chavín and the Origins of Andean Civilization*. Thames and Hudson, London.
Burkert, Walter
    1983   *Homo Necans: The Anthropology of Greek Sacrificial Ritual and Myth*. Translated by
            Peter Bing. University of California Press, Berkeley.
Butler, Judith
    1999   Performativity's Social Magic. In *Bourdieu: A Critical Reader*, edited by Richard
            Schusterman, pp. 113–128. Cambridge University Press, Cambridge.
Carrasco, David
    1990   *Religions of Mesoamerica*. Harper, San Francisco
    1999   *City of Sacrifice: The Aztec Empire and the Role of Violence in Civilization*. Beacon
            Press, Boston.
Carter, Jeffrey
    2003   *Understanding Religious Sacrifice: A Reader*. Continuum, New York.

Ceruti, Constanza
　　2004　Human Bodies as Objects of Dedication at Inca Mountain Shrines (North-Western Argentina). *World Archaeology* 36(1): 103–122.

Chapdelaine, Claude
　　2001　The Growing Power of a Moche Urban Class. In *Moche Art and Archaeology in Ancient Peru*, edited by Joanne Pillsbury, pp. 69–87. Studies in the History of Art 63; Center for Advanced Studies in the Visual Arts, National of Gallery of Art, Washington D.C., Symposium Papers 40. Yale University Press, New Haven.
　　2002　Out in the Streets of Moche: Urbanism and Sociopolitical Organization at a Moche IV Urban Center. In *Andean Archaeology I: Variations in Sociopolitical Organization*, edited by William H. Isbell and Helaine Silverman, pp. 53–88. Kluwer Academic/Plenum, New York.

Chilton, Brice
　　1992　*The Temple of Jesus: His Sacrificial Program within a Cultural History of Sacrifice*. Pennsylvania State University, College Station, PA.

Clendinnen, Inga
　　1991　*Aztecs: An Interpretation*. Cambridge University Press, New York.

Combs-Schilling, M. Elaine
　　1989　*Sacred Performances: Islam, Sexuality, and Sacrifice*. Columbia University Press, New York.

Cordy-Collins, Alana
　　2001　Decapitation in Cupisnique and Early Moche Societies. In *Ritual Sacrifice in Ancient Peru*, edited by Elizabeth P. Benson and Anita G. Cook, pp. 21–34. University of Texas Press, Austin.

Daly, Robert J.
　　1990　The Power of Sacrifice in Ancient Judaism and Christianity. *Journal of Ritual Studies* 4(2): 181–98.

de Bock, Edward K.
　　2005　*Human Sacrifices for Cosmic Order and Regeneration: Structure and Meaning in Moche Iconography, Peru, AD 100–800*. British Archaeological Reports International Series 1429. John and Erica Hedges, Oxford.

de Heusch, Luc
　　1985　*Sacrifice in Africa: A Structuralist Approach*. Translated by L. O'Brian and A. Morton. Indiana University Press, Bloomington.

Derrida, Jacques
　　1995　*The Gift of Death*. Translated by David Wills. University of Chicago Press, Chicago.

Desmond, William
　　1992　*Beyond Hegel and Dialectic: Speculation, Cult, and Comedy*. State University of New York Press, Albany, NY.

Detienne, Marcel, and Jean-Pierre Vernant (editors)
　　1989　*The Cuisine of Sacrifice among the Greeks*. University of Chicago Press, Chicago.

Dietler, Michael
  1999   Rituals of Commensality and the Politics of State Formation in the "Princely"
         Societies of Early Iron Age Europe. In *Les princes de la protohistoire et l'émergence de
         l'état,* pp. 135–152, edited by Pascal Ruby. Actes de la Table Ronde Internationale,
         Centre Jean Bérard et l'Ecole Française de Rome, Naples, 27–29 Octobre 1994.
         Centre Jean Bérard, Naples; Ecole Française de Rome, Rome.

Donnan, Christopher B.
  1978   *Moche Art of Peru.* Museum of Culture History, University of California, Los
         Angeles.
  2001   Moche Ceramic Portraits. In *Moche Art and Archaeology in Ancient Peru*, edited
         by Joanne Pillsbury, pp. 127–140. Studies in the History of Art 63; Center for
         Advanced Studies in the Visual Arts, National of Gallery of Art, Washington D.C.,
         Symposium Papers 40. Yale University Press, New Haven.

Donnan, Christopher B., and Luis Jaime Castillo
  1994   Excavaciones de tumbas de sarcedotisas Moche en San José de Moro, Jequetepeque.
         In *Moche: Propuestas y perspectivas*, edited by Santiago Uceda and Elias Mujica, pp.
         415–424. Travaux de l'Institut Français d'Etudes Andines, Lima

Eilberg-Schwartz, Howard
  1990   *The Savage in Judaism: An Anthropology of Israelite Religion and Ancient Judaism.*
         Indiana University Press, Bloomington.

Elias, Norbert
  1994   *The Civilizing Process: The History of Manners, and State Formation and Civilization.*
         Blackwell, Oxford.

Evans-Pritchard, Edward Evan
  1954   The Meaning of Sacrifice among the Nuer. *Journal of the Royal Anthropological
         Institute* 84: 21–33.

Farmer, Paul
  1996   On Suffering and Structural Violence: A View from Below. *Daedalus: Journal of the
         American Academy of Arts and Sciences* 125(1): 261–283.

Fischer-Lichte, Erika
  2005   *Theatre, Sacrifice, Ritual: Exploring Forms of Political Theatre.* Routledge, London.

Flannery, Kent V., and Joyce Marcus
  1983   *The Cloud People: Divergent Evolution of the Zapotec and Mixtec Civilizations.*
         Academic Press, New York.

Foucault, Michel
  1977   *Discipline and Punishment: The Birth of the Prison.* Translated by Alan Sheridan.
         Pantheon, New York.
  1978   *The History of Sexuality: An Introduction.* Translated by Robert Hurley. Vintage,
         New York.

Franco, R., C. Gálvez and S. Váquez
  1994   Arquitectura y decoración Mochica en la Huaca Cao Viejo, Complejo el Brujo:
         Resultados preliminares. In *Moche: Propuestas y perspectivas*, edited by Santiago
         Uceda and Elias Mujica, pp. 147–180. Travaux de l'Institut Français d'Etudes
         Andines 79, Lima.

Frazer, James C.
   1981 [1890]   *The Golden Bough*. 2 vols. Gramercy, New York.

Freud, Sigmund
   1950 [1905]   *Totem and Taboo: Some Points of Agreement between the Mental Lives of Savages and Neurotics*. Routlege, New York.

Futrell, Alison
   1997   *Blood in the Arena: The Spectacle of Roman Power*. University of Texas Press, Austin.

Geertz, Clifford
   1980   *The Theatre State in Nineteenth-Century Bali*. Princeton University Press, Princeton.

Girard, René
   1977   *Violence and the Sacred*. Translated by Patrick Gregory. Johns Hopkins University Press, Baltimore.

Godelier, Maurice
   1999   *The Enigma of the Gift*. University of Chicago Press, Chicago.

Gordon, Richard
   1990   The Veil of Power: Emperors, Sacrificers, and Benefactors. In *Pagan Priests: Religion and Power in the Ancient World*, edited by Mary Beard and John North, pp. 177–198. Duckworth, London.

Green, Miranda J.
   2001   *Dying for the Gods: Human Sacrifice in Iron Age and Roman Europe*. Tempus, New York.

Hamann, Byron
   2002   The Social Life of Pre-sunrise Things: Indigenous Mesoamerican Archaeology. *Current Anthropology* 43(3): 351–82.

Hamerton-Kelly, Robert G. (editor)
   1987   *Violent Origins: Walter Burkert, René Girard, and Jonathan Z. Smith on Ritual Killing and Cultural Formation*. Stanford University Press, Stanford.

Hammoudi, Abdellah
   1988   *La victime et ses masques*. Éditions du Seuil, Paris

Handelman, Don
   1990   *Models and Mirrors: Towards an Anthropology of Public Events*. Cambridge University Press, Cambridge.

Heinsohn, Gunnar
   1992   The Rise of Blood Sacrifice and Priest Kingship in Mesopotamia: A Cosmic Decree? *Religion* 22: 109–134.

Herrenschmidt, Olivier
   1982   Sacrifice: Symbolic or Effective? In *Between Belief and Transgression: Structuralist Essays in Religion, History, and Myth*, edited by Michel Izard and Pierre Smith; translated by John Leavitt. Chicago University Press, Chicago.

Herskovits, Melville J.
   1967   *Dahomey: An Ancient West African Kingdom*. Vols. 1 and 2. Northwestern University Press, Evanston, IL.

Heyman, George
  2007 *The Power of Sacrifice: Roman and Christian Discourses in Conflict*. Catholic University of America Press, Washington, D.C.

Hoskins, Janet
  1993 Violence, Sacrifice, and Divination: Giving and Taking Life in Eastern Indonesia. *American Ethnologist* 20(1): 159–178.

Hubert, Henri, and Marcel Mauss
  1964 *Sacrifice: Its Nature and Function*. University of Chicago Press, Chicago.

Humphrey, Caroline, and James Laidlaw
  2007 Sacrifice and Ritualization. In *The Archaeology of Ritual*, edited by Evangelos Kyriakidis, pp. 277–288. Cotsen Advanced Seminars 3. Cotsen Institute of Archaeology, University of California, Los Angeles.

Inomata, Takeshi
  2006 Politics and Theatricality in Mayan Society. In *Archaeology of Performance: Theaters of Power, Community, and Politics*, edited by Takeshi Inomata and Lawrence S. Coben, pp. 187–222. Altamira Press, New York.

Inomata, Takeshi, and Lawrence S. Coben
  2006 Overture: An Invitation to the Archaeological Theater. In *Archaeology of Performance: Theaters of Power, Community, and Politics*, edited by Takeshi Inomata and Lawrence S. Coben, pp. 11–46. Altamira Press, New York.

Jay, Nancy
  1992 *Throughout Your Generations Forever: Sacrifice, Religion, and Paternity*. University of Chicago Press, Chicago.

Joyce, Arthur
  1997 Ideology, Power, and State Formation in Oaxaca. In *Early Urban Societies*, edited by Linda Manzanilla, pp. 133–68. Plenum, New York.
  2000 The Founding of Monte Albán: Sacred Propositions and Social Practice. In *Agency in Archaeology*, edited by Marcia-Anne Dobres and John E. Robb, pp. 71–91. Routledge, New York.

Kojève, Alexandre
  1980 *Introduction to the Reading of Hegel: Lectures on the Phenomenology of Spirit*. Cornell University Press, Ithaca.

Lambek, Michael
  2007 Sacrifice and the Problem of Beginning: Meditations from Sakalava Mythopraxis. *Journal of the Royal Anthropological Institute* 13: 19–38.

Lathrap, Donald W.
  1982 Jaws: The Control of Power in the Early Nuclear American Ceremonial Centers. In *Early Ceremonial Architecture in the Andes*, edited by Christopher B. Donnan, pp. 241–268. Dumbarton Oaks, Washington, D.C.

Law, Robin
  1985 Human Sacrifice in Pre-colonial West Africa. *African Affairs* 84(334): 53–87.

Leach, Edmund R.
   1968   Introduction. In *Dialectic in Practical Religion*, edited by Edmund R. Leach. pp.
          1–26. Cambridge Papers in Social Anthropology 5. Cambridge University Press,
          Cambridge.

Lewis, Mark E.
   1990   *Sanctioned Violence in Early China*. State University of New York Press, Albany,
          NY.

Lienhardt, Godfrey R.
   1961   *Divinity and Experience: The Religion of the Dinka*. Oxford University Press,
          Oxford.

Lincoln, Bruce
   1991   *Death, War, and Sacrifice: Studies in Ideology and Practice*. University of Chicago
          Press, Chicago.

Maccoby, Hyam
   1982   *The Sacred Executioner: Human Sacrifice and the Legacy of Guilt*. Thames and
          Hudson, New York.

Marcuse, Herbert
   1955   *Eros and Civilization: A Philosophical Inquiry into Freud*. Beacon Press, New York.

Marvin, Carolyn, and David W. Ingle
   1999   *Blood Sacrifice and the Nation: Totem Rituals and the American Flag*. Cambridge
          University Press, Cambridge.

Mauss, Marcel
   1990 [1924]   *The Gift: The Form and Reason for Exchange in Archaic Societies*. Translated
          by W.D. Halls. Norton, New York.

McWilliam, Andrew
   1996   Severed Heads that Germinate the State: History, Politics, and Headhunting in
          Southwest Timor. In *Headhunting and the Social Imagination in Southeast Asia*,
          edited by Janet Hoskins, pp. 127–166. Stanford University Press, Stanford.

Monaghan, John
   1990   Sacrifice, Death, and the Origins of Agriculture in the Codex Vienna. *American
          Antiquity* 55(3): 559–569.
   1995   *The Covenants with Earth and Rain: Exchange, Sacrifice, and Revelation in Mixtec
          Sociality*. University of Oklahoma Press, Norman.

Nancy, Jean.
   1991   The Unsacrificeable. *Yale French Studies* 79: 20–37.

Nietzsche, Friedrich
   1966 [1886]   *Beyond Good and Evil: Prelude to a Philosophy of the Future*. Translated by
          W. Kaufmann. Random House, New York.

Norris, Andrew
   2000   Giorgio Agamben and the Politics of the Living Dead. *Diacritics* 30(4): 38–58.

Oppenheim, A. Leo
   1977   *Ancient Mesopotamia: Portrait of a Dead Civilization*. University of Chicago Press,
          Chicago.

Pizzato, Mark
    2005   *Theatres of Human Sacrifice: From Ancient Ritual to Screen Violence.* State University of New York Press, Albany, NY.

Price, Simon
    1984   *Rituals and Power: The Roman Imperial Cult in Asia Minor.* Cambridge University Press, Cambridge.

Quilter, Jeffrey
    1997   The Narrative Approach to Moche Iconography. *Latin American Antiquity* 8(2): 113–133.

Ray, Benjamin C.
    1991   *Myth, Ritual, and Kingship in Buganda.* Oxford University Press, Oxford.

Read, Kay A.
    1998   *Time and Sacrifice in the Aztec Cosmos.* Indiana University Press, Bloomington.

Robertson Smith, W.
    1894   *The Religion of the Semites.* A. and C. Black, London.

Rosaldo, Michelle Z., and Jane M. Atkinson
    1975   Man the Hunter and Woman: Metaphors for the Sexes in Ilongot Magical Spells. In *The Interpretation of Symbolism*, edited by Roy G. Willis, pp. 43–76. Wiley, New York.

Ruel, Malcolm
    1990   Non-Sacrificial Ritual Killing. *Man* 25(2): 323–335.

Sagan, Eli
    1993   *At the Dawn of Tyranny: The Origins of Individualism, Political Oppression and the State.* Fish Drum Press, Santa Fe, NM.

Samaniego, L., E. Vergara, and H. Bischof
    1982   New Evidence on Cerro Sechín, Casma Valley, Peru. In *Early Ceremonial Architecture in the Andes: A Conference at Dumbarton Oaks, 8th to 10th October 1982*, edited by Christopher B. Donnan, pp. 165–190. Dumbarton Oaks, Washington, D.C.

Scarry, Elaine
    1985   *The Body in Pain: The Making and Unmaking of the World.* Oxford University Press, Oxford.

Schechner, Richard (editor)
    1985   *Between Theater and Anthropology.* University of Pennsylvania Press, Philadelphia.

Schele, Linda
    1984   Human Sacrifice among the Classic Maya. In *Ritual Human Sacrifice in Mesoamerica*, edited by Elizabeth H. Boone, pp. 6–48. Dumbarton Oaks, Washington D.C.

Schele, Linda, and David Freidel
    1990   *A Forest of Kings: The Untold Story of the Ancient Maya.* Morrow, New York.

Schele, Linda, and Mary E. Miller
    1986   *The Blood of Kings: Dynasty and Ritual in Maya Art.* Kimbell Art Museum, Fort Worth, TX.

Scheper-Hughes, Nancy, and Philippe Bourgois
    2004   Introduction: Making Sense of Violence. In *Violence in War and Peace: An Anthology*, edited by Nancy Scheper-Hughes and Philippe Bourgois, pp. 1–31. Blackwell, Malden, MA.

Schobinger, John
    1991   Sacrifices of the High Andes. *Natural History* 100(4): 62–68.

Sered, Susan
    2002   Towards a Gendered Typology of Sacrifice: Women and Feasting, Men and Death in an Okinawan Village. In *Sacrifice in Religious Experience*, edited by Albert I. Baumgarten, pp. 13–38. Brill, Leiden.

Shimada, Izumi
    1994   *Pampa Grande and the Mochica Culture.* University of Texas Press, Austin.

Smith, Adam T.
    2006   The Spectacular in Urartian Images of Performance. In *Archaeology of Performance: Theaters of Power, Community, and Politics*, edited by Takeshi Inomata and Lawrence S. Coben, pp. 103–134. Altamira, New York.

Smith, Jonathan Z.
    1987   The Domestication of Sacrifice. In *Violent Origins: Walter Burkert, René Girard, and Jonathan Z. Smith on Ritual Killing and Cultural Formation*, edited by Robert G. Hamerton-Kelly, pp. 191–205. Stanford University Press, Stanford.

Stager, Lawrence E.
    1992   Carthage: A View from the Tophet. In *Karthago*, edited by Werner Huss, pp. 353–369. Wissenschaftliche Buchgessellschaft, Darmstadt.

Swenson, Edward
    2003   Cities of Violence: Sacrifice, Power, and Urbanization in the Andes. *Journal of Social Archaeology* 3(2): 256–296.

Tambiah, Stanley J.
    1979   A Performative Approach to Ritual. *Proceedings of the British Academy* 65: 113–169.

Turner, Victor W.
    1974   *Dramas, Fields, and Metaphors: Symbolic Action in Human Society.* Cornell University Press, Ithaca.
    1977   Sacrifice as Quintessential Process: Prophylaxis or Abandonment? *History of Religions* 16(3): 208–15.
    1982   *From Ritual to Theatre: The Human Seriousness of Play.* Performing Arts Journal Publications, New York.

Uceda, Santiago
    2001a El complejo arquitectónico religioso Moche de Huaca de la Luna: El templo del Dios de las Montañas. *Revista Arqueologica Sian* 11: 11–17.
    2001b Investigations at Huaca de la Luna, Moche Valley: An Example of Moche Religious Architecture. In *Moche Art and Archaeology in Ancient Peru*, edited by Joanne Pillsbury, pp. 47–68. Studies in the History of Art 63; Center for Advanced Studies in the Visual Arts, National of Gallery of Art, Washington D.C., Symposium Papers 40. Yale University Press, New Haven.

Uceda, Santiago, and Elias Mujica (editors)

    1994   *Moche: Propuestas y perspectiva.* Travaux de l'Institut Français d'Etudes Andines and the Universidad Nacional de la Libertad, Trujillo, Peru.

    2003   *Moche hacia el final del milenio.* Volumes 1 and 2. Fondo Editorial, Pontificia Universidad Católica del Perú and Universdad Nacional de Trujillo, Lima and Trujillo, Peru.

Uceda, Santiago, Ricardo Morlaes, José Canziani and María Montoya

    1994   Investigaciones sobre la arquitectura y relieves polícromos en la Huaca de la Luna, Valle de Moche. In *Moche: Propuestas y perspective*, edited by Santiago Uceda and Elias Mujica, pp. 251–306. Travaux de l'Institut Français d'Etudes Andines and the Universidad Nacional de la Libertad, Trujillo, Peru.

Valeri, Valerio

    1985   *Kingship and Sacrifice: Ritual and Society in Ancient Hawaii.* Translated by Paula Wissing. University of Chicago Press, Chicago.

Veblen, Thorstein

    1953   *The Theory of the Leisure Class: An Economic Study of Institutions.* New American Library, New York.

Verano, John W.

    2001   War and Death in the Moche World: Osteological Evidence and Visual Discourse. In *Moche Art and Archaeology in Ancient Peru*, edited by Joanne Pillsbury, pp. 111–126. Studies in the History of Art 63; Center for Advanced Studies in the Visual Arts, National of Gallery of Art, Washington D.C., Symposium Papers 40. Yale University Press, New Haven.

Weber, Max

    1966   *The Theory of Social and Economic Organization.* Translated by Talcott Parsons. Free Press, New York.

Zuidema, R. Tom

    1977   Shaft-tombs and the Inca Empire: Prehistoric Contact between Mesoamerica and South America: New Data and Interpretations. *Journal of the Steward Anthropological Society* 9: 133–78.

(Un)Dying Loyalty: Meditations on Retainer Sacrifice in Ancient Egypt and Elsewhere

Ellen F. Morris

Those theorists who have most famously spilt their ink on the relationship between violence, civilization, and sacrifice – Walter Burkert, René Girard, and others – have drawn their inspiration from myth, scripture, ritual, and from literature, but less often from ethnohistorical or archaeological records of sacrifice. Thus Abraham's near-sacrifice of Isaac has been discussed far more often than eye-witness accounts of human sacrifice or the many death-pits worldwide that have served as the repositories for corpses ritually killed. This essay is intended partially to redress this imbalance. Moreover, it focuses attention on a particularly under-theorized aspect of human sacrifice, the provision for a dead person of sacrificed retainers – of servants, sex partners, or others whose services the deceased could command in death, just as he or she had commanded them in life.

The type of sacrifice much more frequently discussed is that undertaken by a community to propitiate a deity thought either to be bloodthirsty or, perhaps, simply thirsty for tangible signs of that community's devotion. The gift of life given back to the gods served ostensibly to save life in the future by virtue of abundant harvests, success in war, divine forgiveness of community transgression, and the like. In such cases, the people sacrificed as gifts to the gods were often taken from categories of social actors deemed in some way already alienated from the community at large and therefore expendable (Girard 2005: 12–13; Law 1985: 60; Westermarck 1906: 467). Enemy combatants, criminals, and slaves are classic candidates for such ritual killings. Alternatively, the person whose life was offered up as a gift to the god might – like the quintessential virgin sacrifice – represent a human equivalent to the first-fruits or to the finest, fattest, and most unblemished beast. Souls of the newly slain might also be expected to fulfil a specific function, such as relaying an important message to those in the next world or protecting a structure erected over their own corpses (Davies 1984). In any case, human beings typically constituted the highest form of sacrifice, the most emphatic medium of request or praise it was possible for a community to offer (Ellis 1970: 119).

Attention to retainer sacrifice as a cross-cultural phenomenon has been far scantier – though the related custom of widow inhumation or incineration (as the individual case might be) has received somewhat more attention, due to Britain's former sovereignty over India. Even when retainer sacrifice has been addressed by archaeologists, however, it has rarely been taken farther than where V. Gordon Childe left it in the 1940s. According to him, "Royal Tombs, characterized by magnitude, extravagance of furniture, and the immolation of human victims, were all confined to a transitional stage in social development when a territorial state was replacing barbarian organizations" (Childe 1943: 118; see similarly Childe 1945: 18). Childe's assertion that such displays tend to coincide with sudden leaps in the scope of a polity's political power does indeed seem to fit the most infamous and extravagant displays of retainer sacrifice. One might cite, for example, the royal tombs of Ur, Kerma, Abydos and Saqqara in Egypt, Cahokia, and Sipan. Thus, when such retainer sacrifices are discussed broadly, they are most frequently interpreted as particularly dramatic examples of the conspicuous consumption typical of a state's first florescence. Along with Childe, scholarly opinion seems to hold that violence co-occurs with the rise of civilization. But, because it in itself is not civilized, one finds it typically abandoned or radically curtailed after the passage of only a few generations.

What I would like to do in the context of this necessarily brief essay is to push the discussion of retainer sacrifice a little further by posing three questions (or sets of questions) concerning retainer sacrifice, provoked in part by my own studies of the custom as it is manifested in First Dynasty Egypt and in part from readings on other instances of retainer sacrifice known from archaeological or historical records. The first asks how distinct a practice retainer sacrifice was from human sacrifice, given that – although scholars contrast the two traditions – they frequently occurred at the same ceremonies. The second asks questions concerned with the nature of the relationship – ideal *and* real – between the deceased and those sacrificed as part of his or her entourage. According to the official view, were lives sacrificed willingly out of love or fealty? Or were retainers viewed as functionally equivalent to grave goods – i.e., as possessions indicative of the deceased's wealth and power, objects to be disposed of freely? The third and final set of questions examines whether or not the trajectories of retainer sacrifice provide evidence that – despite the best efforts of elite ideologies – retainer sacrifices were viewed as violent by those who gave their lives, by those whose loved ones did, and by society at large.

I preface my contribution to this volume with a disclaimer. As an Egyptologist, I am well versed in the instances of retainer sacrifice that occurred in Egypt and in Kerma. It is my interest in these sacrifices that prompted me to look outwards to find other instances in which the motivations for participants in the ceremony of retainer sacrifice were even more clearly articulated than they were in Egypt. Seeking seemingly analogous situations, however, necessitates engaging with evidence from societies about which I have only a superficial knowledge. The questions posed herein are intended, thus, to provoke discussion, rather than to settle it. No claims are made as to the universality of the ideas or trends discussed. While the core of the investigation resides in Egypt, the essay ranges far and wide in the societies that it draws upon for inspiration, but it does not claim that all sacrificial events can or should be encompassed under the same theoretical framework. While eye-witness accounts of ritual killings are inevitably biased, and culture-specific subtleties will always remain obscure, I believe even flawed attempts at understanding cross-cultural patterning are preferable to a dogmatically imposed tunnel vision. In my view, then, this is not so much a study as it is a meditation on an under-served subject. If it has goals, it is to ask a series of generative questions and to address these, however incompletely or ineffectively, by looking out at the world at large.

Question One

Retainer sacrifice is often viewed as "essentially different" from the ritual killing of prisoners of war (Trigger 1978: 161), yet history and archaeology complicate this picture. Are the two practices indeed so different?

I would argue that they are not necessarily so. Childe's generalization – that retainer sacrifice is a practice that peaks in the period of instability initiated by a quantum leap in the power of a polity – holds true for Egypt, as it does in so many cases. And the birth of a new order, of course, is also a period often typified by state violence. New lands are forcibly conquered, internal rivals joust for power, and incipient rebellions must be constantly quelled. Prisoners of war, pictured both before and after their execution, certainly figure prominently in late protodynastic iconography. To take only the most famous example, the Narmer palette appears to commemorate the aftermath of a particularly important battle, and it showcases a deathblow on the verge of being dealt (Figure 3.1). While Narmer's is not the first smiting scene – this occurred in the "royal" Painted Tomb at Hierakonpolis some generations earlier – his hieratic pose was to become emblematic of pharaonic power for nearly 3,000 years.

Figure 3.1. The Narmer Palette. (After Kemp 2006: 84, fig. 27)

Narmer's palette informs us – as do later temple reliefs and battle
narratives – that after the frenzied killing of war came a ritualized and highly
public execution of captives. Narmer is depicted inflicting this punishment
personally on the most obviously important enemy on his palette, while
the execution of a great mass of other prisoners was apparently left to his
agents. Narmer and his officials are depicted inspecting the aftermath of this
work as evident in a field of bound and decapitated corpses. The fact that
each severed head is tucked neatly between the feet of the body it belonged
to demonstrates the meticulously orchestrated spectacle of the event. The
bodies are rearranged in such a precise and disturbing fashion because the
dehumanizing fate of Narmer's enemies was meant to be witnessed, to be
internalized, and to be communicated widely.

Although the meaning of the falcon and the boat carved above the
corpses is unclear, the niched façade surmounted by a Horus-falcon that
seemingly provides entrance to the grisly scene suggests that the captives had
been brought back to the royal capital and that the ceremonial execution
was thus emphatically situated at the very center of Egyptian kingship.
Such scenes of bound captives and ritual execution are staples of Narmer's

pictorial repertoire, and there is little reason to believe that such images were fashioned out of whole cloth. We infer from the vast range of territory in which artifacts bearing Narmer's name were found, from the sophistication of his commemorative artwork, and from the fact that the very next king was indisputably a King of Upper and Lower Egypt, that Narmer's conquests were instrumental in bringing the peoples of the Nile Valley under a single government. Such considerable conquests and consolidations could hardly have been undertaken without an ample application of violence.

So far as it is possible to tell, retainer sacrifice did not begin in earnest until the reign of Narmer's successor, Hor-Aha, although political leaders at Hierakonpolis and perhaps also Nagada experimented with the custom prior to the unification of Upper Egypt (Hoffman 1979: 114–116).[1] With Hor-aha, however, it is clear that just as the king's victory in battle demanded that he sacrifice enemy captives, so the death of the king now necessitated the death of others whose souls would accompany his into the next world. The graves of Hor-aha's sacrificed retainers were arrayed in lines behind his own tomb, as if their inhabitants were processing after the king in strict marching order to battle or court ceremony (Figure 3.2). Behind the triple chambers presumed to have constituted Hor-aha's tomb, there were two largish graves and then eleven rows of three graves each. A double-chambered grave at the rear of the procession originally contained the bodies, not of young men, as most of the others had, but of young lions, killed to enhance the ostentatiousness of the entourage (Dreyer et al. 1990: 86–89). Moreover, each successive First Dynasty ruler emulated Hor-aha's heir in surrounding the tomb – and in some cases the funerary enclosure – of their predecessor with rows upon rows of sacrificed retainers.

In Egypt, the physical evidence so far analyzed from these graves appears consistent with what we would expect for sacrificed retainers. The bodies were interred intact in an apparently respectful manner and were most often provisioned with grave goods of some sort. The bones that have been analyzed bear no signs of trauma, other than perhaps a pinkish tinge of the teeth that may be indicative of death by strangulation (Galvin 2005: 120). If these bodies were indeed strangled, it is possible that this mode of death, as in the Asante kingdom, was viewed as aristocratic "because blood is not shed and there is not any mutilation" (Rattray 1927: 109). Certainly, no bodies were without their heads, and no heads bore the crushing impact of a blow from a mace. There is, however, evidence from three First Dynasty labels that may indicate that other deaths, besides those of retainers, heightened the pageantry of the royal funeral (Figure 3.3).

Two of the labels were discovered in Hor-aha's tomb complex (Petrie 1901: pls. 3.4, 3.6) and depict the ritual killing of a person – pinioned in the manner

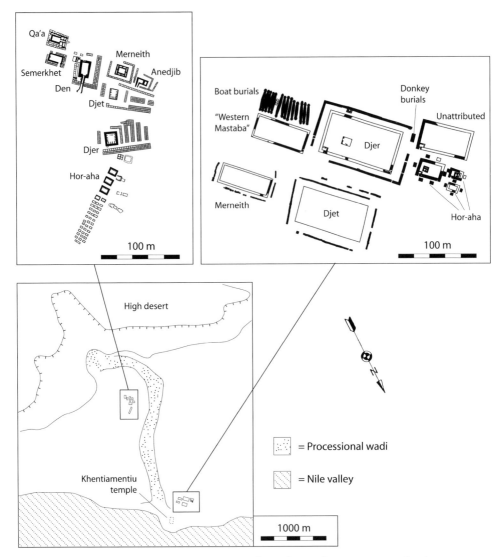

Figure 3.2. First Dynasty Abydos. (Courtesy of Laurel Bestock; Morris 2007a: fig. 1)

of a prisoner of war – just outside the royal palace. Underneath the label "receiving (from) Upper and Lower Egypt" (šsp šm ʿw mḥw), the executioner plunges a dagger into the chest of the victim and catches his blood with a bowl, in the same manner as countless butchers in tomb scenes and models catch the blood of cattle. Just to the right of the sacrifice is a standard bearing

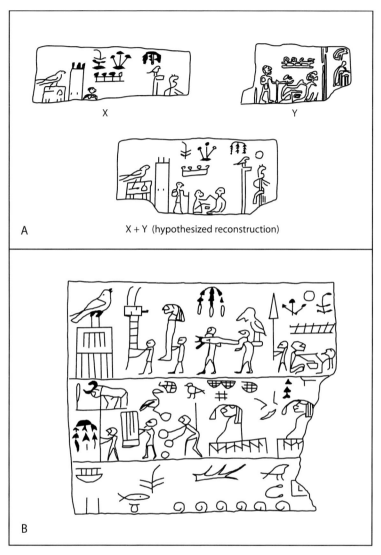

Figure 3.3. Labels showing human sacrifice. (A) from Hor-aha's tomb at Abydos; (B) from mastaba 2035 at Saqqara. (After Crubézy and Midant-Reynes 2000: 30; Emery 1938: 35; Morris 2007a: fig. 3)

the royal god Horus and an imy-wt fetish. This fetish, versions of which were also fashioned in the reigns of the First Dynasty kings Den and Semerkhet (Wilkinson 2000: 196, 242), is closely associated with the god Anubis, who oversaw the king's transition at death into a full-fledged god. It is tempting to speculate that the associated annotation – "ms(t)" (meaning "to create") – may indicate that the sacrifices of individuals taken from the south and the north coincided with the fashioning of one or both royal fetishes and thus that, like the famous nail fetishes of the Bakongo, these religious foci were animated or enriched by the souls of sacrificial victims (Gell 1998: 59–61). The third label, discovered in the most massive mastaba of its time at Saqqara (3035; Emery 1938: 35), shows the same šsp šm ʿw mḥw-ceremony of sacrifice. This time, it occurs in conjunction with what looks to be the "ms(t)"-creation of funerary images, perhaps corpses wrapped in linen. The line of humans bearing these images processes towards the name of King Djer. While it is not certain that these scenes of sacrifice take place in conjunction with a royal funeral, the central imagery surrounding the rite is linked to the "fashioning" of powerful entities that perhaps aided in the spiritual transfiguration of the deceased king.

If the evidence for the co-occurrence of retainer sacrifice and the sacrifice of prisoners of war in conjunction with royal funerals in Egypt is admittedly tenuous, this practice is well attested in archaeological and ethnohistoric records from other societies. Certainly, in the royal tombs of Late Shang China, in Mound 72 at Cahokia, and perhaps even at the Feathered Serpent Temple at Teotihuacan (if, as some scholars have suggested, the sacrifices there were meant not only to dedicate the building, but also to equip a royal burial), bound and/or decapitated corpses shared company with others, whose bodily integrity and arrangement, associated accoutrements, sex, age, and/or regional affiliation present a stark and meaningful contrast.

In the Shang royal tombs at Anyang, sacrificed retainers were generally interred just outside the tomb chamber on ledges and niches. These burials were respectfully laid out in relatively close proximity to the main burial, and the bodies were often equipped with grave goods. Guards, occasionally armed with jade or bronze weapons and accompanied by a dog, were found in the waist pit, closer to the outer extremity of the tomb. In contrast to these bodies, carefully arranged and equipped, excavators also found numerous dismembered bodies at the entrances and extremities of the royal tombs. These were frequently headless and had their arms tied behind their backs in much the same manner as the sacrificial victims on the Narmer palette and the Egyptian labels. Such corpses were either arranged in rows or splayed about in what looked to be death-pits, and grave goods were notably absent (Campbell 2007: 231–234, 239).

Rod Campbell's (2007: 234) study of Shang burials at Anyang suggests that what distinguished the royal burials from others in the cemetery (in addition, of course, to their greater size and opulence) was the presence of large-scale human sacrifice. While retainer sacrifices were found in both large and medium graves (and, very rarely, in small graves), bound and dismembered corpses were associated in appreciable numbers only with the largest tombs. Thus, counter-intuitively, the killing of social outsiders at one's funeral and at commemorative events afterward appears to have been more prestigious (in the sense of being socially restricted) than retainer sacrifice. Perhaps this indicates that the victims had been prisoners of war and so represented tangible symbols of the king's prowess in battle. Alternatively or additionally, the royal co-option of human sacrifice may indicate that human lives represented the most prestigious gift it was possible to offer the ancestors and so access to such sacrifices needed to be strictly regulated (Campbell 2007: 183–184).

The sacrificial victims interred in conjunction with high-status burials at Mound 72 in Cahokia offer an interesting parallel to the Shang burials, although the relationship between the high-status burials, contemporary sacrifices, and commemorative sacrifices is more difficult to disentangle. Mound 72 appears to have been constructed over a period of 50 years at most, during which time some 265 corpses were distributed into 25 burial units. It appears that at least 161 of these individuals had been sacrificed at the death of other higher-status personages. The deaths of the retainers, arranged carefully about the main burials, seem to have been supplemented by the deaths of numerous young women. These females, interred in four mass graves in two careful layers separated by matting were mostly between 15 and 25 years of age. Dental morphology suggests that many came from outside the community – perhaps as tribute, as captives, or as wives drawn from subject populations. Four men buried together overlooking one of these mass graves were also sacrifices, but these men lacked heads and hands. Further, a jumbled mass of 39 people interred below a series of respectful litter burials had been carelessly tossed into their pit. The projectile point wounds and decapitations of some of these victims suggested that they came from a population of war captives. So here again, especially prominent individuals had been buried together with others, killed on the occasion of their death and also, apparently, afterwards in commemoration of it. As with the Shang royal tombs, the sacrificial victims at Cahokia were sharply divided into those treated with care and others whose corpses had been deliberately disrespected (Fowler et al. 1999: 3, 11, 63–82; Pauketat 2004: 87–92).

To supplement the picture gained from archaeology, the practice of slaying both retainers and prisoners of war together at royal funerals is attested in reports concerning Dahomey and Asante, in addition to other West African kingdoms. After Dahomey had conquered its former overlords, the ritual killings associated with royal funerals purportedly skyrocketed. At the funeral of King Kpengla in 1789, reports suggest that over a period of two years some 1,500 people were killed. These included 595 wives and numerous prisoners of war. Sixty-eight captives were killed on the royal corpse's journey to the capital, 48 on the way to his tomb, and 300 at the tomb itself. Then, at the Grand Customs held the following year to commemorate the funeral, a further 500 men, women, and children were killed (Dalzel 1793: 204–205, 224, 226; Law 1985: 68). While these numbers appear exaggerated – and may indeed have been – the many hundreds of sacrificial victims discovered in the individual interments of Egyptian, Nubian, and Chinese rulers, demonstrate that such a flagrant expenditure of human life in the course of a royal funeral is not entirely inconceivable.

Like the kings of Dahomey, Asante rulers were accompanied in their death by wives, officials, and servants, but also ritually murdered slaves and criminals killed by the hundreds and (purportedly) thousands. Such sacrifices gave certain royal centers the reputation of being "cities of blood." Although the bodies associated with the Asante royal graves have not been excavated, the observation that the wives and retainers were sent to their deaths dressed in their finest clothes, stupefied with intoxicants, and strangled suggests that they would not have been difficult to discern from the many hundreds of prisoners and criminals summarily executed at the same funeral and interred outside the royal tomb (Law 1985: 70; Parrinder 1956: 113).

So what accounts for this relatively frequent pairing of retainer and human sacrifice, given that the underlying rationales behind the two types of deaths seem so disparate? I would argue that two factors in particular may lie at the heart of this unusual combination. First, there is the desire of those heavily invested in the success of a new kingship to cope with the death of its figurehead by simultaneously enhancing, dematerializing, and rendering royal authority eternal. The second factor may be the urge of a new – or newly threatened – polity to construct and model in microcosm a world order in which the state is all-powerful, and both internal and external realms are properly pacified. As I will argue below, indulging in human and retainer sacrifices is one way to accomplish both sets of goals. It should be stated, however, that in both cases one of the prerequisites and prompts for choosing such a strategy may have been an exponential increase in subjects and in enshackled enemies due to intensified military activity.

Rulers who practiced mortuary sacrifice with the greatest abandon seem to have been those who were experimenting, as Childe suggested, with ways to express their greatly increased power and to keep a firm grip upon it in this life and the next. For First Dynasty Egypt, Shang China, and Cahokia, this assessment makes sense. Conquests had radically augmented the size of these kingdoms and a royal mandate had been established to continually expand, consolidate, and protect them (Campbell 2007: 9; Hoffman 1979: 279; Pauketat 2004: 167). It also holds true for the Asante and Dahomey kingdoms, although it is fascinating that funerary sacrifices in these two regions were ratcheted up again when suppression of the slave trade left their rulers with the equivalent of human overstock (Law 1985: 69–70, 74, 77–78; Wilks 1993: 227).

Orlando Patterson (1982) argues that in many societies prisoners of war turned slaves were viewed as socially dead, for they had been spared death only in order to completely devote themselves to the service of another. Although undoubtedly violent, the large-scale killing of prisoners of war at a king's funeral or in the type of public ceremony depicted in the aftermath of wars on the Narmer Palette and on Egyptian pylons may not have been viewed as untoward by onlookers. The battlefield execution of such prisoners had essentially been deferred until the desired audience could be mustered to witness it. Indeed, Richard Burton observed in the 1860's that the Dahomey ceremonies showcasing human sacrifice "are, in fact, the yearly execution, as if all the murderers in Britain were kept for hanging on a certain day in London" (quoted in Law 1985: 60). Interestingly, in the Asante Kingdom there was an entire village of prisoners who lived their lives under a death sentence and thus constituted an available pool of victims to be sacrificed when occasion demanded (Rattray 1927: 106). Moreover, Chinese lexical evidence suggests that this type of prisoner, who lived only in order to die spectacularly, may have had equivalents in the *fa*-captives of Shang times. Referred to collectively as "those-to-be-decapitated," this subset of the population was defined both by the inevitability and the precise manner of their death (Campbell, Ch. 4, this volume).

The death of a king – which occasioned such sacrifices in certain societies – is the single greatest cyclically recurrent point of vulnerability for a kingdom. This is especially so if the power of the state is not yet internalized as an unalterable fact of life. At his death, the royal authority of the old king is dematerialized, and the power of his heir has yet to be established. In the context of a young kingdom, then, sacrifice is a way to simultaneously advertise the power of the new king and to perpetuate the power of the old king. Societies that practiced retainer sacrifice evidently believed that it was essential for the king to arrive in the next world attended by dependents who would continue their services and/or devotions eternally. To modern minds, the "continuance theory" underlying retainer sacrifice requires little imagination to comprehend. But why provision the king with the sacrifices of other human beings in addition to his servants and loved ones?

The answer almost certainly has to do with the potential of human sacrifice to dramatically mark the royal apotheosis, the king's transfiguration into an entirely different order of being. Even in an established divine kingship like Egypt, the king only unambiguously attains the status of a god after his death.

When the king is not divine on earth, death represents an even more important transition, for it is only when he enters the realm of the ancestors that he can affect great wonders (Cannadine 1987: 8; Richards 1968: 27). The funeral of a king can thus be viewed as akin to the fashioning of a new idol – much like the Egyptian labels discussed above seem to depict. Fetishes and idols in many cultures required the gift of human lives to activate and sustain them. Further, the king, as an ancestor, now required sacrifices in an analogous manner to other people's ancestors and to gods. If ordinary people offered sacrificial animals to ordinary ancestors, however, and if dead kings needed to be distinguished from ordinary ancestors, what better way to accomplish this than by violating the taboos against taking a human life that extend to all others but the king and his delegates (Campbell 2007: 183–184; Herskovits 1938: 54–55; Law 1985: 74–76)? If violence is a jealously guarded Weberian monopoly of the state, the violence toward people that has the power to transform them into escorting souls, on the one hand, and sustenance on the other, showcases the power of the dead and living king alike – at least at first. The ultimate effectiveness of this experiment will be addressed in subsequent sections.

In the aftermath of the sort of conquest that fashions a great kingdom, there is typically no shortage of prisoners of war or of those caught attempting to break newly imposed rules. Sacrificing prisoners of war is one answer to a dilemma of what to do with large quantities of people whose potential for domestication appears limited. Killing such people not only eliminates the problem that they themselves constituted, but, as an act of terror, it serves as a lesson to all who might act against the state. The thousands killed at the death of Dahomey King Kplenga have been discussed above. In this practice, however, his heir was simply following Kplenga's own lead. This king rationalized his employment of human sacrifice to a European observer, stating: "you have seen me kill many men at the customs… This gives a grandeur to my customs, far beyond the display of fine things which I buy. This makes my enemies fear me, and gives me such a name in the bush" (Dalzel 1793: 220). Such a sentiment is similar to one offered by a nineteenth-century Asante king, who stated simply "If I were to abolish human sacrifices, I should deprive myself of one of the most effectual means of keeping the people in subjection" (Wilks 1975: 594). Clearly, the real function of sacrifice for these kings was its utility in establishing and maintaining a terrible awe among the populace. To quote Bruce Lincoln (2012: 84), by means of such elaborate human sacrifices these rulers were "producing – and perpetuating – a docile, compliant, and semi-objectified state among the community of the fearful."

The killing of prisoners of war at the death of a king, then, perhaps was not at all separate from the killing of retainers, but rather a perfect counterpart. One act of violence communicated the king's power in life and death over those frightening and chaotic entities outside his realm. The other demonstrated his all encompassing power over the very core of his kingdom and the tenet that his, indeed, was a state worth dying for. As Campbell (Ch.4, this volume) has concluded with respect to the Shang, the simultaneous, performative act of human and retainer sacrifice "instantiate(d) and reproduce(d) hierarchies of being fundamental to the Shang civilizational order." Moreover, it "fed the honor and status of the sacrificer at the expense of the sacrificed even as their relative status was marked in the permanence of death" (Campbell 2007: 184). Indeed it is fascinating to see this ideological juxtaposition of insider vs. outsider embodied in the positioning of the representatives of these categories at death. In Shang royal tombs and at Cahokia, for instance, retainers ringed the core burials, while sacrificed foreigners and societal outsiders occupied the periphery. Thus tomb became realm, and the ruler retained his rightful place at its dead center for all eternity.

Question 2

If retainers symbolize a ruler's relationship with his or her subjects – the inhabitants of the kingdom's core – what is the nature of that relationship? Is it akin to the love and devotion offered by a wife or a child to the head of a family? Or are the ruler's subjects literally or figuratively slaves – property that can be possessed and taken to the grave?

Undoubtedly, Childe would have espoused the latter view. In his observations on directional changes in funerary practices over the last 50,000 years, he concluded first that state stability correlated with a societal-wide decrease in the conspicuous consumption associated with funerals and, second, that stability also led to the curtailment of retainer sacrifice (Childe 1943: 117–118). The notion that sexual partners and servants were viewed as possessions and that their souls simply supplemented a ruler's other grave-goods finds support in certain ethnohistorical accounts of retainer sacrifice. The functionaries called to accompany the king to his death in Baganda, for instance, included the chief cook, the chief brewer, the chief over the herdsmen, as well as women in charge of cooking, brewing, the bed chamber, the water, the king's clothing, and the king's milk. About these individuals it was said, for instance, "Her beer-gourd is broken, for whom should she draw beer?" (Roscoe 1966: 106). In Asante too, palace employees and slaves were killed in order to accompany the king, and chiefs provided the dead king with humans to be sacrificed in addition to (other) sumptuous grave goods (Rattray 1927: 109–112). Similarly, at the Grand Customs of Dahomey "a representative of each army corps, a weaver, a smith, a woman potter, a cloth-worker, a wood-carver, a farmer, and a man and woman from each village in the kingdom were sacrificed" in order to provide the dead king with services in the next world (Herskovits 1938: 53).

This utilitarian attitude towards retainer sacrifice was not restricted to African kingdoms. At the funeral of the Maharaja of Jaipur in 1818, the royal barber was one of the 36 victims burnt upon the pyre, so that he might continue to shave his lord in the next world (Thompson 1928: 38). Further, according to Herodotus, Scythian kings were buried together with a complete domestic staff.

> Then they strangle one of the king's concubines and also his cupbearer, his cook, his groom, his principal servant, his courier, and his horses, and they bury them all in the remaining open space of the grave, along with the prized possessions dedicated by others… After they have done all this, everyone enthusiastically joins up in building up a huge mound, which they strive together to make as large as possible. One year later, they attend to the rites again. They first choose the most suitable of the surviving servants; these are native Scythians, for all whom the king orders to become his servants must do so, and servants are not bought and sold among these Scythians. Of these they strangle fifty males, and also fifty of the king's best horses…. After arranging these horsemen in a circle around the burial site, they ride away [Herodotus IV.70–71].

The recent discovery of a Scythian burial with roughly 1,000 people arranged along its perimeter suggests that in this case, at least, Herodotus' reports may not have been exaggerated.[2] Very similar satellite retainer burials have been discovered around Mongolian graves of the nomadic Xiongnu culture from roughly the same period (Allard et al. 2002). Shang soldiers, interred with their weapons and their dogs, provide yet another archaeological example of such functional death attendants, although the Royal Tombs at Ur still provide the most fuel for the imagination. The differing roles of the retainers in these Mesopotamian tombs were easily distinguished by virtue of their association with harps, lamps, oxen-drawn chariots, weapons, and other evocative accoutrements (Woolley 1965: 52–81).

In Egypt, where the majority of retainers seem to have been provisioned with grave goods from a central store, such functional differences are difficult to discern. An unusually massive mastaba at Saqqara (3503), contemporary with the reign of Merneith, is an interesting exception. This monument was surrounded with subsidiary graves, and based on the individualized nature of their contents the excavator felt sure the inhabitants of each had plied a particular trade: boat-builder, artist, vasemaker, potter, butcher, and the like (Emery 1954: 142, 1961: 67–68, 139). Such differentiation is less visible in the subsidiary tombs at Abydos, because of their extremely disturbed state and sparse records. Graves with arrowheads, animal skins, and other seemingly meaningful artifacts, however, did cluster in specific areas of the subsidiary graves at Abydos. Thus, it is not unlikely that retainers had originally been grouped together according to their specific roles or occupations (Bestock 2009: 34–35, 49–50).

As an additional line of evidence, the limestone stelae that served as memorials for specific Abydene retainers are particularly useful. The stelae preserve titles suggesting that these individuals ranged from soldiers to moderately high religious and/or palace officials, although the correlation of duties with titles in the latter cases is often obscure (Petrie 1925: 3; Kaplony 1963: 364–376). Further, it is fascinating to observe that different monarchs seem to have had differing ideas of who they desired to be surrounded by in death. Hor-aha's retainers, buried prior to the tradition of fashioning memorial stelae, appear from skeletal evidence to have been virtually all males, killed at the peak of their physical prowess (Dreyer 1993: 11). His successor, however, evidently preferred to surround himself with women, if the ratio of 76 stelae of females to 11 of males is at all reflective of reality (Kaplony 1963: 215). In the reign of the next king, King Djet, the pendulum evidently swung back the other way, for data suggest that his retainers were primarily male (Bestock 2009: 36). The relatively consistent inclusion of dwarves in the entourages of deceased kings – witnessed in both epigraphic and physical evidence – is also worth remark. These individuals almost certainly belonged to the corps of "palace dwarves," known from Old Kingdom texts, whose job it was to attend the king (Kaplony 1963: 374–375; Petrie 1900: 13 and pl. 60; Petrie 1901: pl. 28; Strudwick 2005: 247).

So, here in Egypt as well, rulers were buried with categories of individuals who could perform specific services for them in the afterlife, just as their slain hunting dogs might accompany them on future hunts, and the donkeys and boats buried outside select funerary enclosures would no doubt aid in transporting them by water and land. If the differing observed instances of porotic hyperostosis in the burials surrounding the kings' tombs and their funerary enclosures are meaningful, this too may suggest that the interment of sacrificed retainers patterned according to the nature of their backgrounds and duties (Keita and Boyce 2006: 70–71). Certainly, the fact that the walls of many subsidiary graves bore the names of their intended occupants indicates that significant forethought went into which individuals (or categories of individuals) would accompany the king and where such people would be most appropriately placed.

If, according to Bruce Lincoln (2012: 83), "we can best theorize violence as the deployment of physical force in a manner that tends to convert subjects – individual or collective, but in either case fully human actors – into depersonalized objects," retainer sacrifice should indeed be classified as a violent act. It is likely safe to say that the bakers, brewers, and soldiers interred with the king were required to die and that their own thoughts on the matter mattered little. People and things in such burials were equated – both interred because of their potential utility to the dead and also (as will be discussed shortly) because the wealth and power it took to procure such things and such people-things inspired awe.

But this is not the sole story, even within specific large-scale instances of retainer sacrifice. Ethnohistoric records from India, China, and Africa indicate that popular ideology in these societies held that at least a core of wives and retainers sacrificed their lives willingly, even ecstatically, out of overriding emotions of love, fealty, and deep personal grief. In Dahomey, for instance, it was stated that "as soon as the king expired, the women of the palace commenced breaking up the furniture, ornaments, and utensils, and then proceeded to destroy themselves" (Ellis 1970: 128). The women killed in these (ostensibly) grief-stricken frenzies could number in the hundreds. Likewise, the wives of the Asante king, said to have lost their desire to live once "the great tree had fallen, compelled their relatives to slay them by swearing the great oath that they must do so, thus not leaving them any option but to carry out their wishes" (Rattray 1927: 107). The suicides of women, whose reason to live had died with their husband or lover, are found wherever retainer sacrifices are – and some of the more (in)famous instances from India and China will be discussed in greater detail below. In New World societies, as in those of the Old, women followed men to the grave because of the intensity of their love – or so the stories go. Indeed, so many royal wives purportedly volunteered to accompany the Inka king in death that some were denied the privilege (de la Vega 1871: 113).

In these societies, the self-sacrifice of a wife was deemed more noble than that of a female servant by virtue not only of her higher status, but also of her higher love (theoretically at least). Analogously, the death of a chief minister meant more than that of an overseer of herdsmen, presumably because of the grandee's greater freedom to choose his destiny and also the correspondingly greater splendor of all that he willingly left behind. In the eyes of others, then, his self-chosen death was the greater sacrifice. This concept is aptly illustrated by a mournful Chinese poem (also discussed by Campbell, Ch. 4, this volume), which was written in honor of three of the 177 victims who perished at the funeral of the Zhou Period ruler Duke Mu of Qin in 621 B.C. "Who went with Duke Mu to the grave? Yen-hsi of the clan Tzu-chü. Now this Yen-hsi was the pick of all our men; But as he drew near the tomb-hole his limbs shook with dread. That blue one, Heaven, takes all our good men. Could we but ransom him there are a hundred would give their lives" (quoted in Chang 1974: 6–7). Each of the three most worthy men who followed Duke Mu to the death, then, was worth a hundred others. It was their deaths that were construed as tragic, not those of the 174 lesser-status retainers whose collective sacrifice did not merit a mention.

The self-sacrifice of male as well as female intimates of the king is reported for many societies that practiced retainer sacrifice. Among the Yoruba, for instance, it was part of the job description of the King's Friend to poison himself out of grief at the death of the king. Perhaps not surprisingly, this office was a particularly lucrative one while the occupant and his king lived, for the King's Friend was awarded first pick from any gifts or booty that the king distributed to his nobles (Morton-Williams 1967: 56). Moreover, among the Asante, individuals who volunteered to die with the king were especially honored in life and allowed not only to choose their manner of death, but also the articles that they wished to take with them, and their funerary rites were fully funded (Rattray 1927: 109; Bowdich 1966 [1819]: 291). Undoubtedly, the quality of the grave goods and the pomp of the funeral would have been far greater than such individuals could have otherwise expected.

This ranking and explicit acknowledgement that some deaths were worth more than others is aptly materialized in Hor-aha's complex, wherein the first two graves following his were significantly larger than the others. Moreover, both the size of the tombs and the amount of grave goods interred within them steadily decreased the farther back one moved in the rows (Dreyer et al. 1990: 63, 66). From one of the especially large front graves came a number of ivory items, including a comb and box that bore the only name besides Hor-aha's found in the entire complex. Bnr-ib can be translated as "Sweetheart" and is generally presumed to have designated a secondary wife of the king, although this cannot be proven. Certainly, the name is reminiscent of some borne by women who had burnt on the funerary pyres of the Bikanir Rajas, such as Love's Delight, Virtue Found, Soft Eye, Comfort, Love-lorn, Eye-play, Love-bud, Glad Omen, or, especially, Dear Heart (Thompson 1928: 47). If Laurel Bestock, who has excavated the two funerary enclosures that complimented Hor-aha's enclosure, is correct in her theory that these installations honored family members of the king, it may have been that part of the compensation for a royal woman to give up her life to accompany her husband in death – in this reign at least, when the practice was new – was the provision of a funerary enclosure, complete with sacrificed retainers of her own (Bestock 2009: 100). Interestingly, where it was possible to tell at Abydos, the largest and richest subsidiary graves located closest to the king's chamber tended to belong to women (Bestock 2009: 26–27; 33–35).

Due to its relative lack of disturbance, an even more nuanced understanding of the rankings of First Dynasty death attendants can be ascertained in the cemetery at Saqqara informally known as Macramallah's rectangle (Figure

3.4). Here some 230 burials laid out in meticulous rows flanked an empty area that Werner Kaiser (1985) has argued, with good reason, was occupied by King Den's body while it lay in state, but before it fared southward for burial at Abydos. If Kaiser is correct, the richest group of burials by far was located to the right of where the king's body would have been, i.e., the traditional place of honor, as the cemetery was oriented toward the south (Group E; see Figure 3.4). Groups A and F ranked next in status and were amply provided for, while the poorest graves – excavated with the least care, provided with the fewest grave goods and the shabbiest protection for the body – were situated at the very back (Groups B/C and especially D). From this vantage, if all the death attendants were envisioned as alive and standing at a ceremony, these individuals would hardly have been able to see (Morris 2007a).

Such elaborate choreography seems also to have been present in the subsidiary burials at Abydos, where on the basis of architecture alone one can easily identify graves that would have been the equivalent of box seats – final resting places that were larger than the others and closer to the king (Bestock 2009: 35, 36; Reisner 1936: 106–107). In the funerary enclosure complexes too, there were particularly posh subsidiary graves, and these generally were located to either side of an ever-present and presumably ritually important gap in the eastern corner of the subsidiary graves (O'Connor 1989: 80–81; Bestock 2009: 60). Similarly, as at Saqqara, retainer graves in the royal cemetery got smaller and poorer the farther they were situated from the king's own grave (Bestock 2009: 27–28, 32, 34–35).

These staged performances of death, as seem to be preserved eternally in Macramallah's rectangle and around the royal tombs at Abydos, perhaps offer a clue as to the motivations of those who were able – to some extent at least – to make up their own minds as to whether to accompany their sovereign to the grave. In return for giving up their earthly life, certain benefits were no doubt offered: the biggest graves and most grave goods, perhaps, for those who were perceived as making the biggest sacrifice; memorialization for those who otherwise would receive no monument to their passing; an afterlife in the shining retinue of the one person whose soul who would surely receive an afterlife, if such existed (see Campbell, Ch. 4, this volume, for similar speculation about the Shang sacrificial burials). And, finally, a key supporting role in one of the greatest spectacles that any given individual was likely to witness in his or her lifetime, that is if one is allowed extrapolate on analogy with eye-witness accounts of the highest-tier suttee ceremonies in India, China, and elsewhere, and from Woolley's "gaily dressed crowd" of royal retainers at Ur (Woolley 1965: 72; see also de Groot 1967: 736, 748–749; Johnson 1966: 54–57; Parrinder 1956: 113, 117; Rattray 1927: 108–111; Swanton 1911: 139–141; Thompson 1928: 51).

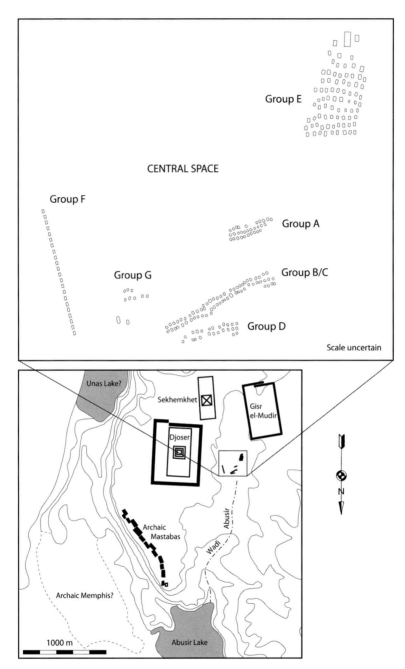

Figure 3.4. Macramallah's cemetery at Saqqara. (After Macramallah 1940: pl. 2; Lehner 1997: 83; Morris 2007a: fig. 4)

Given the material rewards bestowed upon those who appear to have sacrificed their lives willingly in Egypt, one wonders whether there was also a reflected glow of praise once the decision had been made that bolstered the resolve of the royal wife or retainer. The honors laden upon Chinese widows who resolved to sacrifice their lives, for instance, were numerous:

> Such self-destruction of wives and brides… have always been greatly encouraged by public opinion. Moralists vied with each other in extolling such women to the skies… The greatest distinction that can be conferred on mortal man in China, viz. rewards and honors from the Son of Heaven himself, have been bestowed upon many suttees. We read of imperial emissaries being commissioned to worship the suttee woman in her house… But since the fifth century it has become more especially customary for emperors to glorify sutteeites by conferring upon them an honorary inscription, to be written or engraved upon a tablet suspended over the door of their dwelling or the gate of their village; and from this arose the custom of erecting special gates for the exhibition of such tablets [de Groot 1967: 745–746].

Hindu widows received similar memorials (Thompson 1928: 30–32, 46). Indeed, according to sacred scriptures, a widow through her sacrifice could simultaneously save her husband from great sins, sanctify her ancestors, and achieve the highest honors imaginable (Mukhodpadhyay 1957: 102). As Thompson writes in his study on the custom of widow sacrifice, "about the death of a sati there was so much pomp and noise of applause, and about the memory of one such praise and exaltation, that often a psychological intoxication upheld her till she had passed beyond the reach of succour" (Thompson 1928: 50). Such public approbations, especially when lavished upon those unused to applause, undoubtedly helped recruit and retain death attendants in other cultures as well.

When posing the question of who benefitted from the custom of retainer sacrifice, the net may widen to encompass not only the ruler and those retainers that chose to accompany him and were duly compensated, but also quite likely the families that surrendered members to the sovereign's service in the hereafter. The family of a Chinese self-sacrificing widow – even one whose husband was not royal – received state help defraying the costs of the funeral and often much-coveted visits from imperial emissaries (de Groot 1967: 746, 749). A rise in the status of the families of royal death attendants is certainly noted among the Yoruba. Further, if a death attendant lost heart, he or she was apt to be strangled by a relative so that the family would not fall into disgrace and lose the honor accrued to them (Johnson 1966: 57; Parrinder 1956: 117). In an even more explicit example of social promotion, families of those individuals who joined the posthumous retine of the brother of the Great Sun of the Natchez peoples of Mississippi in 1725 executed their relatives themselves and were accordingly raised from the level of "Stinkards" to that of "Honored men" (Swanton 1911: 145–146).

In addition to social advancement in life, the families of death attendants may also have desired to provide themselves with an intercessor, whose spirit could speak to that of the dead king on their behalf. Baser motives yet, however, likely motivated some families, for the personal property of the deceased attendant was in many cases redistributed to living family members to compensate them for their loss. A report from the 1867 edition of the *Calcutta Review* summarizes the complicated web that enabled and exacerbated such sacrificial excesses. By virtue of participation:

> …the son was relieved from the expense of maintaining a mother; the male relatives, reversioners in the absence of direct issue, came in at once for the estate which the widow would have held for her life; the Brahmins were paid for their services and were interested in the maintenance of their religion; and the crowd attended the show with the savage merriment exhibited by an English crowd at a boxing match or a bull-fight [Quoted in Thompson 1928: 47–48].

In one widely reported instance, a royal widow issued a scathing rebuke to her relatives and court officers just prior to ascending the pyre, exposing publically their avarice and lack of empathy (Thompson 1928: 84–85). In general, however, such pecuniary motives remained well cloaked in an ideology that trumpeted sentiments of honor, fealty, and great love.

Question 3

If so many benefited from retainer sacrifice – at least in theory – why should the practice have been abandoned in those societies that persisted beyond their first florescence? Similarly, is it right to consider retainer and/or widow sacrifice a violent act?

To take the second question first, I would argue that once the invisible line between an elected and an expected practice has been crossed, and once the scale of sacrifice has been expanded to include not just a small circle of intimates but an entire cast and crew, the likelihood of the harmonious melding of the real and the ideal dramatically decreases. A typical trajectory for retainer sacrifice is impossible to ascertain, given imperfect records, the accident of conquest or colonial interference, and cultural differences between various societies. It does seem, however, as Childe (1943, 1945) noted long ago, that the scale of retainer sacrifice ratcheted up significantly with a sudden increase in the size and power of a polity. Rulers, who had previously not belonged to a dramatically different class from the upper crust of their subjects, worked hard to distinguish themselves after such an expansion – funding wildly elaborate funerals and sacrificing different orders of beings to their ancestors, for instance.

At the same time in many societies, the practice of retainer sacrifice could be emulated by the inner circle of the wealthiest and most powerful elites. This set off its own dynamic, whereby elites vied with one another to emulate royalty, and royalty felt the need to distinguish themselves from the upper echelons of their followers. Thus, the wasteful expenditure of human life – of the life of the lower classes – became a strategy in conspicuous consumption.

> The increasing scale of human sacrifice evident in some West African societies can therefore be linked to the increasing concentration of wealth, in the form of wives and slaves, in the hands of wealthy and powerful individuals. In some instances, it is true, slaves were purchased specifically for sacrifice rather than (or as well as) being selected from the household of the deceased, but this practice obviously also reflects the same process of the concentration of wealth. Funeral sacrifices increased in scale not merely as an incidental by-product of this concentration of wealth, but also as a means of advertising wealth to the community and thereby ensuring that it conferred commensurate prestige. Human sacrifice can be seen as a particular form of the conspicuous consumption in which wealthy men in pre-colonial West Africa habitually indulged in the quest for social standing [Law 1985: 73].

As Olfert Dapper (1998 [1668]: 16) observed with regard to seventeenth-century Benin, "nobody important dies there without it costing people blood." Sometimes, the cost in blood was labelled clearly. In fifth-century B.C. China, for instance, the sage Mo Tzu stated that "in the case of a Son of Heaven anywhere from several ten to several hundred persons will be sacrificed, while in the case of generals or high ministers the number will be from several to several tens" (Mo Tzu et al. 1967: 67). This carefully calibrated scale of sacrifice exposes the role of this practice in helping to distinguish kings from grandees and grandees from those who served them. The evident need for clearly stated sumptuary regulations, however, suggests that certain members of the elite had a vested interest in blurring boundaries.

Now even if afterlives were viewed as continuations of this life and if retainers willing to sacrifice themselves were rewarded with good burials and praise, once the practice of retainer sacrifice became an exercise in the conspicuous consumption of human lives, there must have been growing numbers who sought to avoid their fate. Certainly, historical documents from China, Africa, the Americas, and India tell of slaves fleeing *en masse* at the death of their master and of active revolts among individuals destined for sacrifice. In Old Calabar in 1852, a cadre of armed and dangerous farm slaves invaded the capital just after the death of the king and only withdrew after securing a guarantee that "no more persons should die, in any way, for the late king" (quoted in Law 1985: 80). Earlier revolts against the extravagant scale of human sacrifice were also recorded in Benin and Asante (Law 1985: 70, 81).

If the king's slaves, who were essentially cognized as objects, were reluctant to die, this could perhaps be chalked up to a general reluctance of slaves to be submissive – worrisome, but theoretically solvable by the application of more violence to cow them into proper submission. What was more problematic ideologically was when the high officials who were supposed to follow the king to their deaths out of love and fealty refused to do so, and their participation in the project needed to be secured by a ruse. In Dahomey, some victims were awarded the titles and insignia of major officials just before being killed (Argyle 1966: 113), and this type of victim substitution was likely common practice. Chinese texts also tell of elite dissatisfaction with sacrificing their own – of delegations of family members attempting intercession, and of the empathy induced in onlookers at the sacrifice of noble men (Chang 1974: 6–7; de Groot 1967: 722–723).

China offers a rare opportunity to study retainer sacrifice over the *longue durée* in order to determine the ways in which it was viewed as time progressed and the practice lost its novelty. Here, the custom ebbed after the mid-twelfth century B.C. in tandem with a number of trends. Military campaigns were less frequent, as the emphasis changed from conquest to consolidation, and when the Shang kingdom was conquered by the Zhou, polities were smaller and could bring fewer resources to bear. War yielded far fewer captives, lessening the expendable mass of prisoners that had previously provided the means to dramatize Shang dominance over the chaotic world around them. Moreover, the normalization of the presence of the state and its attendant class hierarchies may have lessened the need for these hierarchies to be instantiated – performed at the deaths of kings and members of the elite (Campbell 2007: 202, 209–210).

The custom of burying the living with the dead still persisted at certain times in certain kingdoms during the Warring States period, especially at points at which a kingdom's power peaked. Due to increased literacy, however, intellectual debates about the practice are for the first time accessible (see Campbell, Ch. 4, this volume). For the most part, sentiments seem to have turned against the practice, and it was summed up as "not a good rite" by those who chose to abandon it (de Groot 1967: 727). A number of anecdotes are recorded of wise men who succeeded in talking dying grandees or their heirs out of their intention to sacrifice others to accompany the dead (de Groot 1967: 727, 729). It is fascinating to note, however, just as Childe might have suspected, that much of the reaction against retainer sacrifice was encompassed in a growing condemnation of the wastefulness of ostentatious funerals generally (Mo Tzu et al. 1967: 67, 105).

The cultural dynamics that went into the diminishment of retainer sacrifice toward the end of the Warring States period are complex. Arguments against the practice by intellectuals such as Hsün Tzu and Mo Tzu no doubt played an important role. Changing popular sentiment – as perhaps exemplified in the mournful poem about the death of the three retainers – likely also contributed. And, to evoke Childe again, by the beginning of the Han period, the intense internal fragmentation and rivalry that characterized the Warring States period had been repressed by a stable state. What remained, however, and was much slower to die out was the custom of widow suicides, in which the ideology that a sacrifice was freely given out of love was far easier to maintain. Yet, even in this case, the division between what was elected *by* and what was expected *of* these women was not at all clear-cut, and here too the practice was finally officially condemned after competition for that precious reflected glow of honor among families drove the numbers of women pressured into such situations alarmingly high (de Groot 1967: 733–736, 746–749). Indeed, one Chinese emperor, who opposed the practice, publically announced his decision in 1729 to cease awarding honors to such suicides and further enumerated the many ways in which a widow is more noble and self-sacrificing alive than dead (de Groot 1967: 746–747).

In India too, widow sacrifice was not popularly perceived to be a problematic act of violence until the competition among elites became so intense that a great many women burnt on the same pyre, and even reluctant widows were forced to their death by relatives or armed soldiers, as their refusal to cooperate was judged an affront to the honor of the dead (Thompson 1928: 28–29, 35–36, 46, 90–106). Further, widow-burning had become something of a spectator sport. As one eyewitness reported,

> Should utter indifference for her husband, and superior sense, enable her to preserve her judgement, and to resist the arguments of those about her, it will avail her little – the people will not be disappointed of their show; and the entire population of a village will turn out to assist in dragging her to the bank of the river and in keeping her down on the pile. Under these circumstances nine out of ten widows are burnt to death [quoted in Thompson 1928: 5].

The custom of widow suicide ranged far further than India and China, of course, and with the Asante as well we have records of wives who fled at the news of their husband's death and who had to be replaced "by other girls, who, painted white, and hung with gold ornaments, sat around the coffin to drive away the flies – and were strangled at the funeral" (Rattray 1927: 111).

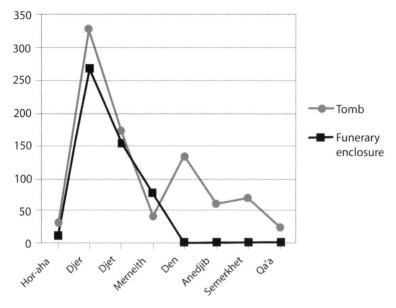

Figure 3.5. Numbers of subsidiary burials at Abydos

Like China, First Dynasty Egypt offers an undisturbed trajectory that may provide a window into otherwise inaccessible debates. Certainly, evidence for the abandonment of large-scale retainer sacrifice in Egypt is dramatic, for after a sharp peak in the first few reigns of the First Dynasty the decline is precipitous (Figure 3.5). The numbers rose to their zenith – 599 – with the second king of the First Dynasty, King Djer, whose retainers were split between his tomb and funerary enclosure. The numbers of death attendants had dwindled to 26, however, by the reign of King Qa'a, the last king of the First Dynasty (Petrie 1925: 3). Rather than being an outlier, Qa'a's low body-count fits into a trajectory in which a steep decline followed King Djer's excesses.

Although retainer sacrifice persisted until the end of the First Dynasty, the emphasis moved from quantity to quality as the reigns progressed from Djer onward (Kaplony 1963: 222–226; Reisner 1936: 104, 115–117).[3] According to the Chinese lament, one noble was worth 100 ordinary men, and so the situation may have been cognized in Egypt. As sacrifices became fewer with the last couple of rulers at Abydos, tombs for retainers moved into the structure of the royal tomb, and the titles on their stelae grew longer. The stele of Sabef, discovered in a burial chamber near to that of King Qa'a, was far larger and better made than those of the retainers sacrificed before him.

The stele depicts Sabef standing and holding a long staff, which was the usual posture of a high official. His titles matched his stance: Foremost of the Audience Chamber, Governor of the Great Estate, Overseer of the King's Sed-Festival, Smr-companion, priest associated with the cult of Anubis, and others less well understood (Petrie 1900: 26, pl. 30; Wilkinson 1999: 133, 135, 137, 140). A stele of an official bearing similar titles was discovered in association with the unusually elaborate subsidiary tomb in a contemporary mastaba (3505) at Saqqara, which suggests that this converse relationship between quantity and quality was a trend that extended to the elite northern cemetery as well (Morris 2007b: 183–184; O'Connor 2005).

The fact that the apparent cessation of the custom of retainer sacrifice in Egypt coincided with a change of dynasty is fascinating, for it suggests that the practice had grown unpopular enough that the new ruling family saw fit to abandon it altogether. The rulers of the Second Dynasty may have anticipated Hannah Arendt (1970) in the realization that although violence is often instrumental in gaining power, its excessive use in the maintenance of power is self-defeating. Self-sustaining power is psychological, not physical, and obedience borne of fear alone is tenuous and seldom uncontested. Following the Early Dynastic period, the same desire to equip important individuals with a support staff in the afterlife was satisfied by non-violent means: the invention of servant statues, figural tomb decoration, and the construction of court cemeteries in which the state built the tombs but patiently awaited the natural death of their intended occupants.

In China, as well, the decline of retainer sacrifice in the Shang period coincided with a development in the idea of magical substitution. Now, instead of interring full-size grave goods in a tomb, small models replaced their prototypes and fulfilled the same purpose, being transformed in the next life (Campbell 2007: 260). While this development can be viewed as symptomatic of a movement towards restraint and cost-saving, the 8,000 clay soldiers of Emperor Qin Shi Huang Di (ca. 210 B.C.) demonstrate that this ethos of burying simulacra – and thereby saving lives – was internalized by even the richest and most powerful man in China's world system. It is, however, worthy of note that while vast quantities of soldiers were spared in this manner, members of the emperor's harem apparently were not – perhaps for the reasons discussed above (Sima Qian 1993: 63).

A narrative contained in the Nihongi, a manuscript of the eighth century A.D., purports to explain the origin of an analogous development in Japan. According to the tale, the personal retinue of an emperor's brother was buried alive at his funeral in 2 A.D. The sound of their wailing so upset the emperor that he pronounced the custom of retainer sacrifice a bad one. Thus, when his wife died the following year, a councillor advised the emperor to command clay workers to fashion miniatures of men, horses, and various objects. A dictate was issued: "Henceforth these clay figures must be set up at tumuli: let not men be harmed," and from then on it became the custom to arrange effigies of men, animals, and objects in a circle around the corpse in royal tombs (Munro 1911: 378–379). Human nature is difficult to reign in, however, and in a fascinating twist, conspicuous consumption of these small effigies in China's Sung Dynasty became so intense that sumptuary rules had to be enacted. According to the Rules for Family Life, wooden carts and horses, servants, followers, and female attendants should all "resemble living beings, but be of smaller dimensions. Thirty-seven are allowed for officers of the fifth and sixth degree, twenty for those of the seventh and eighth rank, and fifteen for such people as have not been raised to the dignity of official servant of the dynasty" (de Groot 1967: 710). Such effigies were especially popular in China from 500 B.C. to roughly 1500 A.D., at which time the custom changed to the graveside burning of paper effigies, including "Hell money." Whether other long-lived independent societies followed a similar trajectory – from many sacrificed retainers, to "a few good men," to figural substitutes – is unclear, but ethnohistorical accounts are suggestive (Westermarck 1906: 469–470, 475; Davies 1981: 39–40).

The evolutionary lineage that displaced violence from human to effigy is not entirely unproblematic, as Confucius recognized. In his day, the custom of burying effigies existed alongside the custom in certain kingdoms at certain times of the immolation of wives and retainers. According to Mencius (1, A, 4.6; de Groot 1967: 807), Confucius strongly condemned wooden and terracotta burial effigies for their realism, "for was there not a danger of their leading to the use of living victims?" Because of this potential slippage between the sign and its referent, Confucius would deign to condone only highly abstract straw models of people. Otherwise the difference between the interment of a servant statue and that of a real servant was too close for comfort. If civilization was idealized as the antithesis of violence, then such reminders of violence done unto others was not civilized.

Concluding Thoughts on Retainer Sacrifice, Violence, and Excess

According to René Girard (2005: 8, 10), human sacrifice – like the animal sacrifice of which it is essentially an extension – serves to suppress dissensions within a community, to restore harmony, and to reinforce the social fabric. Because it is inevitable, unpredictable, and mysterious, death exerts a communal fascination. The executions of criminals, captives, and potentially disruptive social outsiders have formed the center of spectacles for any number of societies. The deaths of these people serve as object lessons and also as happy endings – points at which order has triumphed over disorder and the threat of danger has been quelled. When prisoners of war are offered up to the gods to thank them for victory, in the same way that the first fruits are laid upon the altar to thank the gods for a successful growing season, there is a satisfying internal logic. Likewise, when the lives of those who violate laws or norms are sacrificed in order to strengthen the souls of the most powerful ancestors, then their sacrifice benefits the entire kin-group and wider community of the faithful.

The human sacrifice that is stranger and more troubling is that of an innocent, whose only reason for death is that he or she exists in a socially subordinate position to another individual. With regard to slaves, who by virtue of their slavery are seen as socially dead (Patterson 1982), the notion that a person might double as a grave good to fulfil a function in the afterlife and to be conspicuously consumed might render retainer sacrifice somewhat palatable to a dispassionate observer. Likewise, if the drama of the death is augmented with suitably awe-inspiring trappings of ritual theater and encased in an ideology that this life is but an instant before an eternity spent in a shining retinue, a retainer might be seen to be embarking at death upon an exalted journey. Servants, wives, and officials, however, exist in a complex web of human relations where ties to others than their social superior – their children, parents, spouse, friends, neighbors, etc. – are of vital importance and where such ties are only reluctantly severed, whatever compensation or ideological explanation a state might offer. When such people are called to the grave or the pyre by the hundreds, the tragedy of that waste cannot be disguised.

Retainer sacrifices thus do appear to be an experiment undertaken by rulers and their innermost circle at the very beginning of their ascension to great power or in its final beleaguered throes. In Benin, for example, some of the most horrible excesses in human sacrifice – mistakenly interpreted by European observers as typical – occurred as the king was attempting to reassert the ritual powers of his monarchy amidst increasingly dire economic and political difficulties. Other notable excesses in retainer sacrifice were perpetrated by usurpers, who had a strong desire to insinuate themselves into rites that promoted royal legitimacy (Law 1985: 75).

As was argued above, it seems that retainers buried with their king symbolized the properly submissive core of his kingdom that would happily die in the service of the state. It is deeply ironic, then, that the more emphatically this metaphor was driven home, the more such sentiments were sapped. Perhaps then, those rulers who abandoned the practice of retainer sacrifice realized, as Hannah Arendt (1970: 56) put it, that "violence appears where power is in jeopardy, but left to its own course it ends in power's disappearance." Just as the Giza pyramids are often taken as the crowning achievement of the ancient Egyptian state – but from an emic perspective appear to have been intentionally avoided by subsequent rulers and damned by tradition – so too the hundreds of retainers slain at the funerals of First Dynasty kings were an aberration of power, abandoned when the violence of the state toward its own threatened to undermine any legitimacy it had succeeded in establishing.

Notes

1. Recent work at Hierankopolis has uncovered further evidence of retainer sacrifices at that site. For useful overviews of human sacrifice in Egypt, see van Dijk 2007 and volume 10 of the journal *Archéo-Nil*.
2. See in the website, Russian Life, http://www.russianlife.com/article.cfm?Number=153, accessed October 15, 2013.
3. Merneith and Anedjib both possessed relatively small burials with a large proportion of small-sized retainer graves, but the first was a queen regent and the second appears to have been treated by his successor as to some degree illegitimate (Emery 1961: 80). I am thus considering these two reigns as somewhat anomalous.

References

Allard, Francis, Diimaajav Erdenebaatar, Natsagyn Batbold, and Bryan Miller
    2002 A Xiongnu Cemetery Found in Mongolia. *Antiquity* 76(293): 637–638.

Arendt, Hannah
    1970 *On Violence*. Harvest Books, New York.

Argyle, William J.
    1966 *The Fon of Dahomey: A History and Ethnography of the Old Kingdom*. Clarendon Press, Oxford.

Bestock, Laurel
    2009 *The Development of Royal Funerary Cult at Abydos: Two Funerary Enclosures from the Reign of Aha*. Otto Harrassowitz, Wiesbaden.

Bowdich, T. Edward
    1966 [1819] *Mission from Cape Coast Castle to Ashantee*. Cass, London.

Campbell, Roderick
    2007 Blood, Flesh and Bones: Kinship and Violence in the Social Economy of the Late Shang. Unpublished PhD dissertation, Departments of Anthropology and East Asian Languages and Civilizations, Harvard University, Cambridge, MA.

Cannadine, David
    1987 Introduction: Divine Rites of Kings. In *Rituals of Royalty: Power and Ceremonial in Traditional Societies*, edited by David Cannadine and Simon R.F. Price, pp. 1–19. Cambridge University Press, New York.

Chang, Kwang C.
  1974 Urbanism and the King in Ancient China. *World Archaeology* 6(1): 1–14.
Childe, V. Gordon
  1943 Directional Changes in Funerary Practices during 50,000 Years. *Man* 43: 117–118.
  1945 Directional Changes in Funerary Practices during 50,000 Years. *Man* 45: 13–19.
Crubézy, Eric, and Béatrix Midant-Reynes
  2000 Les sacrifices humains à l'époque prédynastique: l'exemple de la nécropole d'Adaïma. *Archéo-Nil* 10: 21–40.
Dalzel, Archibald
  1793 *The History of Dahomy, an Inland Kingdom of Africa.* T. Spilsbury and Son, London.
Dapper, Olfert
  1998 [1668] *Olfert Dapper's Description of Benin.* Amsterdam. 1998 facsimile ed. African Studies Program, University of Wisconsin, Madison, WI.
Davies, Nigel
  1981 *Human Sacrifice in History and Today.* William Morrow, New York.
  1984 Human Sacrifice in the Old World and the New: Some Similarities and Differences. In *Ritual Human Sacrifice in Mesoamerica*, edited by Elizabeth H. Boone, pp. 211–226. Dumbarton Oaks, Washington, D.C.
de Groot, Jan Jakob Maria
  1967 *The Religious System of China*, Vol. 2, Book I: *Disposal of the Dead.* Ch'eng-wen Publishing, Taiwan.
de la Vega, Garcilaso
  1871 *First Part of the Royal Commentaries of the Yncas*, Vol II. Translated by Sir Clements R. Markham. Hakluyt Society, London.
Dreyer, Günter
  1993 A Hundred Years at Abydos. *Egyptian Archaeology* 3: 10–12.
  1990 Umm el-Qaab: Nachuntersuchungen im frühzeitlichen Königsfriedhof. 3./4. Vorbericht – Mit Beiträgen von Joachim Boessneck und Angela von den Driesch und Stefan Klug. *Mitteilungen des Deutschen Archäologischen Instituts* 46: 53–89.
Ellis, Alfred Burdon
  1970 [1890] *The Ewe-Speaking Peoples of the Slave Coast of West Africa, Their Religion, Manners, Customs, Laws, Languages, &c.* Anthropological Publications, Oosterhout N.B.
Emery, Walter B.
  1938 *The Tomb of Hemaka: Excavations at Saqqara.* Government Press, Cairo.
  1954 *Great Tombs of the First Dynasty* II. Egypt Exploration Society, London.
  1961 *Archaic Egypt.* Penguin Books, New York.
Fowler, Melvin L., Jerome Rose, Barbara Vander Leest, and Steven R. Ahler
  1999 *The Mound 72 Area: Dedicated and Sacred Space in Early Cahokia.* Illinois State Museum Society, Springfield, IL.
Galvin, John
  2005 Abydos: Life and Death at the Dawn of Egyptian Civilization. *National Geographic* April 2005(4): 106–121.

Gell, Alfred
    1998 *Art and Agency: An Anthropological Theory*. Clarendon Press, Oxford.

Girard, René
    2005 *Violence and the Sacred*. Translated by Patrick Gregory. Continuum, New York.

Herodotus
    2007 *The Landmark Herodotus: The Histories*. Edited by Robert B. Strassler; translated by
          Andrea L. Purvis. Pantheon Books, New York.

Herskovits, Melville J.
    1938 *Dahomey: An Ancient West African Kingdom,* Vol. 2. J.J. Augustin, New York.

Hoffman, Michael A.
    1979 *Egypt Before the Pharaohs*. Dorset Press, New York.

Johnson, Samuel
    1966 [1921] *The History of the Yorubas: From the Earliest Times to the Beginning of the
          British Protectorate*. Routledge and Kegan Paul, London.

Kaiser, Werner
    1985 Ein Kultbezirk des Königs Den in Sakkara. *Mitteilungen des Deutschen Archäologischen
          Instituts* 39: 47–60.

Kaplony, Peter
    1963 *Die Inschriften der ägyptischen Frühzeit*, I. Otto Harrassowitz, Wiesbaden.

Keita, Shomarka O.Y., and A.J. Boyce.
    2006 Variation in Porotic Hyperstosis in the Royal Cemetery Complex at Abydos, Upper
          Egypt: A Social Interpretation. *Antiquity* 80(307): 64–73.

Kemp, Barry J.
    2006 *Ancient Egypt: Anatomy of a Civilization*. Routledge, New York.

Law, Robin
    1985 Human Sacrifice in Pre-colonial West Africa. *African Affairs* 84: 53–87.

Lehner, Mark
    1997 *The Complete Pyramids: Solving the Ancient Mysteries*. Thames and Hudson, New
          York.

Lincoln, Bruce
    2012 *Gods and Demons, Priests and Scholars: Critical Explorations in the History of Religions*.
          University of Chicago Press, Chicago.

Macramallah, Rizkallah
    1940 *Fouilles à Saqqarah: un cimetière archaïque de la classe moyenne du peuple à Saqqarah*.
          Imprimerie Nationale, Boulâq, Cairo.

Mo Tzu, Hsün Tzu, and Han Fei Tzu.
    1967 *Basic Writings of Mo Tzu, Hsün Tzu, and Han Fei Tzu*. Translated by Burton Watson.
          Columbia University Press, New York.

Morris, Ellen F.
    2007a Sacrifice for the State: First Dynasty Royal Funerals and the Rites at Macramallah's
           Rectangle. In *Performing Death: Social Analyses of Funerary Traditions in the Ancient
           Near East and Mediterranean*, edited by Nicola Laneri, pp. 15–37. University of

Chicago Oriental Institute Seminars 3. Oriental Institute of the University of Chicago, Chicago.

2007b On the Ownership of the Saqqara Mastabas and the Allotment of Political and Ideological Power at the Dawn of the State. In *The Archaeology and Art of Ancient Egypt: Essays in Honor of David B. O'Connor,* Vol. 2, edited by Zahi A. Hawass and Janet E. Richards, pp. 171–190. Supreme Council of Antiquities of Egypt, Cairo.

Morton-Williams, Peter
1967 The Yoruba Kingdom of Oyo. In *West African Kingdoms in the Nineteenth Century*, edited by Daryll Forde and Phyllis M. Kaberry, pp. 36–69. Oxford University Press, Oxford.

Mukhodpadhyay, Amitabha
1957 Sati as a Social Institution in Bengal. *Bengal Past and Present* 76: 99–115.

Munro, Neil Gordon
1911 *Prehistoric Japan.* Publisher not noted, Yokohama.

O'Connor, David B.
1989 New Funerary Enclosures (Talbezirke) of the Early Dynastic Period at Abydos. *Journal of the American Research Center in Egypt* 26: 51–86.

2005 The Ownership of Elite Tombs at Saqqara in the First Dynasty. In *Studies in Honor of Ali Radwan,* Vol 2, edited by Khaled Abdalla Daoud, Shafia Bedier, and Sawsan 'Abd el-Fattah, pp. 223–231. Publications du Conseil Suprême des Antiquités de l'Egypte, Cairo.

Parrinder, Edward G.
1956 Divine Kingship in West Africa. *Numen* 3(2): 111–121.

Patterson, Orlando
1982 *Slavery and Social Death: A Comparative Study.* Harvard University Press, Cambridge.

Pauketat, Timothy R.
2004 *Ancient Cahokia and the Mississippians.* Cambridge University Press, New York.

Petrie, W. M. Flinders
1900 *Royal Tombs of the First Dynasty, Part* I. Egypt Exploration Fund, London
1901 *Royal Tombs of the Earliest Dynasties, Part* II. Egypt Exploration Fund, London.
1925 *Tombs of the Courtiers and Oxyrhynkhos.* British School of Archaeology in Egypt, London.

Rattray, Robert S.
1927 *Religion and Art in Ashanti.* Clarendon Press, Oxford.

Reisner, George A.
1936 *The Development of the Egyptian Tomb Down to the Accession of Cheops.* Cambridge University Press, Cambridge.

Richards, Audrey I.
1968 Keeping the King Divine. *Proceedings of the Royal Anthropological Institute of Great Britain and Ireland* 1968: 23–35.

Roscoe, John
1966 [1911] *The Baganda: An Account of their Native Customs and Beliefs.* Barnes and Noble, New York.

Sima Qian.

    1993   *Records of the Grand Historian: Han Dynasty.* Translated by Burton Watson. Columbia University Press, New York.

Strudwick, Nigel C.

    2005   *Texts from the Pyramid Age.* Society for Biblical Literature, Atlanta.

Swanton, John R.

    1911   *Indian Tribes of the Lower Mississippi Valley and Adjacent Coast of the Gulf of Mexico.* Smithsonian Institution, Bureau of American Ethnology Bulletin 43. Government Publishing Office, Washington, D.C.

Thompson, Edward J.

    1928   *Suttee: A Historical and Philosophical Enquiry into the Hindu Rite of Widow-Burning.* George Allen & Unwin, London.

Trigger, Bruce

    1978   *Time and Traditions: Essays in Archaeological Interpretation.* Columbia University Press, New York.

van Dijk, Jacobus

    2007   Retainer Sacrifice in Egypt and in Nubia. In *The Strange World of Human Sacrifice*, edited by Jan N. Bremmer, pp. 135–155. Leuven, Peeters.

Westermarck, Edward

    1906   *The Origin and Development of the Moral Ideas.* Macmillan, London.

Wilkinson, Toby A. H.

    2000   *Royal Annals of Ancient Egypt: The Palermo Stone and its Associated Fragments.* Kegan Paul International, New York.

Wilks, Ivor

    1975   *Asante in the Nineteenth Century: The Structure and Evolution of a Political Order.* Cambridge University Press, New York.

    1993   *Forests of Gold: Essays on the Akan and the Kingdom of Asante.* Ohio University Press, Athens, OH.

Woolley, Leonard

    1965   *Excavations at Ur.* Thomas Y. Crowell, New York.

Transformations of Violence:
On Humanity and Inhumanity in Early China

Roderick Campbell

In three seasons of fieldwork between 1934 and 1935, archaeologists from the Academia Sinica uncovered over 670 sacrificial pits in the royal cemetery at Xibeigang, Anyang, shockingly confirming what the fledgling study of the oracle-bones had already suggested: the Shang dynasty had practiced large-scale human sacrifice (Huang 2004). In the decades since those early excavations, archaeological and palaeographic work have only amplified and elaborated that discovery. It is now conservatively estimated that more than 12,000 human victims were interred in the royal cemetery, with another 1,000 or so buried in sacrificial pits in the palace-temple area (Tang 2005). Hu's (1974) count of human sacrifice divinations in the oracle-bones likewise yielded approximately 12,000 victims, the majority from the reign of a king later tradition extolled for his piety and virtue: Wu Ding. Indeed, passages in both the *Book of Odes* and the *Book of Documents*[1] recall the wisdom and justice of Wu Ding's rule, while Mencius comments that due to his sageliness and the merit of his forefathers, "Wu Ding commanded the homage of the various lords and possessed all under Heaven as easily as rolling it in his palm" (Mencius III.1). In the centuries between Wu Ding's reign in the 13th century B.C. and Sima Qian's description of him in the first century B.C. as a paragon of virtuous and diligent rulership, not only had the particulars of Shang kingship been forgotten, they had become unimaginable. And yet, castrated by the Han emperor Wu Di for arguing the case of a disgraced general, and only a few generations beyond the cataclysmic wars that ended the Qin and ushered in the Han, Sima Qian and his contemporaries were no strangers to violence. The question, then, is how what was sanctioned and glorified in the Shang became unimaginable a thousand years later, even as vistas of possibility opened for new forms and logics of visible and invisible violence. Moreover, implicated in these transformations are not only modes of war, sacrifice, and punishment, but also their objects and structuring conditions: namely the contingent formations of humanity and civilization themselves.

In *The Conquest of America*, Todorov (1992) draws a distinction between sacrifice and massacre and their different social-historical conditions of possibility. Sacrifice, according to Todorov, is performed in the name of official ideologies and perpetrated in plain sight in public places. The victims themselves must be liminal, partially incorporated/partially alien figures whose sanctioned deaths testify "… to the power of the social fabric, to its mastery over the individual" (Todorov 1992: 144). Massacre on the other hand, "… reveals the weakness of the… social fabric, the desuetude of the moral principles that once assured the group's coherence; hence it must be performed in some remote place where the law is only vaguely acknowledged…". Unlike sacrifice, massacres take place invisibly, "their very existence is kept secret and denied" (Todorov 1992: 144), and location is crucial to this distinction. Not only do massacres take place far from the *axis mundi* of world-renewing sacrifice, in social terms they belong to the wilds at the edge of civilization, in spaces of translation that can also become spaces of death (Taussig 1987).

> Far from the central government, far from royal law, all prohibitions give way, the social link, already loosened, snaps, revealing not a primitive nature, the beast sleeping in each of us, but a modern being, one with a great future in fact, restrained by no morality and inflicting death because and when he pleases [Todorov 1992: 145].

Visibility, distance/location, and the nature of the victims tie together in Todorov's meta-historical typology of collective violence: from public spectacles of violence at the heart of the metropole enacted on liminal figures in (re)productions of civilization's order, to unacknowledged orgies of death on colonial frontiers, where civilization meets its Other in a space of permanent exception (Schmitt 1988; Agamben 1998). His is a meta-narrative that leads from the steps of the Aztec Templo Mayor (Carrasco 2000), and the scaffolds of Seville, to the gas chambers of Auchwitz, via a colonial heart of darkness. Superficially at least, the epithets "sacrifice society" and "massacre society" would seem to apply to the Shang and Qin cases respectively, but Todorov's account is missing both the articulations between forms of violence and the specifics of socio-political orders, and how, beyond the advent of colonial projects, practices of violence change over time. The historical dynamics of the visibility and location of collective violence and its constructions of humanity and society remain to be investigated in detail.

Part I: Shang Rites of Blood

Beginning with Shang human sacrifice, the first issue is legibility. Shang sacrificial practices are, of course, no less unimaginable for us than they were for Sima Qian, perhaps more so. Nonetheless, the scale, longevity, and resources expended on Shang sacrifice mutely testify to their contemporaneous importance, to the logic these rituals held for at least some Shang people, a logic that must be reconstructed if we are to investigate seriously how regimes of violence were transformed over time.

The Shang is the second of Traditional Chinese historiography's Three Dynasties: the Xia, Shang and Zhou. Archaeologically speaking, the Shang I will refer to is the polity centered at the "great settlement Shang" near the modern city of Anyang and is known through roughly 3,000 years of textual transmission, 100 years of epigraphic study and 80 years of archaeological investigation. The period of Anyang's pre-eminence is known as the Late Shang, Anyang, or Yinxu period in Chinese archaeology, and it dates to roughly 1250–1050 B.C. Viewed from the perspective of monumentality and the focus of social energy, Shang civilization is characterized by large rammed-earth courtyard structures, rich burials, bronze feasting vessels, symbolic weapons of bronze and jade, oracle-bones and large-scale sacrifice. Collectively, these were the sites, implements, and media of ancestor veneration centered on practices of sacrifice and war (Figure 4.1).

Though frequently lumped together in archaeological reports, Shang human sacrifice can be broadly divided into two archaeologically distinct phenomena. The first, which might be termed "death attendants", are found in approximately 2% of the burials at Anyang (Campbell 2007), usually in the larger, richer graves, but also occasionally in relatively small tombs as well.

Death attendants can be distinguished from other human sacrificial victims that can also appear in Royal and high-elite tombs by their receiving what might be termed a proper Shang burial (except for being interred in someone else's tomb), bodies intact, laid out neatly, sometimes with coffins and/or grave goods (Huang 2004; Campbell 2007). Whether the bonds of obligation that brought them to have their lives cut short to accompany a patron in death were received lightly and willingly, or whether they were forced upon them, may have been individually variable, but it is at least notable that death attendants show no obvious signs of violence on their bodies. In stark contrast is the case of human sacrifice proper. Based on inscriptional evidence, these were apparently mostly war captives. Their remains can be found hacked, decapitated, burned, or buried alive in sacrificial pits primarily in the royal cemetery and palace-temple district as well as in royal and high elite burials

Figure 4.1. Shang civilization. From left to right, top to bottom. Chariot burial with horses and two charioteers, Anyang (ca. 1250–1050 B.C.) (from ZSKY 1998: pl. 16). Reconstruction of a palace-temple structure, Erlitou foundation 1, Erlitou period (ca. 1850–1650 B.C.) (from Yang 2005: fig. 5). Yue-axe of royal consort Fu Hao, Anyang, Anyang period (ca. 1250–1050 B.C.)(from ZSKY 1980: pl. 13.1). High elite tomb with death attendants, Anyang, Anyang period (ca. 1250–1050 B.C.)(from ZSKY 1994: pl. 12). Bronze ritual vessel, the Simuwu ding, Anyang, Anyang period (ca. 1250–1050 B.C.)(from Chang 2002: fig. 6.22). Ge dagger-axe with jade blade, bronze backing and turquoise inlay, Anyang, Anyang period (ca. 1250–1050 B.C.)(from ZSKY 2005: 187). Jade-bladed, bronze-socketed spear, Anyang, Anyang period (ca. 1250–1050 B.C.)(from ZSKY 2005: 184). Foundation sacrifice, Anyang, Anyang period (ca. 1250–1050 B.C.)(from ZSKY 2002: pl. 34.2). Sacrificial pit, Hougang, Anyang, Anyang period (ca. 1250–1050 B.C.)(from ZSKY 1994: pl. 17.3). Sacrificial pit in royal cemetery, Anyang, Anyang period (ca. 1250–1050 B.C.)(after ZSKY 1994: pl. 15.1)

(Zhongguo shehuikexueyuan kaogu yanjiusuo [ZSKY] 1994; Huang 2004). Not only are these two forms of Shang ritual killing distinguishable physically, they also operated in distinct logics.

Logic of Human Sacrifice/Captive Sacrifice:
War as Divinely Sanctioned Punishment

In the case of human sacrifice, the victims must be understood in the total context of Shang warfare and the hierarchy of ancestral authority. The Shang kings at Anyang represented themselves as occupying a privileged position in a hierarchy of authority that extended from the lowest creatures, through the king and his royal ancestors to the high god Di, and the powers of the land. The king laid discursive claim to the four quarters of the world, pacifying its dangers with his expeditions, hunts, and sacrifice – at once binding local rulers to him with bonds of tribute and reward, with marriage, as well as ritual and military protection. In reality, however, the political landscape was fractured, coercive capital widely distributed, and warfare endemic (Lin 1982; Keightley 2000; Campbell 2007, 2009).

As rightful mediators of Di's authority on earth, the kings' military endeavors were, therefore, figured in terms of punishment as suggested by the terms *zheng* (cognate with "correct") and "*zhi*" (cognate with "straight"), both meaning "to undertake a military expedition". Thus, *zheng* and *zhi* connote the "rectification" or "straightening out" of an enemy.

> Cracked on Gengshen day, Ke tested: this calendrical cycle(?) the King should mount an expedition against (lit. "straighten") the Tu Fang *heji* 6399 [Guo 1978].

> War, moreover, was undertaken with the blessing, if not commandment of the royal ancestors and higher gods, its legitimacy secured through the cycle of divinations and sacrifices that preceded and continued through any military endeavor [Keightley 1999, 2000].

> Cracked and tested on Dingmao day by the King (meaning of phrase unclear): I will join with the many dian and bo-lords to mount an expedition against (lit. "rectify") Dan, the bo-lord of Yu… From the upper and lower spirits through the sacrificial altars we will receive divine aid. There will certainly be no harm [or disasters]. Announce this to the Great Settlement Shang, there is no harm in the omen cracks. The King examining the cracks said: extended auspiciousness. (Recorded) in the tenth month, upon the day of (ancestor) Da Ding's Yi ritual. *heji* 36511 [Guo 1978].

In this divinely sanctioned moral economy of violence in service of the world order, those rebels or barbarians defeated and brought back to Anyang as captives not only received just punishment, but were put to good use in the community-preserving sacrificial domestication of uncertainty and danger. The actual process through which this occurred, however, took two distinct paths depending on the status of the captive enemy.

The Reduction of Enemies to Nameless Sacrificial Capital

For rank-and-file captives, a progression can be seen in the oracle-bone inscriptions of war and sacrifice. In divinations concerning war, enemies are first referred to by Shang political or ethnic terms; in divinations concerning capture, they are more frequently referred to as variants of the term captive; and in sacrificial divinations, they are referred to as captives, or by their manner of execution (e.g., *fa: those-to-be-decapitated*) (Campbell 2007). This suggests a logic of reduction as dangerous enemies were stripped of identity, becoming, in the end, mere sacrificial objects interchangeable with livestock as the near minimal pair below suggests.

> … (we should) offer a *liao*-burning sacrifice to the Earth (using) **qiang-captives**, *yi*-sacrifice small penned-sheep. *heji* 32118 [Guo 1978].

> … (we should) *liao*-sacrifice to the Earth (using) **one bovine**, *yi*-sacrifice penned sheep. *heji* 14396 [Guo 1978].

The relative value of nameless rank-and-file captives apparent in the sacrificial calculus of the serial divination below, moreover, was below that of cattle:

a) … (what is) offered up to Ancestor Jia should be… specially-reared bovines and one bovine, use.
b) Perhaps X (meaning undeciphered) three specially-reared bovines. Auspicious.
c) Perhaps five specially-reared bovines.
d) *Qiang*-captives, ten people.
e) Ten people and five.
f) Twenty people. Great auspiciousness. Use this. *tun* 2343 [ZSKY 1980, 1983].

Trophies for the Glory of the Ancestors

The case of leaders was, however, different. They were generally named in divinations concerning sacrifice, not to mention sacrificed separately and usually singly, indicating a logic of commemoration and trophy-taking, as these two rare examples of sacrificial divinations inscribed on human skull fragments suggest:

> … Fang leader use (in sacrifice) …   *heji* 38759 [Guo 1978].
> … *Fang* leader …Ancestor Yi decapitate … *heji* 38758 [Guo 1978].

If Elias' (1994) "civilizing process" postulates an initial stage of internal pacification, the Shang sacrifice of war captives was a doubly pacifying practice – focused not only on the elimination of military threats but also the maintenance of ontological security in general. War and sacrifice, moreover, did not found Shang civilization with their violence, but rather constituted its order. The capture and sacrifice of enemies was not merely a military and sacrificial economic convenience; the defeat, degradation, and final ancestral consumption of war captives operated in a negative dialectic of violence, with *kudos* passing from defeated to victor. This transference was not merely temporarily constitutive of enhanced personal honor but, through the institution of sacrifice, the ancestral capital of one lineage was expended for the sustenance of another – indelibly marking the simultaneous enhancement of the one at the expense of the other in the permanence of social, physical, and ancestral death. Much as Carrasco (2000) argued that Aztec sacrifice performed the city of Tenotchitlan, Shang human sacrifice performed the Shang world order – both negotiating and maintaining its hierarchies of being through a negative, inter-subjective, but socially structured and sanctioned dialectic of violence.

On the negative dialectic of violence encapsulated in the concept *kudos* Girard (1979: 152) wrote that it:

> … signifies an attitude of triumphant majesty, a demeanor characteristic of the gods. Man can enjoy this condition only fleetingly, and *always at the expense of other men*. To be a god is to possess kudos forever, to remain forever a master, unchallengable and unchallengable.

To this I would add that the opportunity for the acquisition of *kudos* is in general not equally available to all, but rather structured in social fields of power, and that the categories of "men" and "gods" are not givens or absolutes, but rather run a socio-physically constructed spectrum, a hierarchy of being constituted partially in this very dialectic of violence. For, as Patterson (1982: 11) noted with slavery, violence is an inter-subjectively constitutive relationship: "What was universal in the master-slave relationship was the strong sense of honor the experience of mastership generated, and conversely, the dishonoring of the slave condition". Shang sacrificial violence then, was not merely about reinforcing or reproducing an abstract social order, but rather a patterning practice that inscribed bodies (sometimes literally) with the terms of the King's hierarchy, even as it stratified the category of human – from the near divine and soon to be apotheosized kings, to the "bare life" (Agamben 1998) of human livestock, socially dead and soon to be ancestrally extinguished.

Death Attendants – Social Economy of Burial

If the sacrifice of war captives illustrates the Shang hierarchy of being on an "international" scale, then it has no starker instantiation on a "domestic scale" than in the practice of death attendants. Given the importance of the ancestors and ancestor veneration as the principal feature of Shang religiosity (Keightley 1998), fundamental to the social and spiritual order, to be killed and be interned in the grave of another is all the more striking in its radical subordination of being made existentially manifest and permanent beyond death.

Looking at the total range of Late Shang burials, their division into kin-based groupings (Tang 2004) and their significance in the construction of the ancestors (Campbell 2007) – if we can argue that the social construction of being for Shang people was predicated on position within a social matrix of living kin, ancestors, and descendants (Keightley 2000; Zhu 2004) – then burial, as signifier of ancestral place, as first step in the pacification of the dangerous dead and through them the ancestral domestication of the socio-physical landscape, becomes a matter of crucial importance. Shang burial was a game that was played by all, but with drastically different resources, creating a radically hierarchical structuring of being. This hierarchy was tangibly instantiated in the use of other members of the community as mortuary capital. For those who were death attendants either through loyalty or obligation, service in the retinue of a powerful individual may have been a better option than an impoverished burial marking an insignificant place in the lineage, or worse, consignment to the midden and ancestral oblivion.

What the practice of Shang retainer sacrifice had in common with war captive sacrifice was not merely that they were both varieties of ritual killing, or even that they both participated in a ritual complex of ancestral veneration, but rather that they instantiated and reproduced hierarchies of being fundamental to the Shang civilizational order. If Late Shang civilization can be thought of more as an unfolding ordering than a fixed order, if its ceaseless processes of internal pacification were as much directed toward a whole panoply of spiritual, environmental, social, and cultural dangers, as to the military ones suggested by Elias (1994), then the extreme instances of structural and spectacular violence performed in the sacrifice of war captives and retainers were central features of these civilizing processes. Violence in the Shang, then, was not so much removed behind the scenes, as Elias (1994) would have it, as transformed and put to use in the service of civilization, its moral economies of violence and hierarchies of being (Campbell 2007, 2009) (Figure 4.2).

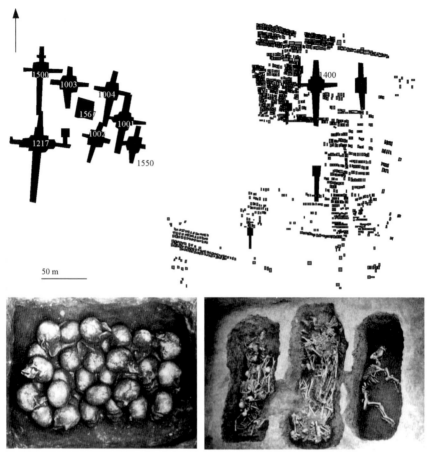

Figure 4.2. Shang royal cemetery and sacrificial pits. From top to bottom, left to right.
    Royal tombs and sacrificial pits at Xibeigang, Anyang, Anyang period
    (ca. 1250–1050 B.C.). The large black shapes are royal and high elite tombs, the
    small rectangles are sacrificial pits (after Tang 2004: fig. 7.5). *Skull pit*, royal
    cemetery, Anyang, Anyang period (ca. 1250–1050 B.C.)(from ZSKY 1994:
    pl. 13.1). *Human and animal sacrifices*, royal cemetery, Anyang, Anyang period
    (ca. 1250–1050 B.C.)(from ZSKY: pl. 16.1).

Part II: Civilization's Triumph?

If human sacrifice and its related practices of war, burial, and ancestor
veneration were so essential to Shang civilization's order, the obvious
historical question is "what happens to human sacrifice after the Shang?"
The usual answer is that, whether seen in terms of captive sacrifice or death
attendants, human sacrifice drops off sharply with the Zhou conquest and

in the following centuries gradually disappears, fading out of all memory but that of myth and fable. In fact, a more accurate description would be that captive sacrifice is transformed and displaced in changing practices and logics of war and religion. Death attendants, on the other hand, remained a stubborn if increasingly rare and condemned practice through Imperial times – repressed by new configurations of human relationships with the living and the dead, yet supported by the increasing power of rulers and ideologies of gendered hierarchical obligation (Huang 2004).

As the Shang case suggests, Early Chinese captive sacrifice must be generally understood as an intersection of war, politics, and religion. While it is true that there is no evidence that the Western Zhou kings used human captives in their sacrificial offering on the scale of the Shang kings, it must also be noted that neither the palace-temples nor the royal cemetery of the Zhou kings have ever been found. Those Western Zhou tombs that have been found show evidence of human sacrifice not significantly different than that found in Shang tombs of a similar class (Huang 2004). Nevertheless, the trend apparent since the mid-12th century B.C. was toward a reduced use of human victims in sacrifice, accompanied by a systematization of royal ritual in general (Chang 1987; Huang 2004; Campbell 2011). Evidence of Zhou royal ritual from bronze inscriptions reflects this trend. The late 11th-century B.C. Western Zhou bronze Xiao Yu Ding, for instance, though badly preserved and only partially legible, records a Zhou victory over the Gui Fang and the subsequent display of captives and trophies taken in battle: 4 leaders, over 5000 left ears, more than 13,000 live captives, 130 chariots, over 100 horses, 355 head of cattle and 28 sheep. The fragmentary inscription suggests that the leaders were sacrificed or executed, while the captives and left ears were displayed then presented to the ancestors in the temple. A fragment of the inscription reads,

> "… people (captives?) and left ears, entered (were brought through) the gate and displayed in the west corridor. …entered and (were used in (?)) the *liao*-burning ritual (at) Zhou…" [Xiao Yu Ding, author's translation].

Here, in Western Zhou practice, rather than bringing back live captives to sacrifice to the ancestors in their tens to hundreds, the left ears of slain enemies were offered at the shrines of the ancestors, while live captives were divided up among the victors along with lands and other spoils.[2]

Although it has been argued that the Western Zhou hegemonic network differed from that of the Shang in being more decentralized and perhaps less rigidly hierarchical (Li 2006), what the Zhou gained control over was, nevertheless, a political landscape that continued to be composed of segmentary lineage polities tied together with bonds of ancestral sacrifice and war. War continued to be figured as a service to the ancestors, and social, political, and religious place continued to revolve around the lineage. Western Zhou war functioned as a tool of punishment conducted in a moral idiom of divinely sanctioned lineage vengeance. The ritualized execution or enslavement of captives was, therefore, simultaneously the world-ordering duty of the Son of Heaven and the precursor of state legal apparatuses. As in the Shang, war and punishment meant, for the loser, political, religious, and social reduction, even death. In order to understand the transformation of Shang and Western Zhou non-persons from sacrificial offerings and bonded dependents to Qin massacre victims or convicts, we must investigate the ways in which war, religion, and the polity changed over the first millennium B.C. However, the sea-changes that reshaped the relationship between humanity, polity, and divinity over the course of this time are perhaps best brought to light through a discussion of death attendants.

Death Attendants

The use of death attendants, unlike captive sacrifice, remained a widespread practice in Western Zhou mortuary ritual (Huang 2004). Indeed, there are prominent examples of tombs equipped with more than a hundred death attendants as late as the 6th century B.C., as in the case of M1 at Yongcheng, believed to be the tomb of Duke Jing of Qin, which contained a total of 166 death attendants (Han and Jiao 1988) (Figure 4.3). Perhaps the most famous Eastern Zhou example, however, is the burial of Duke Mu of Qin, nearly one hundred years before Duke Jing.

In 621 B.C., or roughly four centuries after the demise of the Shang court at Anyang, Duke Mu of Qin, a powerful ruler of the westernmost polity in the Zhou sphere, died and is said to have been buried with "three good men", an event supposedly lamented in the poem "Yellow Birds" from the 6th B.C. *Book of Odes*. The first of three stanzas of "Yellow Birds" reads,

> They flit about, the yellow birds,
> And rest upon the jujube trees.
> Who followed duke Mu [to the grave]?
> Ziju Yanxi.
> And this Yanxi
> Was a man above a hundred
> When he came to the grave,
> He looked terrified and trembled.
> Thou azure Heaven there!
> Thou art destroying our good men.
> Could he have been redeemed,
> We should have given a hundred lives for him.
> [Legge 1994 (1871): 198].

Figure 4.3. Tomb M1 at Yongcheng. Believed to be the tomb of Duke Jing of Qin
          (ca. mid-6th century B.C.), Yongcheng, Shaanxi (from Chang 2002:
          fig. 8.9). Inset: *Death attendant in coffin,* tomb M1 at Yongcheng
          (from Chang 2002: fig. 8.11).

The pattern is repeated in each stanza with each of the three victims,
lamenting the loss of a life for whom the people would have gladly traded
a hundred lives.

The *Zuo Zhuan*, a 4th-century B.C. collection of earlier historical
anecdotes, also records the deaths of the three sons of the Ziju clan noting
that the people of the "state mourned them". The commentary castigated
the long-dead duke Mu stating,

As for Duke Mu of Qin's not becoming a hegemon, it is only appropriate. In dying he abandoned the people. When the former kings left the world they left behind [the legacy of] their laws, how could one instead take away good men?… By this the gentleman knows that Qin will never again march east in conquest. [*Zuo Zhuan wengong* 6, author's translation].

Here the commentator, passing judgment on what he perceived to be Duke Mu's selfishness and ritual excess, implied that the Duke's straying from the righteous ways of the former kings meant not only failure to achieve leadership of the Zhou states, but doomed his polity to future obscurity. The irony, of course, is not only that the prediction about Qin's future could not be more wrong, it was the commentator and not Duke Mu who had forgotten the ways of the former kings. Indeed, what is interesting in the earlier *Book of Odes* poem is that it was not the practice of killing the living to serve the dead that was so lamentable, but rather the worth of the victims – victims, the poem tells us, for each of whom a hundred lesser lives would have gladly been exchanged. The *Zuo Zhuan*, though castigating Duke Mu, does so not on the basis of universal principles of human worth, but rather in terms of a ruler's duty to leave his state strong. This is a case of wasting important state resources for selfish ends.

The story is retold with only minor differences in the early 1st-century B.C. *Shiji*. The differences, however, are fascinating. The *Shiji*, unlike the earlier texts which only mention the three good men, notes that 177 people were buried with Duke Mu. The *Shiji*, moreover, in an earlier passage, claims that previously, in the 7th century B.C., Duke Wu of Qin inaugurated the practice of burying the living with the dead, with 66 death attendants. Based on the 186 death attendants excavated in the tomb of Duke Jing of Qin, 177 seems a plausible number for Duke Mu. From the vantage-point of archaeology, the 1st-century B.C. claim that death attendants were a 7th-century Qin invention is as ludicrous as it is interesting. Why did the early texts make no mention of the other 174 killed for Duke Mu's tomb? How did death attendants become so problematic that their ancient tradition was forgotten and instead had to be ascribed to the relatively recent invention of a semi-barbarous polity? Apparently, by the last half of the first millennium B.C. killing even ordinary people to serve the dead had come to be seen as monstrous. How did this come to pass?

Returning to the larger politico-religious narrative of the first half of the first millennium B.C., the Zhou royal court became increasingly weak over the centuries after the Shang conquest, as power increasingly devolved to the regional polities (Li 2006; Shaughnessy 1999). One material reflection of the court's attempt to shore up its weakening position can be seen in the early (Rawson 1990) or perhaps mid- (von Falkenhausen 2006) 9th-century "ritual revolution", during which the bronze vessels that had served as the central paraphernalia of ancestor veneration became simplified in form and produced in standardized sets. Rawson (1999: 438) writes,

> The very regularity of the bronzes in number and design suggests a need for some sort of visible ordering, one much more explicit than that of the earlier ritual system… [I]f the visual order was so explicit, so perhaps was Zhou aspiration to social order through ritual.

Rawson further notes that the uniformity and rapid spread of this revolution suggests a "strong centralized control of ritual" (1999: 438). It was, however, a reorganization belying the political weakness of the center. The late Western Zhou ritual revolution was an attempt to impose a new level of legibility on Zhou religious hegemony at a time when that hegemony was losing its political and military basis.

In the early 8th century B.C., the Zhou royal house was struck a crippling blow as they were driven eastward from their former power base and reduced to a merely symbolic status. With this event, the centripetal, macro-political, integrating function of ancestor veneration lost its practical basis. The ensuing 8th and 7th centuries saw struggles between the regional states for hegemonic status within the Zhou cultural *ecumene*, as well as a series of usurpations and lineage struggles within the polities. By the end of the 7th century, another ritual transformation can be seen in tomb assemblages which:

> allow us to trace… the redefinition of rulers of polities as a social group apart from the ranked elite; and they document strikingly how the fundamental division between ranked and unranked members of lineages, so strictly maintained in Western Zhou and throughout most of the Springs and Autumns period, became obliterated during the Warring States [von Falkenhausen 2006: 290].

In other words, as the former sub-segments of the Zhou political hegemony became truly independent peer-polities in free competition with one another, their rulers cast off their subordinate sumptuary statuses vis-à-vis the Zhou kings. At the same time, in an era of civil wars and usurpations, rulers sought to demarcate their distinction from other elite lineages within their own polities. The rulers' tombs took the form of increasingly large mausolea, frequently covered with tumuli and set apart from the graves of their kinsmen (von Falkenhausen 2006: 328). With the restriction of politically relevant ancestor veneration to the highest elites, the lower elites were excluded from the formerly integrating function of broad-based ancestral sacrifice. Not surprisingly then, during the 6th century B.C. onward, across the Zhou realm, the mortuary ritual of all but the highest stratum of society changed, with the strict ranks laid out in the 9th century blurring, and the focus of religious practice shifting away from ancestor veneration.

Indeed, the diminution of the social and political relevance of ancestors and of lineages in general led in turn to changing relationships with the dead:

> …[I]n a fundamental contrast to Western Zhou- and Early Springs and Autumns-period concepts, later Eastern Zhou tombs emphasize no longer the communality, but the discontinuity between the living and the dead [von Falkenhausen 2006: 301].

This discontinuity was manifested in a number of ways including the increasing physical separation of burials from residential areas, the growing use of cheaper, miniaturized, symbolic funerary artifacts, and the development of tombs as "microcosmic" reflections of an irrevocably separate world of the dead.

These mortuary changes were part of wider political, intellectual, and religious developments taking place in China over the second half of the first millennium B.C. Socially and politically, the 6th to 3rd centuries B.C. were marked by increasing social mobility, economic development, and the institution of reforms aimed at strengthening the remaining polities engaged in intensifying struggles for domination and survival. The transformation from a hegemonic network of lineage polities to warring territorial states was completed in this period, even as the institutional foundations for later empire were laid (Hsu 1965; Lewis 1999).

Intellectually, the 6th to 3rd centuries B.C., also known as the Warring States Period, was a time of unprecedented intellectual and religious ferment. Ancestor veneration was replaced with state cults of the soil and grain in the realm of political religion (Lewis 1999), even as the rituals and practices of the rulers became more distant from that of the ruled. The socio-political transformations of the time opened up new religious and intellectual ground in which the increasing possibilities for upward mobility and lessening importance of birth coincided with new ideas about "humanity" and its relationship with the spirits. If Shang people saw a continuity or hierarchy of being, stretching from captives and animals through lineage hierarchies to the ancestors and ultimately the high god Di, Warring States thinkers envisioned a more fluid chain of being that was less determined by birth than by various possibilities for self-cultivation or even self-divinization (Puett 2002). It is in this context, of expanded human potentialities, concomitant separation of the living and the dead, and the distancing of rulers from the ruled, that we must understand the changing attitudes toward the practice of interring death attendants in the tombs of the powerful. These attitudes were summed up in the 3rd-century B.C. philosopher Xunzi's remarks that:

> To deprive the dead for the sake of the living is niggardly; to deprive the living for the sake of the dead is delusion; to kill the living and force them to accompany the dead is hideous [Watson 1963: 105].

This statement, generally taken as indicative of the humanistic development of Chinese civilization, should instead be seen in terms of a growing separation between the living and the dead, changing understandings of human potential, and, perhaps most ambivalently, novel relationships between the individual and the polity. If violence always has its moral economy, the separation of the dead from the community of the living and the concomitant attenuation of the cultural logic in which it made sense to have followers accompany patrons into the next world made death attendants too morally costly for all but the most despotic of rulers. What was once an invisible violence was made visible when its social, religious and political logics eroded. This, of course, is not to say that while death attendants were being written out of civilization's proper order other practices of violence were not emerging behind the screen of legitimation. If the mutable category of "human" had come to mean something different in the hands of Warring States thinkers, individuals also entered into a new relationship with the territorial, bureaucratic state than existed in previous lineage polities. If "the human" could now become sage or even god through self-cultivation, individuals also became expendable and interchangeable resources of the state in a way they had never been before.

Qin's Reforms

To understand the changed relationships between the individual and the polity in Early China there is no better-documented example than the state of Qin and the reforms instituted there in the middle of the fourth century B.C. The *Shiji* states,

> According to the ordinances, [Wei Yang ordered that] the common people be put in groups of five and ten households with each member of the group guiding and watching the others and each responsible for the others' crimes. Whoever failed to report a criminal would be cut in half at the waist, whoever reported a criminal would be granted the same reward as for beheading an enemy, and whoever hid a criminal would be given the same punishment as for surrendering to the enemy. Commoners with two adult males in their families who did not divide their household would have their military tax doubled. Whoever won military merit would be awarded higher rank according to his accomplishments, whoever engaged in a private feud would receive punishment according to its gravity [Nienhauser 1994: 89].

The Qin reforms, aimed at the organization of the state and its resources for war, attempted to remake the political community institutionally, spatially, and morally. The state was to replace kinship in terms of loyalty enforced with the iron discipline that professional generals were increasingly imposing on

Warring States armies across the Zhou realm (Lewis 1990, 1999). The strict punishments and rewards of the Qin ordinances in effect remade the polity as an armed camp, not only mirroring military organization in the imposition of a state ranking system and division of the population into units of mutual responsibility, but the idiom of reward and punishment was also that of war (Lewis 1999). If the main avenue of advancement within Qin's 23 ranks was the taking of heads in battle, the equal reward for reporting criminals assimilated domestic and external enemies to a single category. Likewise in war, those not simply massacred by Qin's armies were made convicts, serving alongside domestic criminals in state projects (Yates 2001).

Massacre Societies and Establishing Violence

Over the course of the first millennium B.C., war was transformed from service to the ancestors in Shang and Western Zhou lineage polities, to service to the state in the Warring States period. The Shang sacrifice of captives to the royal ancestors and the Western Zhou presentation of the left-ears of slain enemies at the ancestral altars have their direct descendant in Qin's policy of promotion based on heads taken in battle. What in the one was a service to the ancestors becomes, over time, a service to the state. These were, moreover, states for which "the chief activity... was combat" (Lewis 1999: 619).

Indeed, punishment changed not only in form but context over the 800 years between the Shang and the Qin dynasties – as the polity moved from lineage- to ruler-centered bureaucracy, state punishment became increasingly codified in law, and ancestral punishment became a matter of private vendetta. Stories of presenting the head of a murderer at the grave of the victim by avenging relatives can be seen as the lineal descendants of Shang human sacrifice (Huang 2004).

Not surprisingly, along with the nature of polities, punishment, and sacrifice, the practice and nature of war changed dramatically over the 800 years of the Zhou dynasty. Originally conceived as ancestral service and practiced as a means of negotiating place within a hegemonic network of polities, warfare became increasingly bloody, total, and predicated on a logic of total conquest. With mass mobilization, status dependent on taking heads, and finally the 3rd-century B.C. Qin minister Fan Sui's doctrine of "attacking not only their territory, but also their people" (Watson 1993: 138), the final decades of Qin's conquest resulted in killing on an unprecedented scale, including the total destruction of Zhao's 400,000 strong army at Changping following three years of deadlocked combat (Lewis 1999). Whether or not these numbers are accurate, Fan Sui's policy proved effective, Zhao never recovered, and the rest of Warring States history reads like a grim tally of polities extinguished and heads taken by victorious Qin armies – heads taken in the tens of thousands.

Superficially at least, the transformation from "civilization of sacrifice" to "civilization of massacre" was complete by the end of the first millennium B.C. If it was monstrous to offer the living to the spirits of the dead by the 3rd century B.C., if the moral economy of violence could no longer afford human sacrifice, the massacre of whole enemy armies was newly seen as expedient. In Todorov's scheme of things, massacres occur at the edges of civilization, out of sight, in encounters where the normal rules of community are suspended. In some ways this formulation describes Qin war: a state of exception, a suspension of order paradoxically for the defense or establishment of order. At the conclusion of perhaps the greatest killing spree the world had seen up that point, the First Emperor is purported to have stated:

> Insignificant person that I am, I have called up troops to punish violence and rebellion. Thanks to the help of the ancestral spirits, these six kings [of Qin's rival states] have all acknowledged their guilt and the world is in profound order [Watson 1993: 42].

Where Todorov's understanding of massacre falls short, however, is in his claim that it is an "atheistic murder", "without… any ritual meaning" (1992: 144). This echoes Agamben's (1998: 101) formulation of *homo sacer*, non-persons created through the operation of sovereign power, as "life that may be killed but not sacrificed". Implicit in these macro-histories of social violence, however, is a post-Enlightenment understanding of religion distinguished as a particular sort of "perspective," as opposed to supposedly "perspectiveless" atheism or universal reason (Asad 1993; Žižek 2008). While massacres may occur in apparently spontaneous fashion, they are often, as in the Qin case, the product of policy, and in any case not so much outside of civilization's order as implicated in it by their very exclusion. Sub-human barbarians, apostates, or rebels, victims must be first constructed as non-persons before they can be massacred. This discursive work, whether figured as ideology or religion, is the underside of civilization's ordering and its attendant hierarchies of being. In the words of Gulag survivor Solzhenitsin (1974: 174):

> The imagination and the spiritual strength of Shakespeare's evildoers stopped short at a dozen corpses. Because they had no ideology… That was how the agents of the Inquisition fortified their wills: by invoking Christianity; the conquerors of foreign lands, by extolling the grandeur of their Motherland; the colonizers, by civilization; the Nazis, by race; and the Jacobins (early and late), by equality, brotherhood, and the happiness of future generations.

Qin's conquest of all under Heaven provides a stark example of the initial pacification that Elias would see as the foundation of a civilizing process.

It instantiates the monumental cost of establishing a monopoly of violence resulting in the establishment of empire – short-lived in the case of Qin, but ultimately yielding a nearly 400-year Han *pax sinica*. Along these lines, what distinguishes Shang and Qin civilizations is that in the Shang the work of pacification was never done and had to be continually re-enacted in blood. With the Qin conquest and no enemies left to fight but on distant borders, swords could be beaten into ploughshares,[3] or, perhaps more sinisterly, shackles and the tools of heavy labor.

Part III: Leviathan

Qin ended centuries of intensifying inter-polity warfare with the establishment of new political forms and institutions that would lay the foundation for the next two thousand years of Chinese history. The Qin and Han empires largely turned their backs on the overt political-religious violence of the Shang and, for the majority of the population, violence probably did seem to have been "removed behind the scenes," as Elias would have it. Nevertheless, hierarchies of worth and care did not vanish under the Qin. Rather the hierarchies that in the Shang divided up the category of *ren* or "human" into a spectrum ranging from sacrificial livestock to nearly divine kings, the moral economies of which provided human sacrifice with its logic, were transformed from ancestral to state logics, becoming in the process ever more expansive, inescapable, and invisible.

The systematization of violence in law had the double advantage of distancing punishment from the logic of lineage vengeance and the creation of a new class of non-humans: criminals. Nor is this hyperbole: criminals in the early empires were literally *fei ren* – "not human", cut off from society and lineage ritual through their criminal status and the mutilating punishments, from tattooing to amputation, that often accompanied sentences of hard labor. A debater in the 1st-century B.C. Han text *Discourses on Salt and Iron* makes this distinction clearly when he states that "criminals are not human". Commenting on this and similar statements in the text Yates (2001: 299) notes that,

> Humans are humans because they are tied into a network of kin relationships which constitute the world of social life and which define their social being, and in China humans are human because of the direct line and link between themselves and their ancestors or ascendants and their offspring or descendants. A slave and a criminal in early traditional China lost his rights and obligations and relations to his family, both his parents and his children. He was a socially dead person.

While we have seen that the relationship between the living and the dead and the distributed structuring of human being was not a constant in the first millennium B.C., Yates points to another commonality between Early Imperial and Shang punishment: in both cases the victim is alienated and discursively reclassified as something less than human. As Žižek (2008: 72) notes with regards to the performative efficacy of racist ideology, being is social-symbolic and so racist interpretation "determines the very being and social existence of the interpreted subjects". The Early Imperial courts of law socio-symbolically and materially created new categories of sub-human below the hierarchy of ranks that extended humanity in the direction of divinity.

Viewed through the lens of punishment, the Qin and Han state hierarchies concern far more than abstract statuses. Rank moderated exposure to punishment, and sentences could be bought off with a reduction in status, a payment, or the substitution of a more expendable member of the family or a slave (Yates 2001; Lewis 2007).[4] In other words, state hierarchy and penal apparatus operated in tandem as the pistons of a gigantic machine of structural violence, unequally distributing not only worth and status but exposure to physical suffering. As in the Shang, Early Imperial theodicies of victory, success, and privilege worked through structural and symbolic violence to create nearly ontological distinctions of being and worth. Criminals, in being tattooed, shackled and forced to labor, often to the death, were marked and made less than human by the same system that sanctioned the superior status of the non-criminal, inter-subjectively establishing the "humanity" of the people through state violence against their Other. This human/non-human dichotomy and the flourishing of religious and philosophical thought around ideas of self-cultivation and nearly limitless human potential, however, was belied by the practical ranking of all under Heaven into a hierarchy of wealth, privilege, and exposure to suffering. In short, the category of "human" masked a spectrum of existential statuses stretching from the Son of Heaven himself to the collared, shackled, bare life of hard-labor convicts.

The most common punishment for criminals convicted under Qin and Han law were three- to six-year terms of hard labor (Hulsewé 1955; Yates 2001; Barbieri-Low 2007). Unlike the corvée laborers they worked beside, criminals, as non-humans, were treated as expendable, renewable resources performing the most demanding and dangerous tasks. Many did not survive their sentences. Three excavated and partially published convict cemeteries dating from the Qin and Han give an illustration of the conditions under which Early Imperial convicts worked and died (Zhongguo shehuikexueyuan kaogu yanjiusuo Luoyang gongzuodui [ZSKYLG] 1972; Qin 1972; Shihuangling Qin yongkeng kaogu fajuedui [SQYKF]1982; Pan and Han

Figure 4.4. Early Imperial convict cemetery, collar and shackle. From top, clockwise.
Eastern Han (ca. 86–170 A.D.) convict cemetery near Luoyang (from ZSKYLG
1972: pl. 4). Shackle (Western Han, ca. 152–146 B.C.) from convict cemetery
near Emperor Jing's tomb (from Qin 1972: fig. 11). Collar with spike (Western
Han, ca. 152–146 B.C.) from convict cemetery near Emperor Jing's tomb (from
Qin 1972: fig. 7).

1988). The largest of these lies near the 2nd-century B.C. mausoleum of
the Han Emperor Jing (Pan and Han 1988; Barbieri-Low 2007). Like his
fathers before him and his sons after, Emperor Jing had his mausoleum built
by convict and corvée labor. The nearby convict cemetery bears witness to
the human cost of this endeavor. According to one calculation the convicts
died at a rate of one to six per day (Qin 1972; Barbieri-Low 2007), one in
ten from sudden trauma to the head/neck region, some bearing signs of
mutilating punishments (Pan and Han 1988). They were buried far from
their kin with nothing for grave goods but their shackles and a bureaucratic
epitaph scrawled on a potsherd (Figure 4.4). There were an estimated 10,000
convicts buried in the 8 ha cemetery. 10,000 died over the seven years it

took to construct the tomb of one Han emperor, roughly the same number as were sacrificially punished and offered in Shang royal ritual over a period of 200 years. In the latter we can see the operation of a political theatre of divinely sanctioned terror and lineage vengeance; in the former, vastly greater in scale, the invisible and implacable workings of law and state.

Notes

1. The *Shijing* is a collection of early poems and dynastic hymns, while the *Shangshu* is a collection of orations supposedly delivered by kings and sages of the Three Dynasties. These two texts are perhaps the earliest received texts in the Chinese tradition with some parts dating to the early centuries of the first millennium B.C.
2. The exact nature of Western Zhou bondage/dependency is unclear.
3. Literally, "weapons from all over the empire were confiscated, brought to Xianyang, and melted down to be used in casting bells, bell stands, and twelve men made of metal" (Watson 1993: 45).
4. Compare with Scheper-Hughes's (2007) account of living organ donors and the hierarchies of worth on which this contemporary practice operates.

References

Agamben, Giorgio
  1998 *Homo Sacer: Sovereign Power and Bare Life*. Translated by Daniel Heller-Roazen. Stanford University Press, Stanford.
Asad, Talal
  1993 *Genealogies of Religion: Discipline and Reasons of Power in Christianity and Islam*. Johns Hopkins University Press, Baltimore.
Barbieri-Low, Anthony
  2007 *Artisans in Early Imperial China*. University of Washington Press, Seattle.
Campbell, Roderick
  2007 Blood, Flesh and Bones: Kinship and Violence in the Social Economy of the Late Shang. Unpublished Ph.D. dissertation, Departments of Anthropology and East Asian Languages and Civilizations, Harvard University, Cambridge, MA.
  2009 Toward a Networks and Boundaries Approach to Early Complex Polities: The Late Shang Case. *Current Anthropology* 50(6): 821–848.
  2011 Guo zhi da shi: Shangdai wanqi zhong de lizhi gailiang (The Great Affairs of the State: the Late Shang Ritual Reforms). In *Yinxu kexuefajue 80 nian xueshu jinianhui*. Edited by Zhongguo Shehuikexueyuan Kaogu Yanjiusuo, pp. 267–276. Kexue chubanshe, Beijing.
Carrasco, David
  2000 *City of Sacrifice: The Aztec Empire and the Role of Violence in Civilization*. Beacon Press, Boston.
Chang, Kwang-chih, Pingfang Xu, Liangchen Yu, Sarah Allan, et al.
  2005 *The Formation of Chinese Civilization: An Archaeological Perspective*. Yale University Press, New Haven and London; New World Press, Beijing.

Chang Yuzhi
   1987   *Shangdai zhouji zhidu* (Shang Dynasty Weekly Sacrificial System). Zhongguo
          shehuikexue chubanshe, Beijing.

Elias, Norbert
   1994   *The Civilizing Process: The History of Manners, and State Formation and Civilization.*
          Translation by Edmund Jephcott. Blackwell Publishers, Oxford.

Girard, René
   1979   *Violence and the Sacred.* Translated by Patrick Gregory. John's Hopkins University
          Press, Baltimore.

Guo Moruo (editor)
   1978   *Jiaguwen heji* (Collected Oracle-bone Inscriptions). Zhonghua shuju, Beijing.

Han Wei, and Jiao Nanfeng
   1988   *Qin du Yongcheng kaogu fajue yanjiu zongshu* (Summary of the Research on and
          Excavation of the Qin Capital at Yongcheng). *Kaogu yu wenwu* 5–6: 111.

Hsu, Chou-yun
   1965   *Ancient China in Transition.* Stanford University Press, Stanford.

Hu Houxuan
   1974   *Zhongguo nukang shehui de renxun he renji (xiapian)* (Chinese Slave Society's Death
          Attendants and Human Sacrifice [Part 2]). *Wenwu* 8: 56–68.

Huang Zhanyue
   2004   *Gudai rensheng renxun tonglun* (On Ancient Human Sacrifice). Wenwu chubanshe,
          Beijing.

Hulsewé, Anthony F.P.
   1955   *Remnants of Han Law.* Sinica Leidensia 9. E. J. Brill, Leiden.

Keightley, David
   1998   Shamanism, Death, and the Ancestors: Religious Mediation in Neolithic and Shang
          China. *Asiatische Studien* 52(3): 763–832.

   1999   The Shang: China's First Historical Dynasty. In *The Cambridge History of Ancient
          China*, edited by Michael Lowe and Edward Shaughnessy, pp. 124–231. Cambridge
          University Press, Cambridge.

   2000   *The Ancestral Landscape: Time, Space, and Community in Late Shang China.* Center
          for Chinese Studies, University of California at Berkeley, Berkeley.

Legge, James
   1994 [1871]   *The Chinese Classics IV: The She King or Book of Poetry.* SMC Publishing,
          Taipei.

Lewis, Mark Edward
   1990   *Sanctioned Violence in Early China.* State University of New York, Albany.

   1999   Warring States Political History. In *The Cambridge History of Ancient China*, edited
          by Michael Loewe and Edward Shaughnessy, pp. 587–650. Cambridge University
          Press, Cambridge.

   2007   *The Early Chinese Empires: Qin and Han.* Harvard University Press, Cambridge, MA.

Li, Feng
   2006   *Landscapes and Power: The Crisis and Fall of the Western Zhou, 1045–771 B.C.*
          Cambridge University Press, Cambridge.

Lin Yun

1982 *Jiaguwen zhong de Shangdai fangguo lianmeng* (The Shang Dynasty Confederation of States as Seen in the Oracle-bone Inscriptions). *Guwenzi yanjiu* 6: 69–74.

Nienhauser, William H. (editor)

1994 [1st Century B.C., Sima Qian] *The Grand Scribe's Records: Volume VII: The Memoirs of Pre-Han China*. Translated by Tsai-fa Cheng, Zongli Lu, William Nienhauser and Robert Reynolds. SMC Publishing, Taipei.

Pan Qifeng, and Han Kangxin

1988 Luoyang Dong-Han xingtu mu rengu jianding (Analysis of the Human Remains from the Eastern Han Convict Cemetery). *Kaogu* 3: 277–83.

Patterson, Orlando

1982 *Slavery and Social Death: A Comparative Study*. Harvard University Press, Cambridge, MA.

Puett, Michael

2002 *To Become a God: Cosmology, Sacrifice and Self-Divinization in Early China*. Harvard University Asia Center, Cambridge, MA.

Qin Zhonghang

1972 Han Yangling fujin qiantu mu de fajue (The Excavation of Shackled Convict Tombs near Han Yangling). *Wenwu* 7: 51–53.

Rawson, Jessica

1990 *Western Zhou Bronze Vessels from the Arthur M. Sackler Collections*. Harvard University Press, Cambridge, MA.

1999 Western Zhou Archaeology. In *The Cambridge History of Ancient China*, edited by Michael Lowe and Edward Shaughnessy, pp. 352–449. Cambridge University Press, Cambridge.

Scheper-Hughes, Nancy

2007 The Tyranny of the Gift: Sacrificial Violence in Living Donor Transplants. *American Journal of Transplantation* 7: 507–511.

Schmitt, Carl

1988 *Political Theology: Four Chapters on the Concept of Sovereignty*. Translated by George Schwab. MIT Press, Boston.

Shaughnessy, Edward

1999 Western Zhou History. In *The Cambridge History of Ancient China*, edited by Michael Loewe and Edward Shaughnessy, pp. 292–351. Cambridge University Press, Cambridge.

Shihuangling Qin yongkeng kaogu fajuedui [SQYKF]

1982 Qin Shihuang ling xice Zhaobeihucun Qin xingtu mu (Convict Laborer Tombs in Zhaobeihu Village on the West Side of Qin Shihuang's Mausoleum). *Wenwu* 3: 1–11.

Solzhenitsyn, Aleksandr

1974 *The Gulag Archipelago: 1918–1956, An Experiment in Literary Investigation* I–II. Translated by Thomas Whitney. Harper & Row, New York.

Tang, Jigen

2004 The Social Organization of Late Shang China: a Mortuary Perspective. Unpublished PhD dissertation, Institute of Archaeology, University College London.

2005 The True Face of Antiquity: Anyang Yinxu Sacrificial Pits and the Dark Side of "Three Dynasties Civilization". Manuscript on file, Anyang Workstation, Institute of Archaeology, Chinese Academy of Social Sciences, Anyang, Henan.

Taussig, Michael
1987 *Shamanism, Colonialism and the Wild Man: A Study in Terror and Healing.* University of Chicago Press, Chicago.

Todorov, Tzvetan
1992 *The Conquest of America: The Question of the Other.* Translated by Richard Howard. Harper Perennial, New York.

von Falkenhausen, Lothar
2006 *Chinese Society in the Age of Confucius (1000–250 B.C.): The Archaeological Evidence.* Cotsen Institute of Archaeology, University of California Los Angeles, Los Angeles.

Watson, Burton (translator)
1963 [3rd Century B.C., Xunzi] *Hsun Tzu: Basic Writings.* Columbia University Press, New York.
1993 [1st Century B.C., Sima Qian] *Records of the Grand Historian.* 3 Volumes. Columbia University Press, New York.

Yates, Robin
2001 Slavery in Early China: A Socio-Cultural Approach. *Journal of East Asian Archaeology* 3(1/2): 283–331.

Zhongguo shehuikexueyuan kaogu yanjiusuo Luoyang gongzuodui [ZSKYLG]
1972 Dong Han Luoyang cheng nanjiao de xingtu mudi (The Convict Laborer Cemetery in the Southern Suburbs of Eastern Han Luoyang). *Kaogu* 4: 2–19.

Zhongguo shehuikexueyuan kaogu yanjiusuo [ZSKY]
1980 *Yinxu Fuhao mu* (The Tomb of Fuhao at Yinxu). Wenwu chubanshe, Beijing.
1980, 1983 *Xiaotun nandi jiagu* (Oracle-bones from South Xiaotun). 2 vols. Zhonghua, Shanghai.
1994 *Yinxu de faxian yu yanjiu* (The Discovery and Excavation of Yinxu). Science Press, Beijing.
1998 *Anyang Yinxu Guojiazhuang Shangdai muzang: 1982 nian–1992 nian kaogu fajue baogao* (Shang Dynasty Tombs at Guojiazhuang, Yinxu, Anyang: 1982–1992 Excavation Report). Zhongguo da baike quanshu chubanshe, Beijing.
2002 *Anyang, Xiaotun.* Shijie tushu chubanshe, Beijing.
2005 *Anyang Yinxu chutu yuqi* (Jades From Yinxu). Science Press, Beijing.

Zhu Fenghang
2004 *Shang Zhou jiazu xingtai yanjiu* (A Study of the Family Patterns of Shang and Western Zhou China). Tianjin Guji Press, Tianjin.

Žižek, Slavoj
2008 *Violence.* Picador, New York.

Part II

Community

If the variably instantiated concepts of "humanity" and "civilization" are crucial to a historical understanding of violence, their logical point of intersection is "community." That is to say between the category of human beings, thought as a multitude of individuals, and the normative social orders that divide them into absolute or graded distinctions of insiders and outsiders, there must come some concept of community. Analytically, community is not a single thing but rather operates on a number of scales and principles of coherence: the community of family and/or friends, the larger network of familiar people, the political community, the community of "civilized people" or "people like us," and, most abstractly, the community of all humanity or even all living things. Moral economy, distinction, politics, ontology, and hierarchies of care all come together in community. The nested scales of community, moreover, extend individual yet distributed subjectivities to collective action and shared identities and ultimately to a categorical humanity. Changes in how these communities are ordered and thought and how they interrelate to each other over time generate changes in the practice and discourse of both "humanity" and "civilization."

In Campbell's contribution, changes in political community, socializing practices, and ontological order (world) wrought changes in moral economy, humanity, and civilization in Early China over 1000 years. If Shang political community was based on the lineage, Qin completed the centuries-long gestation of the centralized territorial state culminating in empire. These changes effectively reduced the family to site of primary socialization, promoted the supra-identity of the polity, and founded a centralized regime of violence directed more or less invisibly inward as legal discipline, and more or less spectacularly outward as conquest, massacre and mass enslavement. Paradoxically, the boundaries of civilization's community seem to be more sharply drawn between insiders and outsiders in the Eastern Zhou than in the Shang, even while the human community and its potential was expanded by philosophers, and the monopolizing state codified its hierarchies of being and worth into law. "Community" and its moral economies of violence in the Shang and Qin, then, articulated with very different "civilizations" and authored very different political theologies of human being in spite of their shared genealogy.

Community, humanity, and civilization play a central role in Bryen's contribution on Roman violence and order. Beginning with personhood, Bryen upends the usual equation of violence with dehumanization and argues instead that Roman violence was thought as a relationship between humans or more precisely relations between nodes in distributed, hierarchical networks of being. At the heart of this observation is a shift from a Newtonian social physics of billiard-ball individuals to a non-Euclidean topography of distributed being. Moreover, in contrast to Levinas' notions of intersubjective responsibility founded, as is most modern humanistic thought, on assumptions of equality, Roman personhood was constituted in hierarchical, family-based webs of relationship. Violence as an affront to personhood then was legally recognized to affect families as represented by the *pater* even if the injury was to a subordinate. This hierarchical, distributed or attached personhood defined the basic unit of a particularly Roman community. The central insight here is that the precise nature of distributed being or attached personhood in different times and places is crucial for a local understanding of both violence and the "human".

Although the term is only briefly and obliquely referenced in Bryen's paper, *humanitas* is a uniquely revealing term for the topic of Roman violence and community. Translated as "civilization," it shares an etymological connection to the contemporary English "humanity." Heidegger (2003), for one, saw in it the origin of humanism. Yet it is the Roman conception of human in the fullest, cultivated sense, not the common ground of a shared and equal nature, but a normative and delimited community, a hierarchy of being tied to empire and its management of legitimate violence. Thus in Bryen's re-reading of Agricola's and Calgacus' speeches in Tacitus, the cost of joining *humanitas* for barbarians was a loss of agency and acceptance of a servile place in the Roman world order. This hierarchy of being was, moreover, policed with a startlingly high level of acceptable physical violence. The visibility of this violence is what really distinguishes the defense and expansion of Roman *humanitas* from, say, the defense of neoliberal civilization in Bush and Blair's "war on terror." While undoubtedly the invasion of Iraq killed more people than the repression of Calgacus's revolt, the mode and extent to which the public and the state could take pleasure in the dialectic of violence was very different in each case.[1] The crucial insight of Bryen's focus on the management of violent pleasure is the way it foregrounds the linked issues of the aesthetics of power, the politics of acceptable violence and the nature of community.

Concerns about community and its demarcation and creation through violent processes such as war, slavery, and public punishment have inner and outer dynamics as were noted in the contributions on sacrifice. Working through his central insight that Roman civilization was predicated on a shared but hierarchical humanity, Bryen shows how the policing of the boundaries of community in both the physical and discursive senses were central concerns and sites of violence. These observations suggest that the nature of community and the permeability of its boundaries are key issues generally for the historical study of violence and civilization.

If war and slavery could be seen as different processual stages of Roman civilization's dialectical engagement with outsiders, public punishment shows the reverse process: from insider to outsider. In either case, Bryen's examples parsimoniously link together war, slavery, and punishment in a common articulation of community and violence, violence that was largely predicated on the logics of a *humanitas* seen as inherently unfolding in terms of dominance and subordination.

Combining the insights of the various contributions thus far, Bryen's argument concerning emic Roman understandings of humanity and civilization being inherently hierarchical can be combined with the analytic perspectives on the processual nature of the violence dialectic foregrounded in Swensen's contribution or Campbell's notions of hierarchies of being and the duality of contemporaneous notions of the "human." That is to say, that there is no contradiction in a perception, in different contexts, of both shared identity and categorical difference actualizing very different moral demands. A sacrificial victim might, for instance, at various points in the process be enemy outsider, deity, mutilated body, and food. To recognize that local understandings of "human" may be hierarchical and distributed as opposed to individual and egalitarian is a crucial insight, but to it should be added that local discourses on being, community, and civilization are generally multiple, contingent, and often contradictory.

In Fowles' contribution the author begins with the familiar story of violence in the service of empire legitimated as civilizing the uncivilized Other – and then complicates it. The complication lies in Fowles' attempt to understand both the Spanish "excess" as well as the Pueblo response in terms of a comparative anthropology of violence. Thus, rather than merely taking violence as an unexamined category he seeks to understand Spanish and especially Pueblo regimes and moral economies of violence. Fowles drives home the point that what is at stake in his analysis is "how the inevitable flow of violence has been variously canalized and diverted in the construction of the social throughout the human past." This crucial point should not be taken as a rejection of the historical contingency of violent phenomenon or even the existence of historical mutable orientations toward violence but rather that "violence" can not be understood at all without reference to its local cultural logics, social structuration, and politics. In other words, violence is constructed in a matrix of social meaning. If this is the case, then macro-historical claims concerning the reduction of "violence" such as those of Elias (1994) and his sympathizers (Fletcher 1997; Pinker 2011) are not wrong so much as nonsensical from the perspective of a comparative anthropology of violence. The alternative Rousseauian perspective implicit in many anthropologists' equations of violence with the state, moreover, are problematic for the same reason. Using Clastres' concept of "societies against the state" Fowles amplifies the point that the violence of egalitarian societies is neither a reflection of natural propensities nor entirely reducible to the corrupting influences of "the state," but rather action in the service of egalitarian order.

From a *longue durée* perspective, Fowles's contribution adds to the discussion of regimes of violence and their relationship to changing social-political forms with an observation about initiatory violence and small-scale societies. Adding J.Z. Smith's (1987) insights concerning a historical movement from initiation to sacrifice to Todorov's (1992) from sacrifice to massacre, a trend from inward to outward can be seen. Thus, whereas we have already noted an internal/external dynamic in historical regimes of violence and a general trend toward the temporal and geographical externalization of visible forms of violence associated with larger, stabilized social networks and their associated communities of identity[2], the inwardly directed nature of initiatory violence extends the generalization to even smaller-scale societies. Indeed, Fowles is able to tie together Clastres' examples of warfare in service of egalitarianism with Pueblo initiatory violence and witch persecutions to show that similarly organized societies may share similar regimes of violence despite adhering to vastly different worldviews. Despite the gulf between the Amazonian peoples of Clastres' examples and the world of the Pueblos, a shared ethos of egalitarianism underlay both endemic warfare on the one hand and torture as initiation or witch persecution on the other. The apparent contradictions of this statement dissolve when one considers that warfare against similarly organized villages sharing ties of language, culture, and kinship is a violence that works both outwardly to maintain community against enemy Others while at the same time, from a higher-scale perspective, it can be seen as an internal institution of social organization, as Clastres (1989) in fact argued. Fowles likewise uncovers the paradox of initiation's "democratic violence" that nonetheless served to (re)produce gender, age, occupational and even individual status gradations and witchcraft persecution that at once served to eliminate social deviants and power aspirants and yet was conducted as a kind of dangerously mirroring transgression by the very people who stood in greatest risk of befalling the same fate. In a sense, all of the above examples can be considered forms of inwardly directed violence. Moreover, as Fowles notes, in addition to a relatively egalitarian political orientation, the face-to-face nature of "societies against the state" creates different structural possibilities for moral economies of violence than those pertaining to larger-scale socio-political networks. In such situations ontological distance becomes more difficult to maintain, violence's dual edge more visible, and the enemy Other contains an unavoidable reflection of the Self.

Fowles' account of Pueblo torture reveals possibilities for violence and community as radically distinct from those of the modern West as those underwriting Shang or Moche human sacrifice. And while the strong signifier of violence's over-determining tendencies make it difficult to see Shang human sacrifice as anything but loathsome or Pueblo intiatory or persecutory violence as other than tragically misguided, following Asad (2003) and critically expanding on Elias'(1994) and Scarry's (1985) accounts of mutable historical orientations towards violence or the inverse relationship between agency and pain, Fowles' contribution foregrounds the possibility for very different constellations of pain, agency, destruction, and community. This insight has direct relevance for historically contextualizing the dialectic of violence. If agency and pain are not straightforwardly inversely related but operate through dynamic intersubjective webs of meaning, then violent practices cannot be understood in terms of a simple equation. Returning to the issue of distributed being and community, interpersonal violent acts constitute a relationship and intimately link victim and victimizer – the destruction or reduction of the victim then has a ripple effect on the entire network of his or her social being (including the agent of violence). Fowles' examples of the CIA interrogator feeling the taint of his actions and the way Pueblo witch persecution mimetically reproduced the projected violence of the Other can be seen in these terms. Personally and societally, the Other is included in the Self through its exclusion. Being is shaped against and in contact with what it is not and violence helps constitute self and community through the intended and unintended effects of its ambivalent dialectic.

This last point brings us to the issue of excess and the sociality of violence. Fowles raises the issue of both the excess of the Spanish violence against the Pueblos and those of the Pueblo peoples against witches. In both cases, the violence wreaked on the victims far exceeded the goals of simple physical elimination or domination. Instead it could perhaps be argued that the excess violence was aimed not at physical targets but rather the very networks of community. To be sure, as Fowles points out, the intended goals were very different in each case, but in both cases the spectacle does social work: violently remaking community and its moral economies in the one, vehemently reproducing them in another.

Notes

1. Certainly the argument could be made that the management of the media and its presentation of the video-game violence of laser-guided strikes and fireworks of "shock and awe" were very much concerned with allowing the American public to take pleasure in the dialectic spectacle of US military might unleashed and enemies crushed without crossing the (relatively low) contemporary American threshold for acceptable violence (see Lutz this volume).
2. See Campbell (2009) for a preliminary theory of socio-political forms through time in terms of networks and boundaries.

References

Asad, Talal
    2003   *Formations of the Secular: Christianity, Islam, Modernity*. Stanford University Press, Stanford.

Campbell, Rod
    2009   Toward a Networks and Boundaries Approach to Early Complex Polities: The Late Shang Case. *Current Anthropology* 50(6): 821–848.

Clastres, Pierre
    1989   *Society Against the State*. Zone Books, New York.

Elias, Norbert
    1994   *The Civilizing Process: The History of Manners and State Formation and Civilization*. Translation by Edmund Jephcott. Blackwell, Oxford.

Fletcher, Jonathan
    1997   *Violence and Civilization: An Introduction to the Work of Norbert Elias*. Polity Press, Malden, MA.

Heidegger, Martin
    2003   Letters on Humanism. In *From Modernism to Postmodernism: An Anthology*, edited by Lawrence Cahoone, pp. 274–308. Blackwell, Malden, MA.

Scarry, Elaine.
    1985   *The Body in Pain: The Making and Unmaking of the World*. Oxford University Press, New York.

Smith, Jonathan Z.
    1987   The Domestication of Sacrifice. In *Violent Origins: Walter Burkert, René Girard and Jonathan Z. Smith on Ritual Killing and Cultural Formation*, edited by Robert G. Hamerton-Kelly, pp. 191–205. Stanford University Press, Stanford.

Todorov, Tzvetan
    1992   *The Conquest of America: The Question of the Other*. Translated by Richard Howard. Harper Perennial, New York.

Histories of Violence:
Notes from the Roman Empire

Ari Z. Bryen

Ruling the Roman Empire

As the editor's introduction to this volume indicates, there is self-evidently a relationship between civilization – here conceived as a stable, persistent, distinctive social order – and violence, even if their precise interrelationship is problematic or unclear. As the editor also makes clear, the question itself has a distinguished pedigree: while Campbell's genealogy traces it back at least to Hobbes (whose theories provide the most durable analytical framework for modern inquiry), it was similarly a question that held the interest of the Greco-Roman world – appearing in the fifth century B.C. (albeit in a rather crude form) in the introduction to Thucydides' *History of the Peloponnesian War* (1.2) and in Plato's *Protagoras* (322–3).

The question of the interrelationship between violence, order, and empire is similarly an old one, and has proven fruitful for social scientific inquiry not least because it sits at a middle point in scholarly inquiry between some of the most fundamental questions of social science (Why and how is it that certain kinds of inequality are persistent? Under what circumstances are governments instituted and do people allow themselves to be ruled?) and a series of smaller, more empirical questions (Which empires seem to have been most successful at ruling? What were their particular techniques of governance? In what fashion did they involve themselves in the daily life of their individual subjects at the economic, spiritual, or cognitive levels?). In coming up with answers to any of the above questions some concept of violence has often proven useful for modern scholars, even if the concept itself has remained under-theorized, as compared to order.

This is no less true for the ways in which empire was analyzed in the ancient world itself. The question of how it was that, in the phrasing of Polybius of Megalopolis (ca. 203–ca. 120 B.C.), "practically the entire

inhabited world in less than 53 years came under the exclusive control of
the Romans" (1.1.5) was an urgent element of political theodicy in second
century Greece. The way Polybius's contemporary Greeks might have asked
the question ("How could this have happened *to us*?") was clearly different
from the ways that the Romans themselves would have sought to explain
the success of their own empire, and the role of violence in their respective
answers was similarly different. Polybius's explanation was that the Roman
Empire conquered and governed successfully through the combination of
a domestic political structure that prevented internal violence (*stasis*) and a
military structure that was expert at external violence (war). The answer of
Cicero, a Roman senator writing in the first century B.C., sought, in contrast,
to deemphasize the link between violence and political order: according to
Cicero, Roman governance is effective in no small part because the Romans
themselves were substantially *less* violent in their governance than others
– being rather rational and merciful, and resorting to violence only in readily
predictable circumstances.[1]

Though their solutions to the question of what made the Romans
successful were clearly different, both Polybius and Cicero contrast violence
and order. Order is rational – or at least able to be rationalized, and eventually
to become routine. One can describe an order, claim that it is normative, or
at least argue that it is worthy of emulation. A particular order can constitute
an ideology at least in the limited sense that it provides a constellation of
practical truths around which a person or a community can structure its own
behavior, achieve predictable results, and make sense of the complex world
that it inhabits. Violence, in contrast, is merely a technique: one that can
be mastered, controlled, or deployed strategically, to be sure, though usually
only temporarily, like holding a lid on a boiling pot. To the extent that order
is connected to ruling ideology, it is self-evident why it should be improved,
adjusted, or protected. The perfection of violence, however, is only a self-
evident good when the violence is placed in the service of protecting order
or installing a competing order; to strive to excel at violence for its own sake,
or for no particular reason whatsoever, is merely pathological.[2]

It is no accident that Cicero and Polybius are among the ancient thinkers
most influential in the development of modern theories of government:
their contrast between order and violence has largely proven useful for
approaching a variety of questions (Lintott 1999). But while these thinkers
have proven influential for the study of order, they have proven less helpful
for our attempts to understand violence. There was not, in the Roman
Republic, a serious attempt to theorize violence as more than a problem of
political order (though note Lintott 1999b; Riggsby 1999; Thomas 1984).
With the emergence of the Principate, violence became somewhat less urgent

as a political problem, but this should not be taken to mean that violence did not serve as a topic for reflection and discussion. It is unfortunate, however, that the Principate, for reasons perhaps understandable, lacks for a serious political theorist who could have left us a well-theorized account of such developments.[3] The unification of the powers of government in the person of one man was consequential for many aspects of life in the Roman Empire, particularly for the ways in which rule over others was justified and defended (Brunt 1990). At the same time, the advent of one-man rule promoted the standardization and ritualization of types of, and venues for, spectacular violence, in addition to the development of a structured legal discourse concerning what might and what might not count as a judicially redeemable violation. It seems reasonable to imagine that these processes occurred in conversation with one another, and that with the development of serious imperial justifications of the Roman order, there developed an analogous series of changes in the ways that the Romans understood the proper management of violence – even if these were never given detailed elaboration.

In what follows I hope to sketch, albeit in rough detail, a typology of violence in the Roman Empire. The typology I present will seek to organize concepts of legitimate violence in the Roman world by reference to concepts of membership. The main goal in organizing the material in this fashion is to try to accentuate the difference between various types of violence – not only the distinction between legitimate and illegitimate (and whatever horizon might have existed between the two), but also to try to make distinctions between types of legitimate violence. Empires deal in difference and distinction; this is no less true for the ways that members of empires rationalize violence and consume violent imagery. The purpose of offering this typology is to try to bring some order to the mass of material concerning the Principate that might be deemed "violent", and through this to show how attitudes towards violence, and in particular, permissible reactions to violence, served, in the Roman world, as one means of understanding, organizing, and managing a socio-political world system that made claims to divine favor if not to universality. Specifically, by outlining this peculiarly Roman understanding of violence, we can then go on to ask whether or to what extent such an understanding played a role in constituting the political, ethical, and religious world of Rome's subjects. At the level of method, I hope to suggest that, far from being merely the antithesis of order, Roman imperial ideologies of legitimate or legitimizable violence can be subjected to the sort of scholarly analysis that has proven productive in studies of Roman imperial ideologies of peace and order. I focus on three phenomena in particular: war, slavery, and punishment. There is a rich bibliography on all of these phenomena, though (so far as I know) relatively few attempts to place it within a broader framework. It should go without saying that what follows is necessarily preliminary, and makes no claim to be the only possible way in which to organize the diverse, complex, and problematic material.

The Community of Citizens: Distinctions and Interrelationships

Before looking at the typology in greater detail, it is worth clarifying some points about how we should define violence, and in particular how violence was defined within the community of Roman citizens (in the period of the Principate, a small but growing minority of those comprising the Empire as a whole). Bruce Lincoln (2012: 83) has suggested that "we can best theorize violence as the deployment of physical force in a manner that tends to convert subjects – individual or collective, but in either case fully human actors – into depersonalized objects." This is an elegant formulation, and one that has great potential as an ideal-typical claim – that is, a yardstick for comparison. In this formulation, the contrast between violator and victim is mapped onto the categories of human/non-human, human/less-human, or human/object. In this section I will suggest that this definition, while perhaps useful for particular scholarly purposes (that is, from an etic perspective), does not adequately capture what was distinctly "Roman" about violence *within* the community of Roman citizens, where violations of the person were given a particular social and legal status. I will suggest, in the sections that follow, that Lincoln's definition overstates the matter, and that in the Roman Empire an understanding of at least some sorts of violence was predicated on the recognition of the common humanity of both the violator and the victim – at least insofar as only people, not objects, were entitled to feel pain. What is more, the participation in this common humanity was, in turn, predicated on acceptance of the fact of social inequality. That is, in an important sense, sameness (in the sense of membership in a community or an empire) was predicated on recognizing and accepting difference. This is an important difference from modern understandings of full membership in a community. As good egalitarians, we are often accustomed to equate the fact of subordination with evacuations of humanity and harm to human dignity – think, for instance, or the ways that contemporary rhetoric treats questions of "second-class" citizenship. But such ideas would probably have seemed peculiar to the Romans, who, more often than not, took difference and differential privilege, as well as ranked gradations of membership, largely as a given. As far as violence goes, we might add that for any violation of the body (any "deployment of physical force") to be equated with the loss of humanity (conversion to a "depersonalized object"), we must posit that humanity itself is a something which is vested, completely but tenuously, in the individual person (or perhaps in the individual community). We must also posit, in what seems to me a distinctly modern way, that this person exists as an independent atom free from all social bonds and networks while being charged with policing the boundaries of his ever-threatened place in society. Any challenge to these boundaries constitutes an erasure, and any affront to this person's dignity, no matter how minor, results in the evaporation of a part of him.

Now, it can be useful to posit (for legal or analytical reasons) that the solitary person is the fundamental unit of social analysis. But in point of fact most human beings exist within complex webs of interpersonal relationships and occupy distinct and unequal positions with respect to other members of these networks. There is no reason to posit, *a priori*, that the fact of subordination within these relationships or the capacity to count as violated is necessarily based on being more or less human. Unlike the mythical "war of all against all" posited by the theory of the social contract (in which the isolated individual serves as the basic analytical unit), Roman foundational mythology does not envision individual atoms who tentatively come together and cede power to a sovereign as the source of social solidarity. The Romans themselves drew from a different foundational mythology: according to Livy (writing in the first century A.D.), social cohesion starts with the foundation of city itself, and the cooperation of the male citizen founders in the search for wives (whom they abduct from their neighbors). In contrast to the myth of social cohesion that posits the individual person as the basic unit of analysis, in the Roman world the basic units of analysis are the family and the community of citizens.

Where we start the analysis has consequences for where we end up. In contrast to the contractarian theory in which violence further isolates and depersonalizes the individual victim, let me sketch two ways in which violence serves to activate, and thereby confirm, links between individuals at the level of the family and of the citizen community. Both examples are drawn from Roman laws concerning interpersonal violence (*iniuria*). The first is an example of how hierarchical (family) relationships are activated and humanity is confirmed among victims of violence; the second is an instance of how violent action serves to create bonds of obligation and personhood between violators and victims within the civic community as a whole.

We may define interpersonal violence (*iniuria*) as intentional harm to the person of another. Such a definition has certain advantages: primarily, it is a definition that the Romans would have understood. Personhood (*persona*) was understood to be a totality which encompassed not only the physical body (*corpus*) but both the corporeal body and the social body – the reputation.[4] Violence could be felt corporeally, extra-corporeally, or both (Paul *Sent.* 5.4.1). The question of the intentional nature of a particular harm is more vexed: a concept of intentionality is not strictly necessary for a modern definition of violence, but is important for explaining the Roman conception of *iniuria*, at least in the Imperial period.

> We are told that those who can suffer can be equally guilty of *iniuria*. Of course, there are some who cannot be guilty, such as the lunatic or the minor not capable of wrongful intent; they can suffer *iniuria* but not be guilty of perpetrating it. For since *iniuria* consists in the will (*ex affectu*) of the culprit, it follows that these classes, even if they do strike people or shout abuse, will not be regarded as having committed an affront. Thus, someone can suffer an insult, even though unaware, but no one can perpetrate one without knowing what he is doing, even though he does not know to whom he is doing it [*Dig.* 47.10.3pr-2 (Ulpian, *ad Edictum* 56), trans. Watson 1985].

Crucially, this definition is narrower than our definition of violence: *iniuria* does not include violence done during war, politically-motivated violence (*vis*, or *vis publica*), rape or abduction, extortionate threats of violence (*metus*), theft or harm to property. It does not include things that moderns might term structural or symbolic violence. Certain kinds of violence within familial structures would not have counted as *iniuria*, but this is not to say that all violence within familial structures was legally acceptable (it was not; see Westbrook 1999 on *vitae necisque potestas*; Watson 1979 on *parricidium*). It is worth emphasizing that the definitions of *iniuria* here are drawn from Roman *private* law – the law that governs the interactions of members of the civic community. Insofar as the Roman jurists chose to think about this concept, it was by recourse to a very civic framework.

In posing these definitions we are already in the process of mapping distinctions at several levels. At one level, distinctions are made between individual "rough acts" (to use the phrasing of Lincoln); at another, between actors themselves, in particular their positions relative to society as a whole and their capacity for certain types of intentionality. The latter two are undoubtedly connected, even if their precise interrelationship is unclear. The case of children and madmen is instructive: while not capable inflicting *iniuria*, they are capable of feeling it. They cannot inflict it because they lack the requisite capacity for insult, but this does not preclude their familial representative from legal action on their behalf. As *iniuria* has been committed even if they fail to sense it, it stands to reason that someone would be authorized to seek justice for them. But this raises a possibility with stakes that are more than legal: it implies a capacity – in fact, a legal necessity – to feel violence for another, on his or her behalf. Generally the right to sue for *iniuria* done to subordinates was given to the *paterfamilias*, the independent head of the family:

> Again, *iniuria* can be effected against someone personally or through others: personally, when a *paterfamilias* or a matron is directly affronted; through others, when it happens by consequence, as when the affront is to one's children or slaves, one's wife or daughter-in-law; for *iniuria* affects us which is suffered by those who are subject to our power or are the objects of our affection [*Dig.* 47.10.1.3 (Ulpian, *ad Edictum* 56), trans. Watson 1985].

The ability to feel/sue on account of *iniuria* done to family members was, of course, deeply connected to internal hierarchies within the family. The *paterfamilias* could sue for *iniuria* to a child or a madman. Similarly, he would be able to sue for a violent act against a slave, who *was* capable of inflicting *iniuria*, but not capable of feeling it.[5] He could sue for *iniuria* done to his wife, even if she was not in a formal relationship of subordination to him (*quamvis in manu nostra non sint*: Gaius, *Inst.* 3.221). Wives, however, could not sue on behalf of *iniuria* done to their husbands (*Dig.* 47.10.2 [Paul, *ad Edictum* 50]). Grown sons pose an interesting problem: sons could sue when their father is present, but only if the father was somehow incapacitated; otherwise, if the father choose not to sue, the son had no standing – unless it was decided that the father is a "vile" or "abject" person (Dig. 47.10.17.11–13 [Ulpian, *ad Edictum* 57]). But this was true only if the son sued within the scope of the *private* law; if the son chose to sue under the *public* law concerning violence – the *Lex Cornelia de iniuriis* – his father would have no say on his decision, nor could his father sue on his behalf (*Dig.* 47.10.5.6–7 [Ulpian, *ad Edictum* 56]). Such understandings of the proper, civic forms of personhood and obedience worked the other way around, as well, prohibiting suits by *formerly* lower-status members against higher status members of the family. Thus, freed slaves only rarely would be given actions against their former master (their patron), and then only if the patron treated the freedmen like a slave (*Dig.* 47.10.7.2 [Ulpian, *ad Edictum* 57]); children only rarely would be allow to sue their fathers, and only then if the child had been emancipated from the father's *potestas* (*Dig.* 47.10.7.3 [Ulpian, *ad Edictum* 57]).

In the case of *iniuria*, it is the fact of distinctions and subordination that allows pain to be felt among distinctly unequal members of the household, and on behalf of others. But these feelings move only along certain paths, and only in certain directions. In other words, the ability to feel violated on another's behalf is both a claim on the other's person as well as a claim of the other's validity as a member of the order, if only at a subordinate level. The *paterfamilias* is, in the neat and tidy world of the jurists, the final authority: as the only truly independent member of society, he could feel violence through his subordinates, but not his equals (compare *Dig.* 48.10.39 [Venuleius, *Publicorum Iudiciorum* 2]).

While the father cannot feel pain delivered to other heads of households, this civil law system for dealing with violence nonetheless creates other types of links between free and independent people. Most importantly, by emphasizing the intentionality of the violator, it similarly marks the violator as counting as a full person him- or herself. What is more, the result of doing *iniuria* to someone would produce, in Roman law, a relationship of *obligation* between the two parties – that is, a relationship where the insult to one person (or his subordinates) had to be redeemed by pricing the value of the harm done to the violated person. In other words, by classifying this particular sort of violence the way that it did, the Roman legal system demanded that, within the civic community at least, those capable of doing harm to one another – or representing those who harmed others – recognize one another as full and capable human beings with the capacity for intentionality (compare Bryen 2013). The harder matter is to pinpoint in what degree this system was restricted to members of the civic community. Was this recognition of the humanity of both victim and violator really limited just to Roman citizens, either in practice or in theory? This is a very difficult question to answer, not least because, as Clifford Ando (2011) has emphasized, the laws governing interactions between Romans and non-Romans have largely been effaced from what is left of our judicial texts. Suffice to say, in this instance, one can imagine two possible answers to the question: either (1) it would have seemed very strange indeed to Roman jurists to impute to non-Roman peoples the same types of hierarchically ordered familial relations that Romans took pride in thinking exclusively their own (Gaius, *Inst.* 1.55); or (2) as a practical matter, where a non-Roman person violated a Roman, whoever would have been in charge of dealing the this offense would have been under pressure to treat the violator as having transgressed a boundary by harming a full member of an imperial power, and would punish the violator more harshly.

This, however, must remain speculation. What matters more, for the discussion at hand, is merely to note the ways in which the Roman legal system theorized the relationship between violation, personhood, and hierarchical relationships of power and domination. In the civil law, at least, there is a recognition of the sameness, humanity, and interconnectedness of violators and victims. If it occasionally finds itself in tension with hierarchy, it is similarly dependant on it. Within this system pain is transferrable. Modern individuals who live in a system that presumes isolation and equality have no choice but to make do when someone in authority makes a limp and inauthentic claim to feel their pain. In contrast, by presuming family and civic community as the basic levels of analysis, in the Roman system not only are others able to claim that they feel another's pain, they are legally obligated to do so.

States, War, and Membership

Approaching violence through the rules of Roman law provides one way of grappling with the problem of how to analyze the interrelationship between violence and order. But the case of Roman law is telling in another way. Roman law was not considered a universal or generalizable system of moral precepts, and was restricted to a small percentage of the inhabitants of empire until the universal grant of citizenship in 212. Others were understood to be bound by their own laws, which were distinct but inferior (e.g., Cicero, *Leg.* 2.23; *RP* 1.34). But at the same time, two features of the development of Roman private law concerning violence are worthy of note. First, private-law treatments of *iniuria* are interesting, since they emerge from their relatively rudimentary archaic forms to topics of sustained jurisprudential inquiry *pari passu* with the extension of empire and with the development of the Principate, and alongside (if not in direct conversation with) the developing imperial understandings of violence (Hagemann 1998: 64–68, 100–109). Second, the language of personal violation comes, in the late Republic and early Principate, to serve as an important term for thinking about foreign policy – specifically, about the rightness of war. As Susan Mattern (1999: 184–88) has emphasized, the Romans considered it just and decorous to go to war to avenge (*ulciscor*) perceived *iniuria*. This stretching of the vocabulary of private law to the frame of international relations is a critical move, and one of the ways that the study of Roman civil law can be used as a tool for understanding the expansion of empire (see further, Ando 2011). The system that I will begin to outline does not follow precisely the same logic of interpersonal violence sketched above, but it does share similar features. In particular, it is founded on conceptions of a common humanity that is vested in the acceptance of inequality, and linked to understandings of who can rightly be violated and how. In this context, the Roman state appears as the manager of violence, making possible a system in which it can only partially participate. In particular, the state in the Roman world distinguishes between forms of violence by specifying the extent to which one is allowed to take pleasure in the violence done to other members of the imperial order. Whereas pleasure is not part of the equation when considering interpersonal violence between Roman citizens, it is a fundamental part of the ways in which violence against non-citizen members of the Empire were treated. Within this system, there are specific types of violence against different members of the imperial community through which one can take more or less pleasure.

For the purpose of what follows, I will define Empire simply as a system of political organization in which one group of people rules over another group of people; this involves the recognition of differences between peoples, between ours and theirs, or, more appropriately, between three levels: that which is ours, that which is theirs which is now ours, and that which is theirs which is not, or not yet, ours. The means by which "theirs" becomes "ours" is predominantly war and annexation, which was undoubtedly considered a form of violence, albeit a highly problematic one which was inextricably bound together with concepts of membership. Roman conceptions of the process of crafting an empire are complex, in some respects elusive, and changed significantly over time (Brunt 1990; Lintott 1993; Richardson 1991; 2008). Without venturing to present a new analysis, some basic conceptual features can be identified. First, the overwhelming majority of Roman literary and legal sources are unanimous that the empire itself was just; while there may have been regrettable instances of injustice during individual wars, such as the sack of Corinth (Cic. *Off.* 3.11.46, c.f. 1.10.32–33), wars themselves which sought to bring glory to the Roman people were sanctioned by the gods. While undeniably violent, they were also in accordance with the wishes of the divinities that Rome itself both prosper and rule. Second, while the peoples defeated by Rome may have been different and in some respects deficient, they were not thereby less human. It would be a lousy empire indeed that claimed to rule over beasts or objects, rather than men. The evidence itself points to the contrary: while Roman elites were largely disdainful of the character of the provincials and did not hesitate to cast aspersions on them, they were sensitive to the fact that the process of defeat and incorporation into the imperial system weakened and endangered some of the very elements that had made them worthy opponents. The *locus classicus* is in Tacitus' biography of Cn. Iulius Agricola, where he describes the civilizing process that accompanied the conquest of Britain:

> The following winter was taken up with some highly beneficial planning. To make these men, who had previously been geographically dispersed, wild, and therefore prone to war, accustomed to the peace and quiet that comes from pleasures, he [Agricola] gave encouragement in private and support in public to set up temples, marketplaces, and houses. He further encouraged them by praising those eager to do this and punishing those slow in helping. Because of this there was competition for honor instead of compulsion. He even taught the chieftains' children the liberal arts, preferring the temperament of the Britons to the eagerness of the Gauls, with the result that those who had only recently rejected the Latin language now desired to be eloquent. In this way even our clothing became desirable, and the toga became common. Right away they moved on to the charms of vice – to the piazzas, to the baths, to elegant parties. All this, among these inexperienced men, was called civilization (*humanitas*), though it was in reality of part of their enslavement (*servitutis*) [*Agr.* 21].

In response to Agricola's presence, a native revolt broke out in Britain under the leadership of the chief Calgacus. In his narrative, Tacitus has him rally his troops by means of a speech which feels strikingly modern in its condemnation of the Romans:

> They are the plunderers of the world: they pillage the sea now that all of the land has been left in ruins. If the enemy is rich, they're greedy; if poor, they wish to control him; neither the East nor the West will satisfy these men. They are the only people in the world who lust after wealth and poverty with the same desire. Robbery, slaughter, and plunder they falsely call legitimate rule (*imperium*); when they leave the place a desert, they call it peace (*pacem*) [*Agr.* 30].[6]

Calgacus' critique of Roman rapacity is damning, but its inclusion within Tacitus' narrative is more complex than it might seem. Although Tacitus is capable of writing a defense of a native revolt from a perspective that Romans could understand, he never suggests that the endeavors of Agricola were in some way unjust. While the conquest of Britain may have involved great violence, it does not follow that it should not have been conquered. Tacitus offers a number of biting critiques of imperial politics; this does not imply that he was critiquing the fact of empire. There is no reason to presume, *a priori*, that once someone recognizes that what he is doing is "violence" he will necessarily stop doing it: the fact of reducing others to slavery may have involved unpleasant acts, but it was nonetheless the will of the gods for Rome to rule over others. Rather, that such a powerful indictment of Rome itself can be found in the writings of one of its senators suggests that Tacitus recognized that the nature of empire contained an element of tragedy: while necessary and good to conquer others, the conquest robs them of what made them noble in the first place (Liebeschuetz 2012 [1966]: 90–92; Clarke 2012 [2001]: 59). The results of conquest were complex, occasionally unfortunate, and certainly violent; this did not mean that the fact of conquest was not an occasion for celebration (see also Brunt 1990: 314). Tacitus states, seemingly without irony, that Agricola's troops celebrated their decisive victory over Calgacus, no doubt not far from the battleground itself which he earlier described as covered in "scattered weapons, dead bodies, mangled body parts, and blood-soaked soil" (*Agr.* 37). Agricola himself was honored for his victory. To the extent that the conquest itself was unfortunate, it was that, in spite of his virtues and successes, Agricola himself worked within a system that was itself degenerate and harmful to virtue (Liebeschuetz 1966: 138; Lavan 2011).

The immediate joy (or relief) of victory was frequently accompanied by ritualized celebrations within the city of Rome itself. The Triumph (a ritual largely monopolized by the emperor during the Principate), featured processions through the city of Rome featuring the display of conquered peoples (either the captured enemies themselves or visual representations thereof), accompanied by the victorious army, and celebrations in the form of public games. Similarly, the exploits of triumphant generals (in the Republic) and emperors (in the Principate) were monumentalized in the visual culture of the city of Rome itself, such as in the arch of Titus which depicts the spoils of the conquest of the Jews after their rebellion in A.D. 70, or in the *gentes devictae* monuments that appear in Rome starting in the late Republic (Smith 1988: 70–77).[7] While the origins, history, and function of the triumph are obscure, recent restudy of the relevant evidence for triumphal practices by Mary Beard (2007) has emphasized the complexities of the ritual. While it indeed was a raucous affair in which spectators took pleasure in violence done to conquered peoples, Beard notes that the triumphal rituals could similarly embody particular tensions. First, there was the question of what, if anything, to do with the captives who served as a source of pleasure for Roman audiences: while a number of the defeated enemies would have been killed in the fighting itself, and a further number enslaved, some choice individuals (particularly foreign kings, insofar as possible), would be brought to Rome itself. Sometimes they would be executed, but, Beard notes (2007: 140), they could just as easily be humiliated at that moment and later be well-treated by Romans – eventually, in some cases, achieving citizenship. Seen in this light, the immediate pleasure taken in the violence done to others stands in tension with the fact that the enemy was, literally, first at the gates (the *porta triumphalis*, through which the triumph began), and subsequently, within the city itself, to be managed like other members of the empire as a whole – that is, no longer as an enemy, but as a subject, a subordinate member of the imperial community, and one who can potentially receive rights beyond that station.[8]

A second point deserves emphasis: while the populace of the city of Rome (as well as already subordinated members of the imperial order) took pleasure in the parade of captured enemies and the accompanying games and festivities, the emperor himself took only a far more restrained pleasure in his victories. While he may have claimed a monopoly on the triumphal honors themselves, he in no way claimed a monopoly on the pleasures that people were permitted to take in them. For the emperor, the commemoration of defeats of foreign powers was circumscribed: the giving of titles was formally the prerogative of the Senate, which offered titles to victorious (and sometimes, when the system failed, to non-victorious) emperors in a dance of self-legitimizing reciprocity. To be legitimate, to be seen as a "good" emperor, some titles had to be refused, and at most, the emperor was to take just one triumph per defeated enemy, and one title (such as Parthicus,

Germanicus, and so forth; the vicissitudes of the title Imperator are a more complex issue: McFayden 1920: 53–67; Syme 1958; Talbert 1984: 362–64). Because they were gifts of the Senate that attached to individuals rather than to the office, the titles were non-transferable: an imperial successor could not claim a title earned by his predecessor.[9] This controlled system of titulature and credit was limited to emperors; the remainder of the populace was free to erect temples commemorating the violent defeat of others in the empire, to decorate sarcophagi with images of defeated foreigners, and to otherwise appropriate these images (Smith 1988; Zimmermann 2006: 345). Within this system the state manages violence, initiates its benefits, and facilitates its pleasures for others, but less so much for itself; the state itself partakes of only a limited version of these pleasures and then only within clearly delimited chronological boundaries.[10]

Empire and Slavery

The question of the status of conquered peoples speaks to a different type of violence, and one in which there were yet sharper distinctions concerning the types of pleasure that could be taken in violence. The passage from Tacitus' *Agricola* cited above makes the problem plain: the civilizing process – the act of being brought into the Empire – could just as easily be described as a form of slavery.[11] While sources from the Republican era betray a tension between various ways of describing the precise status of members of the imperial order – as clients, allies, or slaves – in the Principate the language of slavery is used by Roman writers with far greater ease.[12] The link between slavery and annexation is one that Roman legal theorists understood on etymological grounds:

> Freedom is one's natural power (*facultas*) of doing what one pleases, save insofar as it is ruled out either by coercion or by law. Slavery is an institute of the law of peoples, whereby someone is against nature made subject to the ownership of another. Slaves (*servi*) are so-called, because generals have a custom of selling prisoners and thereby preserving (*servare*) rather than killing them: and indeed they are said to be *mancipia*, because they are captives in the hand (*manus*) of their enemies [*Dig.* 1.5.4, Florentinus Institutes 9, trans. Watson 1985].

The challenge of providing consistent legal frameworks for a slave system has resulted in a mass of material for modern historians. Questions about ways of managing slaves and their actions infect nearly every chapter of the Roman legal sources; slavery, especially the treatment of slaves, is a common theme in imperial literature (Garnsey 1996; Wiedemann 1981); inscriptions by former slaves (freedmen, *liberti*) and their descendants compose a significant proportion of the epigraphic record (on the epigraphic material, see Woolf 1996: 35–36). Questions about the legal status of violence (*iniuria*) done to and done by slaves are found throughout the juristic discussions of *iniuria*. In the last quarter-century, historians have done away with the notion that Roman slavery was significantly more humane than modern slavery (Bradley 1987, 2000; Hopkins 1993; Watson 1991). With the violence of the institution no longer a matter of serious debate, several further questions present themselves. First, to what degree is there a useful historical analogy between the lives of actual domestic slaves and a line of thinking that describes the process of annexing territory as a form of enslavement? Second, if there is a useful analogy (and I believe there is), then what are the rules and requirements for the conduct of violence within this institution, how do they relate to the structure of the imperial community as a whole, and how do they differ from the rules and requirements of war or those of the relations between citizens?

At one level, slavery provides a durable metaphor for theorizing both hierarchy and obligations. The obligations of the slave to his or her master were essentially absolute. Later in the Principate legal provisions were introduced that allowed slaves suffering under excessive cruelty by their masters to flee to sanctuaries, but how this actually would have worked in practice is unclear: slaves were not permitted to testify against their masters, and so could not offer proof of cruelty (see Watson 1987: 120–121 on J. *Inst.* 1.8.1). Masters' rights were limited only within highly particular areas: castration, for instance, was forbidden by the emperors Domitian and later again by Nerva. Similarly, slaves were at the mercy of owners sexually (legal sources pay particular attention to the status of the offspring of free-slave unions), economically (the slave could be sold as a gladiator, to the mills or to the mines, or put up for rent as a prostitute), and juridically (the slave could be handed over for torture). All that slaves produced was the property of their masters (aside from their *peculium*, a fictive legal carve-out to recognize some forms of *de facto* ownership by slaves). The only thing that one appears *not* to have been able to do with slaves is kill or abandon them:

> When certain men were exposing their sick and worn out slaves on the island of Aesculapius because of the trouble of treating them, [Claudius] declared that all who were exposed became free, nor were they to revert to the master's control if they recovered. But if anyone wished to kill rather than expose he would be liable for murder [Suet. *Claud.* 25.2, citation and translation from Watson 1987: 122].

The situation of the provincials was better than that of slaves: provincials could appeal to governors and sometimes emperors,[13] they were protected by laws, and the imperial government sought to accommodate their quality of life to the degree necessary for the smooth collection of revenues. But the choice of language is telling, and provides one example of how the language of private law – the language that defined the relationships between members of the civic community – can be stretched almost to the point of rupture to define the relationships between subordinate and superordinate members of the imperial community: while provincial governors were asked to treat their subjects well (as were masters of slaves), abandonment and dereliction of duty towards one's charges was acceptable neither legally nor socially.

An analogous link between subjects and slaves is found in the realities or perceptions of the slave's life cycle. While Greek philosophers developed a doctrine of natural slavery, such a doctrine was never a serious part of mainstream Roman legal thinking. Slavery was a condition into which people could and often did fall; similarly, it was one from which people could emerge. Roman slavery cannot be conceptualized adequately without considering manumission: the manumitted slave, barring some exceptions, would emerge from slavery to become the client of his former master, now his patron. He would in most circumstances be granted citizenship – that is, membership in the community, and a participant in the system of shared pain and humanity outlined above: whereas violence done to a slave was counted as violence done to the master, violence done against a freedman could also be felt by the patron, but the freedman would additionally be able to suffer *iniuria* himself (whereas the slave could not). This juristic picture of manumission is, without doubt, more easily apprehended than its actual practice, the evidence for which is complex and sometimes contradictory.[14] But based on the epigraphic attestations of freedmen it is certain that the practice of manumission was a reality for some slaves at least, as was their enfranchisement, sometimes as full Roman citizens. Analogously, the grant of franchise to selected provincials based on meritorious service to Rome was increasingly a reality in the imperial period (Sherwin-White 1973: 251–263).

As fact and metaphor, slavery provided Romans with a powerful (if imperfect) vocabulary for theorizing their relationships with subordinate others at the imperial level, one which was based on a promise (if not a reality) of eventual full membership in a civic community. The promise or possibility of future inclusion seems to have been an important part of the ways in which the violence of this system was managed. But whereas the potential for manumission and inclusion could provide an incentive at the domestic level, at the imperial level authorities feared that including the victims of violence in the civic community would devalue membership. In his biography of the emperor Augustus, Suetonius preserves this notice of legal reforms:

He thought it a matter of great importance to preserve the people pure and untainted by any admixture of foreign or servile blood, giving grants of Roman citizenship most rarely and placing a limit on manumissions. When Tiberius requested [citizenship] on behalf of a Greek client, he made a formal reply that he would only make the grant if the man came in person and explained why he had just cause for requesting it. And when Livia sought citizenship for a Gaul from a tribute-paying province he denied the request but granted the man immunity [from the tribute], saying that he would rather endure that the treasury suffer some loss than to have the honor of Roman citizenship cheapened. Not only did he put many obstacles in the way of slaves seeking freedom, and still more in the way of those seeking freedom with citizenship, by making careful provision as to the number, status, and type of those who were set free, but he also stipulated that no one who had ever been bound or tortured should ever receive citizenship, no matter what their degree of freedom [Suet. *Aug.* 40.3, translation modified from Edwards 2000].

The immediate if chronologically-bounded joy of conquest was transformed into the emperor's anxieties about membership. But if the imperial response was anxious about the membership of both former chattel and conquered foreigners, the slave-holding populace could take pleasure in their domination. Yet in contrast to the full enjoyment of imperial victories and the enslavement of others on a large scale, the pleasures of domestic slavery were themselves bounded – in this case not chronologically, but rather spatially – restricted to the level of the taking pleasures in cruelty in a private, rather than a public setting.

This statement deserves qualification: the particular pleasures of the slave relationship – particularly sexual enjoyment – were fundamentally domestic pleasures. The beatings, shacklings, sales, maimings, brandings, and other creative forms of cruelty were not meant to be a source of pleasure, and literary sources that record these punishments, while anecdotal and moralistic, indicate that it was considered deeply crass to take pleasure in disfiguring one's own slaves (Bradley 1987; Parker 1989). Further, those who made it their business to engage in the degradation of slaves were fundamentally disreputable characters – be they the slave-dealer (*mango*) or the official contracted to handle slave punishments (*manceps*) attested in an inscription from Puteoli whose primary responsibilities were to deal with the dead (Shaw 2000: 391; Hinard and Dumont 2003: col. II, ll.8–9). One may object that the sources which record opprobrium towards these men's cruelty to the slaves of others were composed by slave owners themselves, who may have thought themselves better than others, but who in fact were not. I would agree, but add that this moralizing derives from the fundamentally problematic position of the slave in society, and is an indication of the anxieties about membership outlined above. One could also add that the emphasis in the literary sources in no ways denies violence, but urges its practitioners to manage their consumption of violence tastefully – by treating it as a pedagogically useful correction, rather than as a commodiafiable pleasure: a fitting warning perhaps for men who, by virtue of their position in the master-slave relationship, were to prove capable of using violence indiscriminately.

Rejecting Distinctions: Punishment and Order

The distinction regarding slaves between punishment as correction (something one does to enforce social expectations, and in which one takes no pleasure) and the moral opprobrium placed on taking pleasure in the purposeful disfigurement of the body of one's charges is one that is largely obliterated when considering the public punishments and spectacular violence that begin to appear in the Principate. The brutality and creativity of these public punishments has attracted attention not only by scholars, but also by popular audiences (Coleman 1990; Garnsey 1968; Millar 2004; MacMullen 1990; Shaw 1996, 2003). The question of punishment is one which is complicated not only by the intersection of several forms of evidence, but also by the intersection of multiple social concerns, which include (but are not limited to): how societies choose to define and deal with deviancy, how conceptions of punishment and conceptions of sovereign power develop analogously, and how creative or exemplary punishments serve to constitute judicial and social truths (Gleason 1999).

While the crowds cheering at blood in the arena are the most immediately memorable image of Roman punishment and violence, the arena was not the only way in which the Roman chose to punish. Crucifixion was a similarly public, and in some ways distinctly Roman punishment.[15] Condemnation to the mines or to hard labor were similarly death sentences, albeit ones in which suffering was prolonged and unspectacular (Millar 2004). Most important, however, was the distinction between ways of punishing the elite and the lower classes. Compare two passages from Suetonius:

> When Quintus Gallius, the praetor, paid Augustus his morning greeting while having some tablets concealed in his cloak, Augustus suspected that he was concealing a sword. He did not dare to interrogate him right away, lest something else should be found, but a little while later some soldiers and centurions snatched him from his tribunal, tortured him like a slave, and, when he confessed to nothing, Augustus ordered him to be killed – but not before he ripped out Gallius' eyes with his own hands. Augustus, however, writes [in his autobiography] that he asked for a meeting as part of a plot, and Augustus had him taken into custody and then exiled, but he died after that either in a shipwreck or because he was attacked by bandits [Suet. *Aug.* 27.4].

A few days after he reached Capreae, and while he was taking care of some secret business, he unexpectedly met a fisherman who offered him a large mullet. Terrified that this man had come up the back of the island, through rough and difficult terrain, and approached him, he ordered his face to be scrubbed with the fish. When the man nonetheless gave thanks during his punishment that he had not given the emperor the giant lobster that he had caught, Tiberius ordered his face to be scrubbed with the lobster, too [Suet. *Tib.* 60].[16]

Both anecdotes describe punishments against people who were, in Suetonius' opinion, fundamentally innocent. Both are examples of the paranoia that infects holders of imperial power. And both are chilling, though in different ways: the flaying of the fisherman does its social work by making the fisherman wear the signs of his punishment (Bryen 2008; Thomas 1984); the punishment of Gallius, however, works by insinuation and indeterminacy – compare the modern Latin American or Iraqi experiences of the families of those who "disappeared". The former creates an image that will resonate with the broader public; the latter is a way of using rumor, interderminacy, and terror to exercise social control.

While this is not the venue to present a new theory of Roman punishment (territory that has been well-covered by the bibliography listed above), these two examples of perceived *lèse majesté* offer one way of approaching a particularly Roman genre of punishment – the violence of the arena. The introduction of executions into public games was a phenomenon of the Principate, originating, most likely, with the emperor Gaius (Caligula: Suet. *Gaius* 27). It was a hugely popular innovation, and the private citizens who presented games could purchase individual condemned prisoners to have them executed in public, along with beasts for the staged animal hunts (*venationes*) and gladiators (Millar 1977: 193–5). The link between the creative killing of humans and the creative killing of animals was not accidental. As Coleman (1990) has pointed out, these events, especially when set in Rome, were intimately linked to the growth of the power of the Emperor and the equation between violations of the imperial peace and harm to the Emperor's sovereign body. Flaunting the peace of the Empire by failing to follow its rules was tantamount to rejecting the benefits of civilization (*humanitas*), making oneself animal-like, and worthy of disposal along with the other surplus fauna. Both Coleman and Gleason (1999) have demonstrated, though in different ways, that these instances of punishment use spectacular violence to create consensus between state and subject concerning the boundaries of truth, law, and order in imperial society. It is no accident that one truth that this exercise validated was that of appropriate order, structure, and deference within the hierarchies that were seen as supporting imperial society.

…every category of society was represented and visible, each occupying its own area according to the elaborate seating-divisions imposed by Augustus to reflect his view of the proper social order. These spectators, hierarchically arranged in their tiers of seats, were fringed at the back by those for whom Roman society allowed standing-room only, while at the front in the centre of the long axis sat the emperor, primus inter pares, solidly flanked by the occupants of the most privileged seats [Coleman 1990: 72].

Unlike in the cases of war or slavery, in the realm of punishment the display of imperial power – and the coordinate fear that it would have imparted – placed the state and the public on the same page in their enjoyment of violence; through the destruction of animal-like humans the hierarchies that served to otherwise validate human relations were reinforced. Even if elite historians and biographers thought imperial pleasure at these spectacles crass and unfortunate, it is evident that they thought so because the emperor was enjoying violence in the same way as his subjects, rather than distinguishing himself through a cultivated distaste for such spectacles.

Two additional notes should be offered here. The first concerns bandits, who, as Brent Shaw (1984) has discussed, posed a particular challenge to imperial sovereignty. In contrast to foreign kings, who could be paraded in triumph and perhaps executed, bandits and bandit leaders were criminals who felt the brunt of state power on the cross or in the arena. The line between a bandit and a foreign nation was in practice blurry, and in large measure the imperial state got to choose. But it is telling that there were separate treatments and modes of pleasure for those who bucked the imperial peace and failed to maintain their inherited positions in the world (e.g., Apuleius, *Met.* 7.4) – those who were once members, and then rejected membership – and those who had never been members in the first place.

A second note concerns a different group of citizens who failed to respect their station: the Roman plebs. The story is set in the fifth century B.C., but is narrated by Livy, writing in the age of Augustus, and is a contribution to the creation of a new set of foundational myths for the Roman Principate. The story concerns an incident of mass protest, the secession of the Roman plebs in a time of war. With Rome vulnerable, the senate sent an envoy to the plebs, Menenius Agrippa, who addressed the plebs with a fable:

> "Long ago when the members of the human body did not, as they do now, agree with one another (*non ut nunc omnia in unum consentiant*), but each had its own thoughts and the words to express them in (*suum cuique consilium, suus sermo fuerit*), the other parts resented the fact that they should have the worry and trouble of providing everything for the belly, which remained idle, surrounded by its ministers, with nothing to do but enjoy the pleasant things they gave it. So the discontented members plotted together that the hand should carry no

food to the mouth, that the mouth should take nothing that was offered it, and that the teeth should accept nothing to chew. But alas, while they sought in their resentment to subdue the body by starvation, they themselves and the whole body wasted away to nothing. By this it was apparent that the belly, too, has no mean service to perform: it receives food, indeed; but it also nourishes in its turn the other members, giving back to all parts of the body, through its veins, the blood it has made by the process of digestion; and upon this blood our life and our health depend." The fable of the revolt of the body's members Menenius applied to the political situation, pointing out its resemblance to the anger of the populace against the governing class; and so successful was his story that their resentment was mollified. An agreement was reached (*agi deinde de concordia coeptum*) on the condition that the plebs should have their own magistrates to protect them from the consuls, and that these magistrates should be sacrosanct [Livy 2.32–33, trans. Selincourt 1960, with minor changes].

Livy's insertion of this story in his history of Rome is consistent with a late republican interest in the *concordia ordinum* (agreement of the orders) and the *consensus omnium* (agreement of all – the English language strains to distinguish the two terms). It is both a myth of the origins of the tribunate and the tribunician veto, and, as the jurist David Daube (1972: 138) points out in his commentary on this passage, a version of an ancient *Rangstreitsfabel* – a story of the conflict of classes which seeks to provide a logic for inequality. The logic here is that the social body is a coherent whole with each part connected to the center – in this case, the stomach – which is the source of both extraction (of the labor of the limbs) and redistribution (of the blood that it passively produces but which the subservient members share and require to live). Daube rightly realized that Menenius' fable "is, of course, disingenuous. To reflect on the similarity between a social structure and an anatomical one can be quite stimulating; to treat them as the same is a different matter," adding that "Menenius' audience could well have retorted: 'Right, there must be a belly as well as other parts, only let us be the belly for a spell and undertake the refined tasks, while the senators labor as the eyes, hands, and feet'" (Daube 1972: 133). His sense of justice notwithstanding, I would suggest that Daube underestimates the power of the myth, and misses an important and dark undercurrent.

Livy emphasizes that the members of the body had two abilities: to think and prioritize (to generate their own *consilium*), and to articulate these thoughts as speech (*sermo*). The relationship is causal: through their ability to form articulate thoughts (*consilium*), they are able to conspire with one (*sermo*) another and finally to act (to secede). In an effort to punish the stomach they punish themselves and waste away, until they realize that the stomach's redistribution is keeping them alive in the first place. As a result, *concordia* and *consensus* are restored, and the stomach's bottomless hunger is understood as necessary for the function of the social body. But in Livy's formulation, this would appear to depend on the loss of the *sermo* and *consilium* that had provoked the secession in the first place. The contrast between *consensus* on the one hand and *sermo* and *consilium* on the other brought out in the beginning of Menenius telling of the myth cannot be accidental: to realize inequality and exploitation is to be articulate but starving *disiecta membra*; to come together in agreement is to be silent and to validate the hierarchy on which all are dependant for their common humanity.

The Order of Violence

One could summarize the above argument as a table:

War	Full pleasure	Bounded Pleasure (chronologically)	Membership eventually
Slavery	Bounded pleasure (spatially)	Fear	Membership possible
Punishment	Pleasure/Fear	Full pleasure	Membership revoked
	Public	**State**	**Position of Outsiders**

The typology sketched above is a first attempt at placing evidence into a structure that renders it more easily apprehensible. But this ordering of violence is, to my mind, one distinctive feature of the way that the Romans governed their empire. The categories certainly overlap in places – no society that I know of succeeds in policing the margins of what it hopes to retain as distinct categories (see further Morris, this volume, and Campbell, ch. 1, this volume). This does not mean that they did not try. In the Roman case, the order of legitimate violence – in particular, the violence that could be inflicted against those in various relation to the citizen community – was carefully constructed for negotiating anxieties about membership in the context of an expanding citizen body marked by a state which only claimed a partial, managerial role in the governance of the empire as a whole. In the sense that the pleasures of violence were allowed to the state in some capacities, and to the civic community in other, different capacities, is perhaps not distinctively Roman, but this particular typology seems to be.

Whether or not this typology can withstand further scrutiny (and I do emphasize that this is only a preliminary attempt), what should also be asked is whether, or to what extent, it (or some other version of it) was assented to by the constituent members of the imperial order. The terms of this acceptance – if there was one – and its consequences for the history of violence in the Principate and further into the Christianizing world of late antiquity is indeed an open question.

Acknowledgments

This essay was begun during my time as a Visiting Research Scholar at NYU's Institute for the Study of the Ancient World, and completed during my time at Georgetown University. I thank both institutions for their hospitality. This essay has benefited in particular from comments by Anna Boozer and Kevin van Bladel, and from discussion with Michael Peachin. In addition, I thank the editor for arranging the conference that led to this paper, and to the conference participants for sharing their ideas and comments.

Notes

1. I take this to be the primary thesis of book 6 of Polybius' *Histories*; for Cicero's take, see *ad Q. fr.* 1.1.

2. I explore this relationship – and the ethical content of claims that certain acts constitute "violence" – in Bryen 2013.

3. Specialists will note that I use slightly unconventional terminology: Roman political history is traditionally divided between the Republic (ca. 510–27 B.C.) and the Principate (the period of rule by emperors, 27 B.C. onwards). The latter term has fallen from fashion, and scholars today speak instead of the Empire, as well as of Late Antiquity (a period which, depending on scholarly preference, starts anywhere between ca. A.D. 180 and the conversion of Constantine in A.D. 312). In a discussion of imperialism, these distinctions are somewhat misleading, since Rome acquired an empire long before the advent of rule by a *princeps*. In what follows I have used the terms empire/imperial to refer to the system of rule over others, and use the terms Republic/Principate to refer to the form of government at Rome at a particular time.

   Given the requirements of space, my citations are necessarily selective. I have sought to privilege readily accessible English-language works of a high caliber of scholarship that may prove useful to practitioners of other disciplines.

4. I am, of course, aware that *persona* is a rich term, with a theatrical valence. I use the term here in its legal sense, in contrast to *res* (thing) and action (Gaius, *Inst.* 1.8).

5. The question of the development of the status of the Roman slave, or of Roman slave law, is vexed at best. Buckland 1970 [1908]: 79–82 argues that the action *servi nomine* is a late creation; see also Watson 1987: 61–63. Gaius argues that slaves cannot feel *iniuria*: *Inst.* 3.222.

6. Compare Caes. *BG* 7.77 (Critognatus' speech). The problem of what happens when the barbarians initially win, but are subsequently brought within the Empire, is evident in a text from Late Antiquity: see Jordanes, *Getica* 26, concerning the death of the Emperor Valens at the battle of Adrianople.

7. Visual reminders of defeat could perhaps also be installed to remind the conquered of misbehavior: see Eck 1999:87–88; Eck and Foerster 1999; Bowersock 2003 on the "triumphal arch" at Tel Shalem.

8. The *locus classicus* is the speech of Claudius concerning the admission of provincials from Lyons to the Senate of Rome (Tac. *Ann.* 11.24; a version is preserved also on a bronze tablet from Lyon: *ILS* 212). See also Brunt 1990: 294, citing Cic. *Pro Balbo* 31, that

Rome's strength had come, in part, from her allowing conquered peoples to partake in civic benefits. On citizenship, the standard treatment remains Sherwin-White 1973.

9. For instance, the *Historia Augusta* (Hadrian 6.3) notes with approval that upon Trajan's death Hadrian refused to take a triumph owed to his predecessor, and instead used a picture of Trajan in the triumph itself.

10. The traffic in triumphal honors can be interpreted in at least two ways: Mattern (1999: 168) takes the prolific use of honorary terminology as evidence of prolific enjoyment of victory; I would agree that the general public certainly could do this, as well as with the contention that emperors took pleasure in proclaiming their virtues, but that there was a distinct and well-regulated set of constraints on this system as well.

11. As of this writing, Lavan 2013 was not yet available; I look forward to its publication. See, for now, Lavan 2011.

12. Cicero, at least, deploys a varied and possibly irreconcilable vocabulary for theorizing the relationship between Romans and provincials: I *Verr.* 18; *Off.* 2.8.27, on which compare *Off.* 2.20.69; *de Prov. Cons.* 5.10 (on Jews and Syrians); also Livy 39.37.9, in which Livy places in the speech of Lycortas an acknowledgment that a notionally equal alliance can in practice be a relationship of servile domination.

13. Brunt 1961 collects the evidence, though it strikes me that in practice the appeal against the governor's cruelty would have been severely circumscribed by the realities of imperial governance: I discuss this further in Bryen 2012.

14. On the one hand, evidence for the *promise* of manumission as a way to ensure the good behavior of slaves abounds, while evidence for the realization of the promise is substantially more limited: Wiedemann 1985. On the other hand, examination of the papyrological evidence from Egypt shows few male slaves over 30, and few female slaves over 40, which, according to Bagnall 1993: 213 would seem to indicate the prevalence of manumission at roughly this point in the life cycle of the slave. In his doctoral thesis, Hawkins (2006: ch. 4) emphasizes the profitable economic dynamics of manumission; a revised version of this work will soon be available as a monograph from Cambridge University Press.

15. Though note an inscription (probably Hellenistic) regarding a slave crucifixion discussed in Llewellyn 1998.

16. Compare Leviticus Rabbah 25.5, a similar story from a Jewish (midrashic) context discussed by Hasan-Rokem 2003: 87.

References

Ando, Clifford
    2008 Aliens, Ambassadors, and the Integrity of Empire. *Law and History Review* 26: 491–519.
    2011 *Law, Language, and Empire in the Roman Tradition.* University of Pennsylvania Press, Philadelphia.
Bagnall, Roger
    1993 *Egypt in Late Antiquity.* Princeton University Press, Princeton.
Beard, Mary
    2007 *The Roman Triumph.* Belknap Press, Cambridge and London.

Bowersock, Glen

  2003 The Tel Shalem Arch and P. Nahal Hever/Seiyal 8. In *The Bar Kokhba War Reconsidered: New Perspectives on the Second Jewish Revolt against Rome*, edited by Peter Schaefer, pp. 171–180. Texts and Studies in Ancient Judaism 100. Mohr Siebeck, Tübingen.

Bradley, Keith

  1987 *Slaves and Masters in the Roman Empire: A Study in Social Control.* Oxford University Press, Oxford.

  2000 Animalizing the Slave: The Truth of Fiction. *Journal of Roman Studies* 90: 110–25.

Brunt, Peter

  1961 Charges of Provincial Maladministration under the Early Principate. *Historia* 10: 189–227.

  1990 *Roman Imperial Themes.* Clarendon, Oxford.

Bryen, Ari

  2008 Visibility and Violence in Petitions from Roman Egypt. *Greek, Roman and Byzantine Studies* 48: 181–200.

  2012 Judging Empire: Courts and Culture in Rome's Eastern Provinces. *Law and History Review* 30: 771–811.

  2013 *Violence in Roman Egypt: A Study in Legal Interpretation.* University of Pennsylvania Press, Philadelphia.

Buckland, William

  1970 [1908] *The Roman Law of Slavery.* Reprinted. Cambridge University Press, Cambridge.

Coleman, Kathleen

  1990 Fatal Charades: Roman Executions Staged as Mythological Enactments. *Journal of Roman Studies* 80: 44–73.

Daube, David

  1972 *Civil Disobedience in Antiquity.* Edinburgh University Press, Edinburgh.

Eck, Werner

  1999 The Bar Kokhba Revolt: The Roman Point of View. *Journal of Roman Studies* 89: 76–89.

Eck, Werner, and Gideon Foerster

  1999 Ein Triumphbogen für Hadrian im Tel von Beth Shean bei Tel Salem. *Journal of Roman Archaeology* 12: 294–313.

Edwards, Catharine

  2000 *Suetonius: Lives of the Caesars.* Oxford University Press, Oxford.

Fitzgerald, William

  2000 *Slavery and the Roman Literary Imagination.* Cambridge University Press, Cambridge.

Frier, Bruce

  1989 *A Casebook on the Roman Law of Delict.* Scholars Press, Atlanta.

Garnsey, Peter

  1968 Why Penalties Became Harsher: The Roman Case, Late Republic to Fourth Century Empire. *Natural Law Forum/American Journal of Jurisprudence* 13: 141–162.

1996 *Ideas of Slavery from Aristotle to Augustine.* Cambridge University Press, Cambridge.

Gleason, Maud

1999 Truth Contests and Talking Corpses. In *Constructions of the Classical Body*, edited by James Porter, pp. 287–313. University of Michigan Press, Ann Arbor.

Gordon, William, and O.F. Robinson

1988 *The Institutes of Gaius.* Cornell University Press, Ithaca.

Hagemann, Matthias

1998 Iniuria: *Von den XII-Tafeln bis zur Justinianischen Kodifikation.* Böhlau Verlag, Köln.

Harris, William

2001 *Restraining Rage: the Ideology of Anger Control in Classical Antiquity.* Harvard University Press, Cambridge.

Hasan-Rokem, Galit

2003 *Tales of the Neighborhood: Jewish Narrative Dialogues in Late Antiquity.* University of California Press, Berkeley.

Hawkins, Cameron

2006 Work in the City: Roman Artisans and the Urban Economy. Ph.D. dissertation, Department of History, University of Chicago.

Hinard, François, and Jean-Christophe Dumont

2003 *Libitina: Pompes funèbres et supplices en Campanie à l'époque d'Auguste. Édition, traduction et commentaire de la Lex Libitinae Puteolana.* De Boccard, Paris.

Hopkins, Keith

1993 Novel Evidence for Roman Slavery. *Past and Present* 138: 3–23.

Isaac, Benjamin

2004 *The Invention of Racism in Classical Antiquity.* Princeton University Press, Princeton.

Lavan, Myles

2011 Slavishness in Britain and Rome in Tacitus' *Agricola. Classical Quarterly* 61: 294–305.

2013 *Slaves to Rome: Paradigms of Empire in Roman Culture.* Cambridge University Press, Cambridge.

Liebeschuetz, J. H. Wolf

2012 [1966] The Theme of Liberty in Tacitus' *Agricola.* 73–9. In R. Ash, *Oxford Readings in Tacitus.* Oxford University Press, Oxford. (Originally published in *Classical Quarterly* 16: 126–39.)

Lincoln, Bruce

2012 Sanctified Violence. In *Gods and Demons, Priests and Scholars: Critical Explorations in the History of Religions*, pp. 83–94. University of Chicago Press, Chicago.

Lintott, Andrew

1993 *Imperium Romanum: Politics and Administration.* Routledge, London.

1999a *The Constitution of the Roman Republic.* Oxford University Press, Oxford.

1999b *Violence in Republican Rome.* 2nd edition. Oxford: Oxford University Press.

Llewellyn, Stephen
    1998   *New Documents Illustrating Early Christianity 8: A Review of Greek Inscriptions and Papyri Published 1984–5.* W.N. Eerdmans, Grand Rapids and Cambridge.

MacMullen, Ramsay
    1990   Judicial Savagery in the Roman Empire. In *Changes in the Roman Empire: Essays in the Ordinary*, pp. 204–217. Princeton University Press, Princeton.

Mattern, Susan
    1999   *Rome and the Enemy: Imperial Strategy in the Principate.* University of California Press, Berkeley.

McFayden, Donald
    1920   *The History of the Title* Imperator *under the Roman Empire.* University of Chicago Press, Chicago.

Millar, Fergus
    1977   *The Emperor in the Roman World, 31 B.C.–A.D. 337.* Cornell University Press, Ithaca, NY.
    2004   Condemnation to Hard Labour in the Roman Empire, from the Julio-Claudians to Constantine. In *Rome, the Greek World, and the East, vol. II: Government, Society, and Culture in the Roman Empire*, edited by Hannah Cotton and Guy Rogers, pp. 120–150. University of North Carolina Press, Chapel Hill, NC.

Parker, Holt
    1989   Crucially Funny or Tranio on the Couch: The Servus Callidus and Jokes about Torture. *Transactions of the American Philological Society* 119: 233–246.

Richardson, John
    1991   *Imperium Romanum*: Empire and the Language of Power. *Journal of Roman Studies* 81: 1–9.
    2008   *The Language of Empire.* Cambridge University Press, Cambridge.

Riggsby, Andrew
    1999   *Crime and Community in Ciceronian Rome.* University of Texas Press, Austin.

Sélincourt, Aubrey de (translator)
    1960   *Livy: The Early History of Rome.* Penguin Books, London.

Shaw, Brent
    1984   Bandits in the Roman Empire. *Past and Present* 105: 3–52.
    1996   Body/Power/Identity: Passions of the Martyrs. *Journal of Early Christian Studies* 4: 269–312.
    2000   Rebels and Outsiders. In *The Cambridge Ancient History, XI: The High Empire, A.D. 70–192*, edited by Alan Bowman, Peter Garnsey, and Dominic Rathbone, pp. 361–402. Cambridge University Press, Cambridge.
    2003   Judicial Nightmares and Christian Memory. *Journal of Early Christian Studies* 11: 533–563

Smith, R.R.R.
    1988   *Simulacra Gentium*: The *Ethne* from the Sebasteion at Aphrodisias. *Journal of Roman Studies* 78: 50–77.

Sherwin-White, Adrian
    1973   *The Roman Citizenship.* 2nd edition. Clarendon Press, Oxford.

Syme, Ronald
   1958   Imperator Caesar: A Study in Nomenclature, *Historia* 7: 172–188.

Talbert, Richard
   1984   *The Senate of Imperial Rome*. Princeton University Press, Princeton.

Thomas, Y.
   1984   Se venger au forum: Solidarité familiale et procès criminel à Rome (premier siècle
          av.-deuxième siècle ap. J.C. In *La Vengeance: études d'ethnologie, d'histoire, et de
          philosophie*, vol.3, edited by Raymond Verdier and Jean-Pierre Poly, pp. 65–100.
          Editions Cujas, Paris.

Tilly, Charles
   1984   *Big Structures, Large Processes, Huge Comparisons*. Russell Sage Foundation, New
          York.

Watson, Alan
   1979   The Death of Horatia. *Classical Quarterly* 29: 436–447.
   1985   *The Digest of Justinian*. University of Pennsylavania Press, Philadelphia.
   1987   *Roman Slave Law*. Johns Hopkins University Press, Baltimore.
   1991   Roman Slave Law and Romanist Ideology. In *Legal Origins and Legal Change*, pp.
          279–291. Hambledon Press, London.

Westbrook, Raymond
   1999   Vitae Necisque Potestas. *Historia* 48: 203–223.

Wiedemann, Thomas
   1981   *Greek and Roman Slavery*. Johns Hopkins University Press, Baltimore.
   1985   The Regularity of Manumission at Rome. *Classical Quarterly* 35: 162–175.

Woolf, Greg
   1996   Monumental Writing and the Expansion of Roman Society in the Early Empire.
          Journal of Roman Studies 86: 22–39.

Zimmermann, Martin
   2006   Violence in Late Antiquity Reconsidered. In *Violence in Late Antiquity:
          Perceptions and Practices*, edited by H.A. Drake, pp. 343–358. Ashgate, Aldershot,
          Hampshire.

On Torture in Societies Against the State

Severin Fowles

State sadism. This may be the only way to describe the events of January 1599 in what is now New Mexico, but was then an embattled northern periphery of New Spain. It was less than a year since Don Juan de Oñate thrust his way into the Pueblo world intent on conquest, subjugation, Christianization, and the establishment of what he gambled would be another lucrative Spanish imperial venture. It was less than a year since the Pueblos had been abruptly transformed from autonomous and largely egalitarian communities into the colonized subjects of a royalty who laid claim to their lives from seats of power that, from a Pueblo perspective, might as well have been on Mars. The times were volatile and tragically uncertain, and Oñate's campaign met with understandably strong resistance, not least from Acoma, the most fortified and fiercely independent of the Pueblo communities, who, in December of 1598, rebelled and killed Oñate's nephew along with a party of 30 soldiers under his command.

It was a bold and defiant move, one that could have set a dangerous precedent. Retribution, therefore, came swiftly. Well-armed soldiers were dispatched by an enraged Oñate to wage a war by blood and fire in which many hundreds of Acoma perished. The village was no match for Spanish steel and gunpowder, and it wasn't long before its residents chose submission over annihilation. When the smoke cleared, those still standing were sentenced to 20 years of slavery. But Oñate, in an act that would come to define his historical legacy, further commanded that all men over the age of 25 were to suffer additional disciplinary measures: these men were to have their right feet severed (Hammond and Rey 1953: 477, 614–15).[1]

Two dozen individuals were publicly dismembered in this way, but the wounds festered across the Pueblo world. Still today, 400 years on, they remain potent wounds indeed: "When I think of what Oñate did to the

Acoma Pueblo," said a member of Sandia Pueblo in 1998 during the fourth centennial of his conquest, "I have a vision of Indian men lined up to have one foot cut off. I see the blood pouring from their legs as they crawled or hopped away. I see the bloody pile of feet left behind."[2]

How are we to understand this incident, its memory and historical legacy? In one sense, Oñate's spectacular violence – sanctioned, it must be acknowledged, by the men of the cloth who played a key role in legitimating Spanish conquest of the Pueblos – was the product of a particular colonial mentality in which the "savagery" of the New World seemed both to justify and necessitate a certain military savagery in return. Fire to fight fire. Violence as the sole means of dealing with a pre-rational primitive world that could understand nothing else. It is difficult to gauge the degree to which this particular brand of racism lay behind Oñate's actions; regardless, such explanations only go so far. Indeed, Oñate's cruelty seems far in excess of the "savagery" the Spaniards had suffered at the hands of the indigenous peoples of the New World up to that point. And we are left to deal with the source of this excess.

Another way of understanding the foot incident is to explore the manner in which it adhered to the internal cultural logic of the conquistadors themselves. Such violence, it could be argued, was generally in keeping with the early modern mode of domestic discipline within Europe and was, from this perspective, but another example of what Foucault (1979: 14) referred to as "the great spectacle of physical punishment," "the theatrical representation of pain" within the European penal system focusing on the tortured body of the accused. But this also seems an inadequate explanation of Oñate's actions. Like the other New World indigenous peoples, the Pueblos were viewed by European society as radical Others, and during the sixteenth century it was not at all clear whether one was to view such Others as different peoples or different sorts of animals altogether. It is unlikely that domestic European modes of discipline would have had much salience in a fully alien world that lay outside not only the penal system, but also all known systems of morality.

For Tzvetan Todorov (1984: 143–145), it was precisely this moral void – generated by the extreme alterity of the New World in the eyes of the European – that prompted inhumane acts like Oñate's. Indeed, Todorov argued that the Spanish invasions of the New World were ultimately responsible for ushering in a distinctively colonial mode of violence. Out of Columbus's wake sprang the first true "massacre-society":

> Far from the central government, far from royal law, all prohibitions give way, the social link, already loosened, snaps, revealing not a primitive nature, the beast sleeping in each of us, but a modern being… restrained by no morality and inflicting death because and when he pleases. The "barbarity" of the Spaniards

has nothing atavistic or bestial about it; it is quite human and heralds the advent of modern times. In the Middle Ages, we find that a woman's breasts or a man's arms will be cut off as a punishment or revenge; but such things were done in one's own country… What the Spaniards discover is the contrast between the metropolitan country and the colony, for radically different moral laws regulate conduct in each: massacre requires an appropriate context [Todorov 1984: 14].

This is a compelling account, and I will return to Todorov's understanding of the massacre-society below.

For the moment, though, I want to move away from the rationale behind European violence on the colonial frontier and consider instead the question of why such violence – and here I am thinking in particular of the severing of Acoma feet – was perceived to be so profoundly jarring amongst native societies such as the Pueblos. Why were Oñate's orders so apparently unimaginable in the eyes of the indigene?

Our immediate response to such a question is surely to challenge its very legitimacy. *How*, we might protest, *could it possibly have been viewed otherwise?* How could such systematic maiming of the members of one's society – the maiming of fathers, brothers, and husbands – ever be "imaginable"? How could the bloody pile of feet be anything but "profoundly jarring"? These are entirely appropriate protests, but my concern is that the tendency to simply invert the savage/civilized labels – to underscore the savagery of the European and comparative civility of the Native American – leads us away from, rather than toward, a deeper understanding of the event and its reception. My concern is that it forecloses an important discussion of how the violence of the State locked horns with the indigenous violence of the Pueblos.

Indeed, many archaeologists have been loudly telling us, as of late, that blood and fire had their own prominent place within the indigenous communities of the Southwest. Such scholars have taken it upon themselves to correct a misleadingly sanitized presentation of the ancestral Pueblos that had dominated the literature during the second half of the twentieth century. In contrast, we now find a great deal of attention being drawn to the architectural evidence of defensive settlement orientations, to the iconographic evidence for militarism generally and beheadings in particular, and to the osteological evidence of innumerable "badly treated individuals" (LeBlanc 1999; Lekson 2002; Nichols and Crown 2008; Rice and LeBlanc 2001; Turner and Turner 1999; White 1992). The latter euphemism is a gloss for a great many phenomena ranging from unburied corpses and mass interments, to carefully premeditated acts of dismemberment, to what Kuckelman et al. (2000) refer to as "extreme processing" – another euphemism that describes not only dismemberment but also the breakage, boiling, and burning of human remains in a manner that parallels the treatment of consumed animal carcasses.

The piles of "processed human bone," needless to say, have attracted the greatest controversy. Argument swarms around these remains like flies. For some, the meticulous research into breakage patterns, cut marks, and the like provides proof of anthropophagy, most often interpreted as a strategy deployed by Ancestral Pueblo peoples to degrade and dominate their enemies (Kantner 1999; LeBlanc 1999; Lekson 2002; Turner and Turner 1999). Others read the same remains as evidence of a more internally directed form of violence bound up in the problem of witchcraft accusation and treatment, as it is known to us from ethnographic discussions of the late nineteenth- and early twentieth-century Pueblos (Darling 1998; Ogilvie and Hilton 2000; Walker 1998, 2008; Whiteley 2008). Still others, particularly within the Pueblo community itself, read the inordinate attention given to such remains as simply one more Euro-American effort to dehumanize native peoples and thereby legitimize a history of genocide and continued domination.

Be that as it may, few would deny that the Ancestral Pueblos have come to look far less Apollonian than once thought. The indigenous violence documented in much contemporary archaeological writing, in fact, would seem to suggest that when the Spanish began their bloody campaigns, the Pueblos had seen it all before. No societies, we are now told, have ever lived prior to war (Keeley 1996). Rather, marked social violence seems bound up in the project of being human itself, a structural aspect of all societies, as basic as kinship, politics, economics, or religion. And colonialism comes to be understood as a tragic new form of entanglement between competing modes of violence, rather than the viral spread of European brutality into what had formerly been pre-colonial peaceable kingdoms. Hence, the problem facing anthropology is not about drawing divisions between more or less violent societies, but to understand how the inevitable flow of violence has been variously canalized and diverted in the construction of the social throughout the human past.

What, then, were these competing modes of violence? How did Oñate's cruelty differ from that already known among the Ancestral Pueblos, and in what ways would the latter have found the former novel?

The Labor of Scars/Master Narratives

It is difficult to address such questions seriously without also confronting the evolutionary narratives that continue to guide – as models or foils – so many of our answers. These narratives broadly break down into competing Hobbesian and Rousseauian traditions, underscoring the lingering Early Modern philosophical foundations of much contemporary scholarship. The opposition has always tended toward polemics,[3] and so has stunted critical inquiry into the history of violence at a general level. Still, we cannot help but work through the opposition, if only to transcend it.

Superficially, it would seem that we are dealing with two very different narratives indeed. For Rousseau (1985 [1754]), of course, violence was quite simply irrelevant prior to the evolution of sedentism, property, and the state. In *Discourse on Inequality*, he argued that interactions between primitive men would have been governed by "natural pity" and that interpersonal violence, far from being innate, could have only emerged as a historically contingent construct once society came to have monopolizable resources and statuses to fight over. Humans had to *learn* to suffocate their natural pity, he suggested[4] – a key teaching of civilization that was only emboldened by colonialism – and generations of social critics, particularly in anthropology, have followed Rousseau's lead in using pre-modern or tribal societies to portray, by way of contrast, the modern violence of the State as a dangerous abomination.

Hobbes's (1998 [1651]) master narrative, to which Rousseau largely wrote in response, began quite differently. Where Rousseau saw pity, Hobbes saw an elemental seed of competition that marked both humanity's brutal point of origin as well as a perennial enemy that must be opposed by a strong Commonwealth with its centralized powers, laws and religion. Like a primitive river, violence surged just beneath the surface in the Hobbesian imaginary, ever-threatening to erode the political order, and the civilizing process has evolved, if not to reduce the power of its waters, then to build dams, canals, and levies, so as to domesticate and keep them under control.

One could debate which position, in the end, has had the greater impact within intellectual circles, but the Hobbesian vision of civilization as a grand historical struggle against violent primitive tendencies has clearly come to dominate popular Western discourse. No doubt this is partly attributable to its remarkable versatility, its success in drawing together not only Hobbes's own critique of Europe's bloody religious wars and his plea for strong governing institutions, but also everything from Catholic notions of original sin to subsequent Darwinian principles of phenotypic competition. Needless to say, it also served European interests on the colonial frontier, where indigenous resistance to foreign rule could be spun as the innate violence of the primitive rather than the legitimate struggle of the freedom fighter.

Indeed, it is with this versatility in mind that we must read the work of someone like John Wesley, founder of Methodism and a contemporary of Rousseau, who authored numerous portrayals of American Indians as exemplars of an original, pre-Christian world of violence. "The natural religion of the Creeks, Cherokees, Chickasaws and all other Indians," he wrote, "is to torture all their prisoners from morning to night, till at length they roast them to death... Yea, it is a common thing among them for the son, if he thinks his father lives too long, to knock out his brains" (Wesley 1958: 402). Such claims, their racist underpinnings notwithstanding, went hand-in-hand with the growing European acceptance of an inexorable trend toward human progress. Wesley preached individual perfectionism, the doctrine of a Christian's ability to improve and ultimately transcend his state of original sin, and in this sense paralleled many of his contemporaries' evolutionary arguments for a vast civilizing process in which humankind's original state of violence and irrationality was gradually overcome. And it was only a century after Wesley that Herbert Spencer articulated his own well-known doctrine of evolutionary perfectionism: "providing the human race continues… so surely must the things we call evil and immorality [continue to] disappear; so surely must man become perfect" (Spencer 1883 [1850]: 60).

Ours is a more cynical age, and only the oddest of contemporary idealists would claim that humankind remains steadfast on a developmental trajectory towards perfection. Still, I assume that most in the West continue to regard modernity as an effort to reduce an imagined sum total of violence and suffering in the world (even while acknowledging that the "collateral damage" of this effort is often very high, particularly for non-Western populations). And along with this comes the general opinion that, however violent the current world may be, the pre-modern world was worse.[5] (Cue the scenes of spear-wielding natives in any number of recent films.)

Insofar as a large percentage of the Euro-American population continues to harbor Hobbesian notions of ignoble savagism, many anthropologists have responded either by a retreat into a vague neo-Rousseauian position or by simply distancing their work from a serious investigation of the role of violence in pre-Columbian North American societies. As the recent explosion of media attention to claims of Ancestral Pueblo cannibalism have reminded us, the mere mention of Indians and violence in a single sentence is too often read as an invitation to sensationalization by the press. This does not, however, alter the fact that much is simultaneously lost when we avert our eyes from violence as an anthropological subject. The goal, then, must be to move beyond Enlightenment polemics to explore alternative narratives.

No one understood this more clearly than Pierre Clastres, who argued that anthropology's pacification of pre-colonial societies perverts our understanding to the point of obscuring the very nature of politics in non-state societies. Clastres offered instead a new engagement with Hobbes, accepting his vision of original violence, *but not a violence that opposed society*. Hobbes's mis-step, argued Clastres, was his failure to realize that the "primitive" state of war – far from making society impossible – was precisely the fertile seedbed out of which the egalitarian social order grew and was nourished. Hence, when

Clastres (1994) wrote that "primitive societies are violent societies" or that "their social being is a being-for-war," the image he conjured was not a pre-social Hobbesian savage but rather an anarchist revolutionary, a citizen of the world who used war as a means of subverting despotism:

> What is primitive society? It is a multiplicity of undivided communities which all obey the same centrifugal logic. What institution at once expresses and guarantees the permanence of this logic? It is war, as the truth of relations between communities, as the principal sociological means of promoting the centrifugal force of dispersion against the centripetal force of unification. The war machine is the motor of the social machine; the primitive social being relies entirely on war, primitive society cannot survive without war [Clastres 1994: 166].

Egalitarianism, in short, comes neither naturally nor cheaply. The maintenance of a society free from centralized domination and the state has its own costs and is premised upon its own strategic deployment of violent action.

Of course, Clastres's image of the war machine in non-state societies does not bring us any closer to understanding the Oñate foot incident. In fact, to argue that war is inimical to the state, as Clastres does, introduces its own radical perversion as soon as we return to the brutal war waged by Oñate and his fellow Europeans to gain control of the New World. But there is a second component to Clastres's understanding of violence in non-state societies that I suggest is more useful: his emphasis on the centrality of torture – particularly self-torture – to tribal initiation rituals.

A great many ethnographies and colonial travel diaries have reported with gory fascination the various ways in which pain was often a necessary ingredient in the rites of passage among the "uncivilized savages" famously reconceived by Clastres as societies against the state. Clastres was particularly captivated by George Catlin's accounts of the *O-kee-pa* ritual (a variant of the Sun Dance) of the Mandan on the Great Plains, a torturous four-day trial in which initiates fasted, had their bodies skewered with wooden pegs from which they were then hung (Figure 6.1), and finally were made to run "the last race" until their arm and leg flesh ripped free of the wooden pegs that had been attached to dragging, heavy weights (Catlin 1965 [1841]: 169–76). The goal was to endure. And to "procure honourable scars" (Catlin 1996 [1865]: 105). "Holes pierced in the body, skewers forced through the wounds, hanging, amputation, 'the last race,' torn flesh: cruelty's resources seem inexhaustible," wrote Clastres in response (1989: 181).

For Clastres, however, the most jarring aspect of such cruelty was that it was self-imposed, and he was not alone in this opinion. Many twentieth-century scholars argued for a deep connection between primitivity and auto-mutilation. Bettelheim (1954), for instance, concluded that primitive peoples tend to be

Figure 6.1. The "cutting scene" during the Mandan *O-kee-pa* ceremony, as drawn by
George Catlin (1965 [1841]: 171, pl. 68). In addition to those hanging in the
center of the image, a penitent in the lower right gives thanks to the Great
Spirit in preparation for submitting to an officiant who sits ready to chop off
one of his fingers.

"autoplastic," acting upon their own bodies as a means of influencing the world,
whereas modern peoples are "alloplastic," acting instead upon the external
reality itself (see also Róheim 1925). Bataille (1985: 68–69; cf. Taussig 2006:
162) explored a related theme, linking documented examples of the purposeful
chopping off of one's finger among tribes such as the Blackfoot (Wissler 1918:
266–267) not only to the self-torture of mentally ill Europeans (a common
comparative move in early psychoanalytic theory), but also to evidence in
Upper Paleolithic rock art of hands with missing digits. In this way, Bataille
extended auto-mutilation back to the origins of humanity itself.

   (As an archaeologist, I feel compelled to add that most scholars of the
Upper Paleolithic now dismiss the mutilation hypothesis as an explanation for
the many hand stencils lacking digits at sites like Gargas and Cosquer caves,
arguing that we are instead simply looking at folded over fingers expressing
an unknown symbolic code [Clottes and Courtin 1996: 67–69]. Perhaps
this is the correct interpretation. Perhaps. However, the vigor with which
the mutilation hypothesis is now opposed – and with which the so-called

"rational explanation" of folded-over-finger-signs is defended – strikes me as entirely suspicious. Indeed, the assumption that it is necessarily irrational to inflict pain on one's own body, that such actions are only ever undertaken by a neurotic minority and never by the healthy majority of a society, flies in the face of not only non-Western ethnographic reports [see in particular Bowers 1950: 65–66; Catlin 1965 (1841): 172] but the Medieval history of Europe as well [Asad 2003]. I will return to this issue shortly.)

Regardless, it is worth taking seriously the – admittedly unfashionable – claim that elaborate and painful initiation rites have been most common among small-scale and highly egalitarian peoples. Jonathan Smith (1987) has argued that comparative ethnography largely confirms this correlation. And he adds that elaborate initiations seem to be inversely related to the practice of human or animal sacrifice, which historically has been much more common in larger-scale and more hierarchical societies:

> It is my sense, after surveying a wide sample of literature, that sacrifice and initiation stand in an inverse ratio to each other: where there are elaborate initiatory rituals, sacrifice seems relatively undeveloped; where there are complex sacrificial cycles and ideologies, initiation seems relatively undeveloped. Indeed, I am tempted to suggest that initiation is for the hunter and gatherer and primitive agriculturalist what sacrifice is for the agrarian and pastoralist [Smith 1987: 198].

Here, then, is an alternative genealogy of violence: from that of the initiate who tortures himself, to that of the sacrificer whose violence is directed toward another. In fact, we might add to this by noting that "sacrifice" is commonly granted its own genealogy, progressing from the killing of other humans as gifts to the deity (prototypically seen in God's demand upon Abraham), to the sacrifice of animal substitutes, and finally to the destruction of inanimate offerings. This latter sequence may be more Biblical than empirical, but this is not to say that it fails to reveal a deeper truth regarding the successive projection of violence outwards toward the more distant Other over the course of the evolution of the state.

The critical issue, however, is how one accounts for the patterned relationship between violence and politics. Why, in particular, do torturous initiatory rites so frequently go hand-in-hand with small-scale societies of (more-or-less) equals? And why are they less common among highly stratified societies? Clastres's answer stood at the very heart of his understanding of egalitarianism. Through their willing submission to the pain of initiation, he argued, individuals in egalitarian societies inscribed upon their bodies a powerful statement: "You are one of us. Each one of you is like us; each one of you is like the others... None of you is less than us; none of you is more than us. *And you will never be able to forget it.* You will not cease to remember the same marks we have left on your bodies" (Clastres 1989: 186). The initiate emerges as a marked man: "The scars traced on the body are the inscribed text of primitive law; in that sense, they are *a writing on the body*" (1989: 187; italics in original).

Clastres read the initiate's bodily scars, in other words, as a quasi-legal text that, like all legal texts, is inherently violent, but that nevertheless serves to carve out an egalitarian space within the tribal contexts that so fascinated him. Institutionalized and democratized by its incorporation into the lifecycle of all society's members, the violence of initiation not only leveled the status of individuals; it left a permanent record of that social leveling upon the body. As Mary Douglas (1988 [1966]: 116) put it in her critique of Bettelheim's psychoanalytical thesis, "what is being carved in human flesh is an image of society."

Clastres may have overstated the degree to which initiatory violence serves to establish a society of equals. The standard critiques of egalitarianism apply: that what these rites actually achieve is a solidification of hierarchical divisions, if not between adult males, then between initiates and the not-yet-initiated, as well as between men and women, whose bodies are often marked in very different ways. Furthermore, one must acknowledge the many shamans in earlier tribal societies who used extreme forms of self-induced pain to induce altered states of consciousness. Pain offered access to hidden realities and unseen powers that bolstered their private status vis-à-vis the larger community of non-shamans; pain, in such contexts, was closely linked to privilege (Lewis-Williams and Pearce 2005: 63–64).

Nevertheless, the special relationship between a general ethic of egalitarianism and painful initiatory rites remains important. Indeed, the very distinction between "initiation" in small-scale societies and "sacrifice" in more complex polities identified by Smith provides a useful complication and expansion of Todorov's (1984: 14) distinction between "sacrifice" societies and "massacre" societies.[6] From initiation to sacrifice to massacre, from self-torture to social violence to amoral attacks on dehumanized or objectified others, from autoplastic to alloplastic to what we might call *alter*plastic – this is the grander grand narrative that I suggest we critically consider. In this genealogy, violence is neither early nor late, but its targets, and political and moral valences, vary significantly.

I want to return to the case of early colonial violence in New Mexico, but before doing so, let me attempt to counter a potential criticism of the above discussion. Insofar as the traditions of psychological and social analysis in the modern West have come to be wedded to a definition of rational behavior as action specifically designed to increase personal pleasure and avoid pain, some readers may worry that the conceptual linkage between self-torture and pre-modernity indulges in a dangerous form of primitivism. Surely, to identify an "autoplastic" pattern among small-scale, pre-modern societies is to brand them as irredeemably irrational. Surely, it resuscitates a problematic Freudian tradition in which primitive peoples are equated with modern neurotics no less than it does Lévy-Bruhl's (1926) identification of a distinctively primitive mentality. And surely, this is unacceptable. Should we not, instead, begin with the assumption that pre-modern peoples were just as rational as us? After all, the many early travelers' and ethnographic accounts of self-torture in Africa, Australia, and the New World could be discounted as the products of nothing more than colonial propaganda and Western racism.

This sort of pre-prepared anthropological critique fails us, however. Without question, pre-modern peoples such as the ancestral Pueblos were "rational" in the sense that their actions followed a definite logic. But were they rational "just like us"? More to the point, where is it established that the logic of "rational behavior" in all times and places necessarily moves away from suffering? As Talal Asad (2003) has emphasized, attitudes toward pain are, to a large extent, historical constructions, and the notion that pain is, by definition, undesirable is a very specific characteristic of the secular modern West. And yet, it is common within anthropology and related disciplines to link such culturally specific understandings of the undesirability of pain to universal models of human action: "Although the various usages of agency [as an anthropological category] have very different implications... cultural theory tends to reduce them to the metaphysical idea of a conscious agent-subject having both the capacity and the desire to move in a singular historical direction: that of increasing self-empowerment and decreasing pain" (Asad 2003: 79).

Following orthodox cultural theory, then, the Mandan youth's participation in the torturous *O-kee-pa* ceremony could hardly be seen as a rational act of agency. If it is assumed that, given the choice, individuals will always move away from pain, then one must read the initiate as a victimized pawn, passively accepting his suffering because his culture (allegedly, the true agent) tells him he must. Catlin, for instance, might have repeatedly emphasized that pain was both ostensibly voluntary[7] and a matter of honor accompanied by great spiritual power and social prestige. But he was quick to add that the victim was nevertheless a "poor and ignorant, misguided and superstitious man," one who was ultimately reduced to a "listless silence" (Catlin 1965 [1841]: 232–233). And so the Westerner weeps:

> ... for their ignorance – he pities them with all his heart for their blindness, and laments that the light of civilization, of agriculture and religion cannot be extended to them, and that their hearts which are good enough, could not be turned to embrace *something more rational and conducive to their true happiness* [1965: 183, italics added].

Which is to say that the Mandan youth is not really an agent at all. The very desires upon which he acts seem not to be his own.

There is a vexing irony here. What for the Mandan was regarded as an individual's most profound and willful act of agency – to experience pain deeply and nobly – is reread by the Western analyst as a fundamental example of blind cultural conditioning. The seemingly unbridgeable divide between these two viewpoints results from the fact that no real cultural translation has occurred, no true anthropology has been offered. Instead, the Western analyst has taken a post-Medieval European belief – that the only rational engagement with pain is the act of pushing it away – and made it universal.

Once we place the relationship between rationality, desire, and pain into question, however, the issue of the Mandan sufferer's agency emerges quite differently. Human intentionality always being impossible to demonstrate at an ultimate philosophical level, we are left with no other option than to accept another culture's logic of rational agency on its own terms. Writing of the violence during Sun Dances among the culturally-related Oglala Sioux, for instance, Walker observes:

> One who dances the Sun Dance in its fullest form establishes before the Sun, and in the presence of the people, his possession of the four great virtues, which are: 1. Bravery. 2. Generosity. 3. Fortitude. 4. Integrity. One who possesses these four virtues should be respected and honored by all the people. Thus, the scars made by the wounds and tortures inflicted during the Sun Dance are honorable insignia [Walker 1917: 62].

Here one finds a simple and overt set of motivating principles that I suspect were much closer to those of the nineteenth-century Mandan.

Blood and Fire/Pueblo Auto-Violence

Let us return to the case of the Pueblos and the arguments surrounding the forms of indigenous violence that would have been in place when Europeans arrived on the scene. To what extent did the Pueblos exhibit the particular sort of internally directed, egalitarian violence just discussed?

We can begin by noting that there is no evidence the Pueblos ever scarified or otherwise mutilated their youths. Nevertheless, Pueblo coming-of-age rituals did tend to be elaborate and painful. At Zuñi, boys were whipped both publicly and privately at various points along their initiatory path by the katsina, powerful and intimidating spirits who used masked humans as vessels through which to exert their will. Bunzel wrote:

> At the first ceremony they [the initiates] are severely whipped by the katcina priests to inspire them with awe for these creatures. There is another and

more severe thrashing at the second ceremony. Whipping is the prerogative of the katcinas. It is employed by no other ceremonial group at Zuñi and as a mechanism of juvenile punishment is unknown. The American method of establishing discipline by switching is met at Zuñi with horrified contempt. The katcinas whip to instill awe for the supernatural, but also to remove sickness and contamination. The whipping of katcinas is a blessing. It is administered with the formula, "May you be blessed with seeds"… Therefore outsiders are never whipped [Bunzel 1992: 518].

Whipping was a core part of ritual, and it was designed to inculcate youths physically with a fear and awe of the spirits to whom all humans must submit. But the pain was also considered creative, constructive. It was not only for the initiates' own good. The whipping was goodness itself; violence was a blessing, a gift, a cure.[8] "May you be blessed with seeds," said the katsinas as they flogged young bodies. The resultant wounds were equated with fertility and growth (see also Fergusson 1931: 129).

I want to underscore the sharp line drawn between the whipping of initiates and the whipping of miscreants. Indeed, it is noteworthy that *punitive* pain of the latter sort seems not to have had a place within Pueblo logics of violence (similar to the situation among the aggressively egalitarian Iroquois among whom "young children were never slapped, violently restrained, or reprimanded" [Trigger 1990: 132]). Pain was ritually distributed as a blessing, and this may have precluded its use as a mundane punishment. However, we might also read the Pueblo's "horrified contempt" for the flogging of children as part and parcel of a broader aversion to overt shows of dominance and submission. In ritual contexts, violence might be employed to establish a hierarchical relationship between the gods and society at large, but could not be used to establish dominance between individuals within society – even between parents and children.

Standing in apparent tension with this last observation is the powerful image of the tortured Pueblo witch that has increasingly come to stand as an icon of pre-Columbian cruelty within the archaeological literature (Figure 6.2). Here we seem to be confronted with a mode of discipline that, on the surface, is quite distinct from Clastres's notion of self-imposed "primitive torture." Witchcraft punishment or execution among the Pueblos was fundamentally concerned, after all, with the brutal singling out of individuals who were suspected of using supernatural means against the welfare of the community. In this sense, it was quite distinct from the democratized violence of initiations.

Of course, some have viewed Pueblo witchcraft as a classic example of egalitarian leveling sanctions in which self-aggrandizing individuals were cut (sometimes literally) down to size. Ethnographic anecdotes do suggest that nonconformists or braggarts were particularly susceptible to accusations.

Figure 6.2. "Torturing a sorcerer" from Frank Hamilton Cushing's *My Adventures in Zuñi* (1883).

"Fear of witchcraft," observes Whiteley (1998: 97), "is at least as effective a deterrent as fear of the electric chair" in keeping social deviants in line. What I find more interesting, however, is that witchcraft accusation was also a dangerous possibility for those who stood centrally positioned within Pueblo society and held important priestly positions. Ritual power, we are repeatedly told, was itself intrinsically dangerous, for the same power could be used for either good or ill effect – sometimes unknowingly. As a man from Santa Clara observed: "One must always be alert, because you might think that you were getting good wisdom (power) but discover later this friend was giving you the wrong kind" (quoted in Hill 1982: 312).

This brings us to an important irony: the very ritual specialists charged with the task of dealing with witches in Pueblo society were themselves especially susceptible to being found guilty of witchcraft. Hill's research at Santa Clara Pueblo, for instance, established that members of the Bear Society – the medicine society that who took a leading role in identifying, punishing and executing witches – were also those most likely to be accused of witchcraft, and it is reasonable to assume that a parallel situation prevailed at most if not all the Pueblos. Indeed, Whiteley (1998: 94–95) has written in quite similar terms of the Hopi *pavansinom* or "ruling class" of ritual specialists. The *pavansinom*, like the Santa Clara Bear Societies, were in possession of a power that was profound, but neither intrinsically good nor evil, once again resulting in an unstable moral polarity that could flip as the political force fields of the village shifted. Pandey (1994: 333) acknowledges a parallel pattern at Zuni, where the lay community "often suspected priests of witchcraft, that is, of using 'valuable' religious knowledge for private ends."

The realities of Pueblo witchcraft, then, resulted in a situation whereby individuals, as they moved upward in the ritual hierarchy, approached not only the highest (most valorized) position in society, but potentially also the lowest (most stigmatized) position. This is the Janus face of power – the paradox, encountered in so many societies, in which the strongest leaders also stand in the positions of greatest vulnerability. Little surprise, perhaps, that some individuals were extremely reluctant to accept the positions of ritual leadership offered them or that some established leaders who sought to resign were beaten and violently forced to retain their posts (Hill 1982: 184–185).

If we are to attain a deeper understanding of the underlying logic of violence in societies such as the Pueblos, however, we must push beyond the traditional language of political anthropology where one speaks of leveling sanctions or the prevention of anti-social behavior, for witches were not simply tried and executed in an expeditious or coldly legalistic manner. Their deaths were clearly extreme and need to be appreciated as such. It is true that anthropological knowledge of the specific practices tangled up in the treatment of Pueblo witches prior to the twentieth century is vague and uncertain, a product not only of Spanish and American efforts to outlaw all acts of violence not undertaken by the State, but also of a deep indigenous tradition of secrecy surrounding such events. Nevertheless, both ethnographic and archaeological glimpses into this expansive, if largely subterranean, drama of ritualized violence do exist (see Darling 1998).

We know most about the steps taken to secure a witch's confession. This was a public process, directly observed by Cushing (1883) and a handful of other Anglo-Americans during the late nineteenth century, in which the accused was dragged from his bed or chased down by the appropriate ritual society, hung by his hands or thumbs in the plaza, and beaten until his transgressions were admitted (Figure 6.2). In a number of recorded cases, outsiders intervened to prevent the confession from proceeding to execution. When execution did occur, however, it appears to have been accompanied by excessive acts of violence toward the witch's body that might include stoning, dismemberment, burning, or the extraction and destruction of the accused's heart. Native testimony suggests as much, and the occasional discovery of dismembered, charred, fragmented, or otherwise "extremely processed" human remains in the archaeological record supports the conclusion that such acts were practiced deep into the Pueblo past.

In grappling with such remains archaeologically, our sympathies tend naturally to be directed toward the executed victim or to those in society who stood on the sidelines and shivered in fear as the events unfolded. But what of the executioners themselves? How would they have been affected by the violent excess of witch treatments? What would have gone through the mind of an individual whose priestly position required him to torture, bludgeon, deflesh, dismember, and incinerate the body of someone who may well have formerly stood in his own social position? What was it like to do this to someone who, but for the suspicious mind of one's peers, might *still* be in one's own social position?

To a certain extent, these questions draw us toward the more general problem of the torturer's psychology. In *The Body in Pain*, Elaine Scarry grapples with this problem directly, locating the answer in what she regards as the ever-widening chasm between torturer and victim, between voice and body, and between the powerful extension of self and the stultifying constriction of the sufferer's world:

> Although the torturer dominates the prisoner both in physical acts and verbal acts, ultimate domination requires that the prisoner's ground become increasingly physical and the torturer's increasingly verbal, that the prisoner become a colossal body with no voice and the torturer a colossal voice (a voice composed of two voices) with no body, that eventually the prisoner experience himself exclusively in terms of a sentience and the torturer exclusively in terms of self-extension [Scarry 1985: 57].

> What by the one is experienced as a continual contraction is for the other a continual expansion, for the torturer's growing sense of self is carried outward on the prisoner's swelling pain [1985: 56].

For Scarry, the torturer denies the pain he inflicts, distances himself ontologically from his victim, and swells in power because of this. The implicit frame placed around Scarry's analysis, however, is that she is really only concerned with *modern* contexts in which pain and agency are assumed to be fundamentally opposed. As the pain of the Other increases, the agency of the Self is understood to correspondingly grow. As the autonomous voice of the Other is obliterated and reduced to a mere reflection of one's tormentor, the voice of the Self is doubled in strength.

Now this cannot be the full story even within secular modern societies. We have seen in recent years, for instance, much discussion of the use of torture in the CIA's interrogation of suspected Al Qaeda members. Methods such as waterboarding obviously incur significant psychological trauma on the tortured, but the spectacle of pain and fear has lasting psychic effects on the torturer as well. As one CIA official commented, "When you cross over that line of darkness, it's hard to come back. You lose your soul. You can do your best to justify it, but it's well outside the norm. You can't go to that dark a place without it changing you" (Mayer 2007: 56). In non-modern and especially small-scale egalitarian communities built upon regular, face-to-face interaction, however, those inflicting pain on other members of their community must have registered the torturer's line of darkness more deeply yet, for here Self and Other stood much more closely beside one another.

If torture is textual and if scars are scripts, as Clastres suggests, then the torture and execution of a community member is, in one sense, a kind of bodily erasure, wholly distinct from the initiatory violence discussed earlier. Needless to say, the executed witch has not learned that she or he lives in an egalitarian society. But when our sympathies are extended to those ritual executioners who get the blood on their hands, a broader political significance is revealed. The killing of witches, I suggest, must be regarded as another mode of painfully inscribing the law on society, insofar as violence must always have a recursive quality that acts back upon its perpetrators. The extreme measures taken to destroy the individual body of the witch, then, might be viewed simultaneously as a scarification of the collective body or, borrowing from Bataille (1985: 68), as a form of collective auto-mutilation. Let me emphasize again that the dismembered Pueblo witch – unlike most drawn and quartered criminals of Medieval Europe and even less like the victims tortured by modern intelligence agencies – was a close reflection of his discipliners. In many cases, the witch *was* the priest or medicine man who, in the eyes of public opinion, had crossed the fine line between the positive and negative use of power. There is a sense, thus, in which the executioners, in the act of killing, rehearsed their own murder, practiced their own mutilation. In visceral fashion, such rehearsals would have taught them that power in societies against the state is tenuous and that personal aggrandizement is dangerous.

Pueblo witchcraft executions may have functioned as leveling sanctions, then, but I am suggesting that they did so in a far more complicated and deeply psychological fashion than we are typically led to believe. These were not simply acts against transgression, acts against those who stepped outside the bounds of social convention. Witchcraft executions, I suggest, would themselves have been viewed as dangerously transgressive acts, particularly when "extreme processing" was involved and extensive corporeal mutilation followed the torture and killing of the victim. In the Pueblo tradition, a witch is defined by his or her actions as much as the possession of a "bad heart," and these actions typically involve murder, cannibalism, or some other mistreatment of human remains directed toward a member of one's own social group. "To become a *powaqa*, or witch, one must magically sacrifice the life of a close clan member," observes Whiteley (2008: 191). The specification of a *close* clan member is significant, for the witch embodies transgression, chaos, and assaults on the orderliness of society, and the killing of kin as the most basic rejection of the social contract. The Pueblo witch, through fratricide, is exposed as a dark force standing outside of and opposed to society.

The witch murders and mistreats the corpse of its victim. So too does (did) the Pueblo priest in retaliation. Would not the community on some level have viewed both executed and executioner as walking the same thin red line? Was not violence done unto both executed and executioner (the latter of whom no doubt must have been under a great deal of pressure to undertake the dangerous act in the first place)? Are we not looking at a sacrifice of the killers as well as the killed? Mutilation and also auto-mutilation?

In the end, no amount of bludgeoning, breakage, or burning could ever do away with the witch as a structural position within Pueblo thought, for the act of removing the witch mirrored the act of witchcraft itself (Figure 6.3). But perhaps this was the very logic that lay behind the violence. All societies define themselves by what they are not. All societies demand their anti-societies; they demand their witches. And it is in this sense that we may, perhaps, find greater significance in the "extreme processing" events as necessarily acts both *against* transgression and *of* transgression.

This is the sort of complexity that gets lost when archaeologists bluntly present us with a world of Pueblo terrorists, single-mindedly killing to dominate and instill fear of nonconformity into the hearts of the populace. Lekson (2002: 618) argues, for instance, that during the Chacoan era, when political centralization in the Southwest appears to have been most pronounced, violence was used as "a strong tool... for maintaining the structure of political power." Whether we imagine "political 'death squads'"

Moral enforcer Executioner Priest	Moral transgressor Executed Witch	Anti-Society
Moral community		Society

Figure 6.3. Structural position of witch and witch-killer in Pueblo society.

or witchcraft 'inquisitions',", he writes, "the constant threat of socially
sanctioned violence… would almost certainly create a climate of mistrust and
fear" (2002: 620; see also Bustard 2008: 94–95; Kantner 1999). The claim
here is that Pueblo violence was driven by a basic logic of domination and
hierarchy: one killed to keep others in a subordinate position. While I do
not contest the likelihood that hierarchy lay in the hearts of some ancestral
Pueblo leaders, I suggest that the social realities of Pueblo violence led away,
rather than toward, the possibility of overt domination.

Let me extend this argument one step further. Recent reconsiderations
of Pueblo witchcraft have focused upon the trials of individuals or small
families, but it is clear that witchcraft could manifest at the level of the village
and, consequently, demand a community-wide act of violence. Consider the
well-known destruction of the Hopi village of Awatovi at the start of the
eighteenth century. Spanish accounts indicate that the Awatovi community
had invited the Franciscans to reestablish a church in the village following
the reconquest of New Mexico, and that other Hopi dealt with this affront
to their native religious autonomy through a coordinated assault. A Hopi
destruction of fellow Hopi ensued, leaving the village in smoldering ruins,
the Awatovi men dead, and surviving Awatovi women redistributed among
the attackers. Most scholars acknowledge the probability that many of the
Awatovi victims were also burned and dismembered following death. Hopi
oral history, at least, indicates as much (Fewkes 1893: 366), and Christy
Turner (Turner and Morris 1970; Turner and Turner 1999) has controversially
interpreted the Polacca Wash Site as the very location where the bodies
of at least thirty of the Awatovi victims were "mistreated" and, possibly,
cannibalized (but see Whiteley 2008).

For my purposes here, the most significant element in the story of
Awatovi's destruction is its architect. Hopi oral histories widely concur that
while neighboring communities undertook the assault, it was the Awatovi's
own village chief, Tapolo, who coordinated the event in an effort to purge the
world of an outbreak of sorcery that, he believed, had overtaken his village.
"My children [meaning his people] have become evil," states Tapolo in one
Hopi account. "They are engaging in witchcraft and conspiring with the
Kastilam [Spanish]. I have been thinking about it for a long time and can
see no other solution. My village must be destroyed – razed to the ground,
so that Awat'ovi will be no more" (as quoted in Whiteley 1988: 21–22; see
also Fewkes 1893: 365; Voth 1905: 246–255).

It was an extreme and tragic measure, not only because the resultant
violence was directed against Tapolo's home community, but because it was
directed against the village chief as well. Peter Whiteley learned from his
Hopi informants that:

Tapolo himself would have to die in the process, as well as his sons – this was how such matters were arranged in the Hopi way. So this was an act of great sacrifice on his part, to benefit the rest of the Hopi people. The evil would be rooted out and mankind purified [Whiteley 1988: 22].

Not surprisingly, many have viewed the destruction of Awatovi as a consequence of Spanish colonialism and so have isolated it from discussions of pre-Columbian Pueblo violence. However, there are good grounds for taking native testimony seriously and accepting that such acts of sacrifice were, in an important sense, part of "the Hopi way." As one Hopi oral historian put it in describing a similar incident at Oraibi Pueblo: "This is the way chiefs often punished their children [people] when they became 'bewitched.'… Many people were killed in that way because their chiefs became angry and invited some chief or inhabitant from other villages to destroy the people" (Voth 1905: 256).

One could argue over the degree to which Hopi oral history has simply drawn upon a ready-made cultural storyline to explain an act of violence that had a far more complicated set of historically specific causes. Still, the storyline remains. That the destruction of Awatovi and other ancestral villages has been attributed to acts of auto-sacrifice is itself a fact of Pueblo society, and this fact deepens the contrast with European mode of violence.

"Fair is Fair"/Monumental Torture

Where, then, are we left in our understanding of the Oñate foot incident and its reception? If the pre-Columbian pueblos were already no stranger to blood and fire, what made Spanish violence so unthinkable?

I suggest that whether we are examining Europe's genocidal acts on the colonial frontier, or the killing of witches in Pueblo villages, we must, following Clastres, be centrally concerned with the particular politics into whose service the violence was put. We must attend to the laws that would have been inscribed (both corporeally and psychologically) onto bodies (both individual and collective) as a consequence of the violent acts in question. And it is in this sense that we find Oñate's actions standing in such stark contrast.

In the Pueblo world, war never appears to have been waged as a means of establishing institutionalized relations of hierarchy between conqueror and conquered. There is no indigenous tradition of subjugation in this sense. Elsewhere, I have offered one example in which, I argue, an immigrant population from the Chacoan region at the close of the twelfth century overpowered an autochthonous community in the northern Rio Grande region, killing many (in the local oral history, the victims are sometimes referred to as "witch people"), and eventually incorporating the survivors into a few newly established large towns (Fowles 2005, 2013). However, the result, in this case, was the creation of a community organized around a ceremonial moiety system that expressly embodied an ideology of power-sharing and religio-political parity. Other examples of "conquest" events in the pre-Columbian Pueblo world might be offered (a few Chacoan scholars would, no doubt, enthusiastically offer their own), but there is no reason to conclude that violence ever created or was intended to create a truly subjugated population. More often than not, violence among the ancestral Pueblos would have led away from relationships of domination within the wider social sphere, not toward such relationships.

At a deeper level, I have suggested that this was the case because much of the torture, killing, and corpse mutilation that took place from time to time in the Pueblo past had a decidedly reflexive aspect. If a witch becomes a witch by killing a member of his own kin, what are we to make of the village chief who arranges to kill his own community in an effort to rid it of witchcraft? And if Pueblo witches are notorious for not just killing their victims, but for dismembering, roasting and consuming them as well, then what are we to make of ritual leaders who were expected not only to execute those accused of witchcraft, but also to dismember and otherwise mistreat their corpses? There is a dark symmetry here that underscores the ambivalence toward power in Pueblo society. Leadership, as I have already noted, was dangerous and frequently regarded as undesirable (see also Fowles 2010). In fact, one might say that Pueblo leadership paradoxically involved socially mandated acts of social deviance that would have left the leader in a position perilously close to that of the witch.

Needless to say, the Spaniard stood in a vastly different relationship to his victims. Colonial violence was designed to lead toward, rather than away from, relationships of dominance and submission. Violence was done unto the bodies of indigenous peoples (not only in overt acts of whipping or mutilation, but also in things like the missionaries' efforts to cut the hair of native men) in an effort to create disciplined, lower-class subjects of cross and crown. In some cases, the violence clearly also had humiliation and degradation as its goal; in others cases, extermination was the blunt objective. Regardless, the effect was successively to distance the Pueblos in social space, to make them less legible as autonomous agents, and to render them convincingly as object-like extensions of colonial power.

It is worth adding that part of the process was accomplished through language and the compulsion to make certain speech acts that inevitably accompanied colonial violence. Scarry (1985: 35) writes of modern torture as necessarily consisting of two interlinked components: "a primary physical act, the infliction of pain, and a primary verbal act, the interrogation." The former disintegrates the world of the victim; the latter, as it leads to a confession, fills the void with the extended voice and agency of the torturer: "Intense pain is world-destroying. In compelling confession, the torturers compel the prisoner to record and objectify the fact that intense pain is world-destroying. It is for this reason that while the content of the prisoner's answer is only sometimes important to the regime, the form of the answer, the fact of his answering, is always crucial" (1985: 29). Something similar must have underwritten the conquistadors' repeated insistence that the Pueblos formally proclaim their submission and obedience to Spain. All villages throughout New Mexico were compelled to make verbal oaths in this way, a fact that received much emphasis in Spanish records. Of course, the words spoken had to have been empty, insofar as, even if linguistic barriers were bridged, the notion of being a "vassal" of the crown would have had no real referent. The driving motivation, perhaps, was more that Pueblo victims were simply made to parrot Spanish words. Colonial violence was world-destroying, and the empty oath of allegiance objectified that fact.

"Massacre requires an appropriate context," writes Todorov, and I might have used this essay as an opportunity to explore the degree to which early European brutality in the American Southwest was defined by the fact that it was performed in a moral and social vacuum by men who saw no flicker of themselves reflected back in the eyes of those they aggressed. Oñate and his men were indeed the sort of torturers Scarry (1985) had in mind: separated by a radical gulf, their power and voice was amplified as pain came to replace personhood for their victims. But my focus instead has been on indigenous patterns, and my simple aim has been to counter the archaeological tendency to present Pueblo violence as merely a smaller-scale version of the violence of the State. As I have argued, the underlying logics were worlds apart: hence, the particular horror over Oñate's actions at Acoma.

Eventually, of course, violence always finds its way back to those who deal in it. In the case of Oñate, he was tried and convicted (if later cleared) by the Council of the Indies for his mistreatment of indigenous peoples, as well as his mismanagement of New Mexico's colonization generally. His true trial, however, was a much more recent affair. In 1998, in the context of the controversial celebrations of the 400th anniversary of Oñate's colonization of New Mexico, protesters – presumably Puebloan – secretly attacked a monumental bronze statue of the conquistador at the Oñate Monument Visitor's Center north of Española. They taped a note to the statue reading "Fair is fair". And they left with Oñate's sawed-off right foot.

Notes

1. Two Hopi men, who were also captured during the siege, walked away but with their right hands severed, so as to be a lesson to other potential rebels.

2. This statement by Andres Lauriano appeared in *The Albuquerque Journal* in 1998 (as cited in Brooke 1998).

3. In one recent discussion of pre-modern violence, for instance, Steven Pinker (2002: 56) complains that "many intellectuals have embraced the image of peaceable, egalitarian, and ecology-loving natives. But in the past two decades anthropologists have gathered data on life and death in pre-state societies rather than accepting the warm and fuzzy stereotypes. What did they find? In a nutshell: Hobbes was right, Rousseau was wrong." This sort of polemical argument remains common, particularly in the more popular literature.

4. Printed just a few years prior, Hogarth's *The Four Stages of Cruelty* (1751) offered a dramatic graphic portray of the successive un-learning of natural pity and socialization for cruelty on the streets of London over the course of a man's life.

5. In his *History of Torture Throughout the Ages*, George Ryley Scott expressed the growing cynicism of wartime Europe, accepting that extreme cruelty was a tragic potential written into human nature and therefore a persistent threat to the civilizing process. "If there is one lesson that history teaches," he wrote, "it is that any possibility of abolishing torture is endangered by the existence of cruelty in any form and for any purpose. In all circumstances and at all times cruelty may easily develop into torture" (Scott 1959 [1940]: vii). And yet, argued Scott, one need only look to the supposedly extreme violence of primitive societies – to the anachronistic examples of raw human nature in its "nearness to animal behaviourism" (1959 [1940]: 35) – to confirm that progress has indeed been made. What I find most interesting about Scott's work is its deviance from the purely Hobbesian solution to the problem of innate human violence. Rather than rely on the centralized authority of the State, Scott promoted a radical liberal humanist agenda which sought (1) to altogether strip the State of its ability to distribute corporeal punishment and (2) to encourage civility in the State's citizens purely through the expansion of individual intellectual freedoms and humanitarian teachings in home and school. The primary goal, as he put it, was to overcome "the primeval tendency of the mob," (1959: 312) which only enlightened individualism and not the authority of the State could secure (see Asad 2003: 103 for a different reading). In doing so, Scott offered an unusual mixing of both Hobbes's and Rousseau's positions.

6. Todorov drew his distinction between sacrifice-societies and massacre-societies with the contrast between Aztec and Spanish modes of violence in mind. His interest was not in the non-state societies of the New World, many of which appear to have developed precisely as a rejection of Aztec-style forms of state power.

7. "It is a sort of worship, or penance of great cruelty," Catlin (1965 [1841]: 232) wrote, "with only one palliating circumstance about it, which is, that it is a voluntary torture."

8. There is a natural comparison to be drawn here with Bloch's (1986) well-known discussion of violence as blessing in the Merina circumcision ritual.

References

Asad, Talal
   2003 *Formations of the Secular: Christianity, Islam, Modernity.* Stanford University Press, Stanford.

Bataille, George
   1985 Sacrificial Mutilation and the Severed Ear of Vincent Van Gogh. In *Visions of Excess: Selected Writings, 1927–1939*, edited and translated by Allan Stoekl, pp. 61–72. University of Minnesota Press, Minneapolis.

Bettelheim, Bruno
   1954 *Symbolic Wounds: Puberty Rites and the Envious Male.* Free Press, Glencoe, IL.

Bloch, Maurice
   1986 *From Blessing to Violence.* Cambridge University Press, New York.

Bowers, Alfred
   1950 *Mandan Social and Ceremonial Organisation.* University of Chicago Press, Chicago.

Brooke, James
   1998 Oñate's foot story. Electronic document, http://weber.ucsd.edu/~rfrank/class_web/ES-112A/Onate.html, accessed April 15, 2008

Bunzel, Ruth L.
   1992 [1932] Introduction to Zuñi Ceremonialism. *Forty-Seventh Annual Report of the Bureau of American Ethnology 1929–1930*, pp. 467–544. Smithsonian Institution Press, Washington, DC.

Bustard, Wendy
   2008 Chaco Horrificus? In *Social Violence in the Prehispanic American Southwest*, edited by Deborah L. Nichols and Patricia L. Crown, pp. 70–97. University of Arizona Press, Tucson.

Catlin, George
   1965 [1841] *Letters and Notes of the Manners, Customs, and Condition of the North American Indians*, Vol. 1. Ross and Haines, Minneapolis.
   1996 [1865] An Account of an Annual Religious Ceremony Practiced by the Mandan Tribe of North American Indians. In *Catlin's O-kee-pa*, edited by Colin F. Tylor, pp. 89–111. Verlag für Amerikanistik, Wyk auf Foehr, Germany.

Clastres, Pierre
   1989 *Society Against the State.* Zone Books, New York.
   1994 *Archaeology of Violence.* Semiotext(e), New York.

Clottes, Jean, and Jean Courtin
   1996 *The Cave Beneath the Sea: Paleolithic Images at Cosquer.* Translated by Marilyn Garner. Harry N. Abrams, New York.

Cushing, Frank Hamilton
   1883 My Adventures in Zuñi. *Century Illustrated Monthly Magazine* 6: 28–47.

Darling, Andrew
   1998 Mass Inhumation and the Execution of Witches in the American Southwest. *American Anthropologist* 100(3): 732–752.

Douglas, Mary
   1988 [1966]   *Purity and Danger: an Analysis of Concepts of Pollution and Taboo.* Routledge and Kegan Paul, London.

Fergusson, Erna
   1931   *Dancing Gods: Indian Ceremonials of New Mexico and Arizona.* University of New Mexico Press, Albuquerque.

Fewkes, Jesse Walter
   1893   A-wa'-to bi: An Archeological Verification of a Tusayan Legend. *American Anthropologist* 6: 363–375.

Foucault, Michel
   1979   *Discipline and Punish: The Birth of the Prison.* Vintage Books, New York.

Fowles, Severin
   2005   Historical contingency and the prehistoric origins of Eastern Pueblo moieties. *Journal of Anthropological Research.* 61(1): 25–52.
   2010   A People's History of the American Southwest. In *Ancient Complexities: New Perspectives in Pre-Columbian North America*, edited by Susan Alt, pp. 183–204. University of Utah Press, Provo.
   2013   *An Archaeology of Doings: Secularism and the Study of Pueblo Religion.* School for Advanced Research Press, Santa Fe.

Hammond, George P., and Agapito Rey (editors)
   1953   *Don Juan de Oñate: Colonizer of New Mexico, 1595–1628.* University of New Mexico Press, Albuquerque.

Hill, W.W.
   1982   *An Ethnography of Santa Clara Pueblo, New Mexico.* University of New Mexico Press, Albuquerque.

Hobbes, Thomas
   1998 [1651]   *Leviathan.* Oxford University Press, Oxford.

Kantner, John
   1999   Survival Cannibalism or Sociopolitical Intimidation? Explaining Perimortem Mutilation in the American Southwest. *Human Nature* 10(1): 1–50.

Keeley, Lawrence
   1996   *War Before Civilization: The Myth of the Peaceful Savage.* Oxford University Press, New York.

Kuckelman, Kristin A., Ricky R. Lightfoot, and Debra L. Martin
   2000   Changing Patterns of Violence in the Northern San Juan Region. *Kiva* 66(1): 147–165.

LeBlanc, Steven A
   1999   *Prehistoric Warfare in the American Southwest.* University of Utah Press, Salt Lake City.

Lekson, Stephen H
   2002   War in the Southwest, War in the World. *American Antiquity* 67(4): 597–624.

Lévy-Bruhl, Lucien
   1926   *How Natives Think.* Washington Square Press, New York.

Lewis-Williams, David, and David Pearce
    2005   *Inside the Neolithic Mind: Consciousness, Cosmos, and the Realm of the Gods*. Thames and Hudson, New York.

Mayer, Jane
    2007   The Black Sites. *The New Yorker*, 13 August: 46–57.

Nichols, Deborah L., and Patricia L. Crown (editors)
    2008   *Social Violence in the Prehispanic American Southwest*. University of Arizona Press, Tucson.

Ogilvie, Marsha D., and Charles E. Hilton
    2000   Ritualized Violence in the Prehistoric American Southwest. *International Journal of Osteoarchaeology* 10(1): 27–48.

Pandey, Triloki Nath
    1994   Patterns of Leadership in Western Pueblo Society. In *North American Indian Anthropology: Essays on Society and Culture*, edited by Raymond J. DeMallie and Alfonso Ortiz, 328–339. University of Oklahoma Press, Norman.

Pinker, Steven
    2002   *The Blank Slate: The Modern Denial of Human Nature*. Penguin Books.

Rice, Glen, and Steven A. LeBlanc (editors)
    2001   *Deadly Landscapes: Case Studies in Prehistoric Southwestern Warfare*, University of Utah Press, Salt Lake City.

Róheim, Géza
    1925   *Australian Totemism: A Psycho-Analytic Study in Anthropology*. G. Allen and Unwin, London.

Rousseau, Jean-Jacques
    1985 [1754]   *A Discourse on Inequality*. Penguin Classics.

Scarry, Elaine
    1985   *The Body in Pain: The Making and Unmaking of the World*. Oxford University Press, New York.

Scott, George Ryley
    1959 [1940]   *The History of Torture Throughout the Ages*. Luxor Press, London.

Seefeldt, Douglas
    2005   Oñate's Foot: Histories, Landscapes, and Contested Memories in the Southwest. In *Across the Continent: Jefferson, Lewis and Clark, and the Making of America*, edited by Douglas Seefeldt, Jeffrey L. Hantman, and Peter S. Onuf., pp. 169–209 University of Virginia Press, Charlottesville.

Smith, Jonathan Z.
    1987   The Domestication of Sacrifice. In *Violent Origins: Walter Burkert, René Girard and Jonathan Z. Smith on Ritual Killing and Cultural Formation*, edited by Robert G. Hamerton-Kelly, pp. 191–205. Stanford University Press, Stanford.

Spencer, Herbert
    1883 [1850]   *Social Statics*. Appleton, New York.

Taussig, Michael
    2006   *Walter Benjamin's Grave*. University of Chicago Press, Chicago.

Todorov, Tzvetan
  1984   *The Conquest of America: the Question of the Other*. Translated by Richard Howard. Harper and Row, New York.

Trigger, Bruce G.
  1990   Maintaining Economic Equality in Opposition to Complexity: An Iroquoian Case Study. In *The Evolution of Political Systems: Sociopolitics in Small-Scale Sedentary Societies*, pp. 119–145. Cambridge University Press, New York.

Turner, Christy G., and Nancy T. Morris
  1970   A Massacre at Hopi. *American Antiquity* 35(3): 320–331.

Turner, Christy G., and Jacqueline A. Turner
  1999   *Man Corn: Cannibalism and Violence in the Prehistoric American Southwest*. University of Utah Press, Salt Lake City.

Voth, H. R.
  1905   *The Traditions of the Hopi*. Anthropological Series, vol. III. Field Museum, Chicago.

Walker, J. R.
  1917   The Sun Dance and Other Ceremonies of the Oglala Division of the Teton Dakota. *Anthropological Papers of the American Museum of Natural History* 16(2): 51–221.

Walker, William
  1998   Where are the Witches of Prehistory? *Journal of Archaeological Method and Theory* 5(3): 245–308.
  2008   Witches, Practice, and the Context of Pueblo Cannibalism. In *Social Violence in the Prehispanic American Southwest*, edited by Deborah L. Nichols and Patricia L. Crown, pp. 143–83. University of Arizona Press, Tucson.

Wesley, John
  1958   *The Works of John Wesley*, vol. 5. Zondervan, Grand Rapids.

White, Tim D.
  1992   *Prehistoric Cannibalism at Mancos 5MTUMR-2346*. Princeton University Press, Princeton

Whiteley, Peter
  1988   *Bacavi: Journey to Reed Springs*. Northland Press, Flagstaff.
  1998   *Rethinking Hopi Ethnography*. Smithsonian, Washington D.C.
  2008   Explanation vs. Sensation: The Discourse of Cannibalism at Awat'ovi. In *Social Violence in the Prehispanic American Southwest*, edited by Deborah L. Nichols and Patricia L. Crown, pp. 184–215. University of Arizona Press, Tucson.

Wissler, Clark
  1918   The Sun Dance of the Blackfoot Indians. *Anthropological Papers of the American Museum of Natural History* 16(3): 223–270.

Part III

Terror

If violence is paradoxically always social in its operation and effects, articulating with notions of community and remaking social networks, there is another crucial aspect of violence that has not been discussed thus far: its threat or potential. Indeed, the threat of force is arguably more socially potent than its actual operation. If violent acts send ripples through networks of distributed being, the shadow of their potential is all the more effective as a socializing force for its constant presence. Moreover, beyond the obvious, instrumental uses of potential violence, threats, as products of collective imagination, can generate social effects free from any intentional agency. If Giddens (1981) is correct in his claim that the search for ontological security is a central human concern, variable though notions of security and thresholds of risk may be, then fear and threat must be considered key elements of socio-historical process and potential violence a potent force.

While the most obvious aspect of potential violence is fear, and while anxiety and perceptions of danger have been linked to violence in cases as widely diverse as Aztec sacrifice (Carrasco 2000), Amazonian colonial atrocities (Taussig 1987) and Rwandan genocide (Gourevich 1998), potential violence can also have more subtle social effects. Such indirect effects in contemporary America in the form of the US military institutions and their dominant discourses has been the focus of Lutz's work for the last decade. Lutz has argued that the increasing power of the US military and the ascendance of what she calls the "military normal" has had a corrosive effect on democratic institutions and civil society since the end of World War II, dramatically increasing post-9/11. The imposition of a military perspective has not only promoted military virtues of "obedience, loyalty, duty, honor, and conformity", increasingly shaping discourse on citizenship and moral economy, but also produced profound socio-economic effects through the opportunity cost of bloated military spending and structural violence of its unequally distributed costs and benefits (Lutz 2001). Moreover, Lutz's description of the military normal as the vested perspective of a power-elite promulgated with great effort and expense, shares more than a little with Baines and Yoffee's (1998) notion of "civilization" as the validating ideology and high culture of inner elites. One crucial distinction, however, is that while the "military normal" may be a dominant discourse within the "civilization" that is supposedly being defended in the war against terror, it is crucially tied to various other facets of contemporary American practice and belief including American exceptionalism, individualism, consumerism, and teleological neo-liberal historiography. At the same time, Lutz's brief sketch of the military normal's institutional history points to the importance of understanding macro-scale concepts such as "civilization" in terms of their multitude of components and historical processes.

Another importance of Lutz's contribution (originally written for Engleke 2009) for the present work lies in its startling presentation of the hidden violence of the familiar and the familiar cloaking and distancing of violence from its agents. Thus, despite having the most powerful military the world has ever known and a "political economy centered on making war and preparing to make war", the institutions of the US military normal present their actions as "humanitarian" and able to attain "coercion without blood", founded on cosmologies of freedom, justice, and democracy. Framed by the massive resources expended to maintain and promulgate this perspective, Lutz exposes the absurd contradictions of the "military normal", even while the by-now familiar forms of legitimized, invisible violence in the service of high elites take banal but sinister shape.

What is perhaps most interesting about Lutz's paper from the perspective of long-term trends in violence and civilization, are the actual mechanisms through which the self-image of peace-loving Americans is reconciled with the reality of a large, expensive, and interventionist military. Lutz focuses on the military's management of the media coverage of conflict and domestic pubic relations, crucial links in controlling the narrative of conflict to be sure, but from the perspectives being pursued through this volume there is also the long-term trend of affective and spatial distancing. As Sontag (2003) noted, the remote viewing of others' pain has become a commonplace of contemporary life even as the desensitized virtual violence of videogames is mimetically reproduced in smart weaponry and war from a distance. With the advent of embedded reporters, mouth-piece media organizations, and the virtualization of distant wars fought by professional soldiers with relatively few friendly casualties, it may well be that conventional legitimized violence has reached a near perfect moral invisibility in the post-Cold War era.

The macro-historical narrative of violence and civilization suggested thus far appears teleological – from the intimate, inward violence of face-to-face societies to the spectacular political violence of early polities to the externalizing violence of empires and finally to the perfection of distance and invisibility in post-Cold War virtual war. Yet Bonditti's contribution complicates this perspective. Rather than an end of history, he posits a "deep mutation in the art of governing", predicated on a shift from spatial to temporal coordinates. Tracing changes in the definition of terrorism since WWII, Bonditti maps out its increasing importance and shifting discourse until terror itself becomes the enemy and locus of "radical otherness".

Relating Bonditti's arguments to other papers in the collection, such as Bryen's and Fowles's, he is interested in linking institutional or organizational aspects of violence and its management to modes of community. Thus definitions of terrorism show an institutional *habitus* as well as a vested interest in mapping its coordinates to a topography of sovereign states. In a sense the elevation of transnational terrorism to the highest order of threat is a defense of the sovereign nation-state against emergent forms of political violence, while at the same time betraying the new importance of mobility and temporality. While in the larger scheme of history, preemption, mobility, and time are not new factors in the amelioration of threat or circulation of violence, Bonditti convincingly shows an inter-related shift in technologies, discourses of otherness, and political violence over the last 50 years. Connecting these arguments to Lutz's contribution, it is easy to see how the "defense in depth" strategy of the post-Cold War era attenuates the link between violence and its moral costs, helping to lessen the difficulty of sustaining the "military normal" even while the promotion of terror itself to the status of the new enemy and the blurring of Modern categories of domestic and foreign create new opportunities for the expansion of the military mission (and its demands on resources). At the same time, the blurring of the boundaries of community and otherness threatens to overturn the distancing mechanisms by which the nation state practices violence. The war against terror is both domestic and foreign, the enemy can be anywhere, and threat is omnipresent.

In line with the Eliasian thinking that has served as a critical undercurrent to the discussion of the papers collected here, a connection can be made between the emergence of terror itself as the new enemy of "civilization" and the long-lived, low-risk, physical harm-adverse societies of the contemporary West. As Zygmunt Bauman (2006) has observed, our attempts to rationally master personal danger in all of its forms has had the perplexing effect of multiplying sources of anxiety. Our twin mega-centers of resource expenditure, health and defense, are paradoxically linked in being aimed at pushing sources of individual anxiety as far as possible from those privileged enough to enjoy the benefits of neo-liberal civilization (which is of course, internally as well as externally gradated). Also paradoxically, the fixation with physical, rights-denying harm and the limited moral horizon of community in societies based around the pursuit of personal comfort helps to focus attention on shadowy terrorist networks, while simultaneously motivating vastly more destructive violence at temporal, spatial, and affective distance. Most disturbing, however, is the manner in which these priorities camouflage the massive but invisible harm created by our contemporary world order's systemic violences. Neo-liberal theodicies of privilege and poverty posit a world of unfettered competition producing morally sanctioned victors and condemned losers: a hierarchy of being determined almost entirely by economic status. Paradoxically, Western Civilization's "civilizing process" has attempted to do away with physical suffering (especially of its own citizens) and promote political egalitarianism, even while the increasing commodification of society is creating an ever more liquid and streamlined source of hierarchy. Our local moral economies deny these inequalities the name of violence, but the systemic effects of poverty and inequality worldwide are suffering, sickness, and death (World Health Organization, Commission on the Social Determinants of Health, 2008).

References

Baines, John, and Norman Yoffee

    1998   Order, Legitimacy, Wealth in Ancient Egypt and Mesopotamia. In *Archaic States*, edited by G. Feinman and J. Marcus, pp. 199–260. School of American Research, Santa Fe, NM.

Bauman, Zygmunt

    2006   *Liquid Fear*. Polity Press, Cambridge.

Carrasco, David

    2000   *City of Sacrifice: The Aztec Empire and the Role of Violence in Civilization*. Beacon Press, Boston.

Engleke, Mathew (editor)

    2009   *The Counter-Counterinsurgency Manual: Or Notes on Demilitarizing American Society*. Prickly Paradigm Press, Chicago.

Giddens, Anthony

    1981   *A Contemporary Critique of Historical Materialism*. Macmillan Press, London.

Gourevitch, Philip

    1998   *We Wish to Inform You That Tomorrow We Will be Killed With Our Families: Stories from Rwanda*. Farrar, Strauss & Giroux, New York.

Lutz, Catherine

    2001   *Homefront: A Military City and the American Twentieth Century*. Beacon Hill Press, Boston

Sontag, Susan

    2003   *Regarding the Pain of Others*. Farrar, Straus and Giroux, New York.

Taussig, Michael

    1987   *Shamanism, Colonialism and the Wild Man: A Study in Terror and Healing*. University of Chicago Press, Chicago.

World Health Organization, Commission on the Social Determinants of Health

    2008   *Closing the Gap in a Generation: Health Equity through Action on the Social Determinants of Health. Final Report of the Commission on Social Determinants of Health.* World Health Organization, Geneva.

— 7 —

The Military Normal: Feeling at Home with Counterinsurgency in the United States

Catherine Lutz

The Military Normal

Here were two typical US media moments in July 2008. On Fox News, Brit Hume opened his interview with two advocates of "victory" in Iraq – pundits Charles Krauthammer and Fred Barnes – with video of George Bush explaining rising US casualties in Afghanistan. "One reason why there have been more deaths [recently]," the President declared, "is because our troops are taking the fight to a tough enemy. They don't like our presence there because they don't like Americans denying safe haven." This clip was followed by one of Admiral Mike Mullen, Chairman of the Joint Chiefs of Staff, reminding Americans, "We all need to be patient. As we have seen in Iraq, counterinsurgency warfare takes time and a certain level of commitment. It takes flexibility." Over on radio, NPR's *Fresh Air* program featured an hour-long discussion with Lt. Col. John Nagl, a recently retired Army officer who led tank assaults in the First and Second Gulf Wars, one of the co-authors of the *Counterinsurgency Manual,* and now working with the ascendant, new Democratic-leaning think tank, the Center for a New American Security. Interviewer Terry Gross's gentle questions generally went like this one: "Ethics become very complicated because it's hard to tell who's a friend and who's the enemy. And that must make it hard to tell, too, when it's appropriate to fire and when it's not. Can you tell us about a difficult judgment call you had to make about whether or not to fire on individuals or on a crowd?"

Prevailing mainstream media discussions of counterinsurgency wars in Iraq and Afghanistan have this restricted kind of range, focusing on how the wars are being fought, or should be fought – with what tactics, for how long, and with what level of "success." The pundits, with the populace in tow, debate whether the military is stretched too thin, well-enough resourced or not, or in need of tens of thousands more troops to do the job. They debate whether the Bush administration lied about the reasons for going into Iraq, but not whether the nation should have been there or in Afghanistan under any circumstances. They debate timetables for bringing the troops home, not plans for accountability for illegalities of war and torture.

They do not ask whether the US should have history's most lethal and offensively postured military, one with soldiers garrisoned in thousands of bases around the world, waging wars covert and overt in numbers of countries, and with annual costs to citizens of $1.2 trillion and an arsenal of unparalleled sophistication in ways to destroy people and things. They treat it as a "no brainer" that the security of the United States grows when the military budget or the size of the army grows, and that it is sensible for the federal government to spend more on the military than on protecting the environment, educating children, building transport systems, developing energy sources, agriculture, and job skills in the populace, and getting people into housing – combined. In these discussions, it goes without saying that the military serves the nation and/or the world as a whole, "policing" it for the common good. These stories assume that above all we live in a world of threat and risk, of enemies and allies, and of national and state rather than global and human interests as operative values. They assume that all civilians addressed by those media outlets are American citizens who are happy to pay the Pentagon's bills and who want nothing but victory or honorable withdrawal from fights around the world. The dominant media narrative suggests the values associated with the military as an institution – obedience, loyalty, duty, honor, conformity – should be the primary values of the civilian world as well: it assumes that soldiering builds character more than nursing does.

While polls show the majority of Americans in 2008 wanted US troops to return home from Iraq, the reasons pundits and populace most often gave for this did not question those basic assumptions: they argued the fight was elsewhere, or that the military should be put in a more defensive rather than interventionist stance. Most remain inside the consensus that makes an enormous military normal and acceptable: the most left-leaning think tanks tend to, at most, propose cutting military spending by 10 percent, pulling it back to levels it was at just a few years ago. Whether conservative or centrist, libertarian or liberal, the television, radio and internet sites from which the great majority of Americans get their news share these elements of a foundational narrative about the military, war, empire, and the world "out there," a world whose voices are rarely heard.

For expert comment on security, the media go to generals and civilian Pentagon employees who have made their careers preparing to make war far more than diplomats, humanitarian officials, or civilians about to deal with the catastrophic consequences of war. Many of these experts, the *New York Times* reported in 2008, have been operating on specific Pentagon instructions as to message, with access to Defense Department powerbrokers and, in some cases, money as compensation. These Pentagon mouthpieces are but the tip of a very large iceberg of money invested in convincing the American public to support a government and economy on a permanent war footing, a point to which I return in a moment.

We can call all of this – the massive investments in war and in the public relations of war, and the assorted beliefs that sustain them all – "the military normal."

A Brief History of the Rise of the Military Normal

In his important 1956 book, *The Power Elite*, C. Wright Mills wrote that a military mindset had already, relatively early in the era of permanent war, taken deep hold among the public. He termed this now taken-for-granted world of assumptions a "military metaphysics," or "the cast of mind that defines international reality as basically military." He argued that "The publicists of the military ascendancy need not really work to indoctrinate with this metaphysics those who count: they have already accepted it." He noted that what he called "crackpot realists" had come to rule the day, garnering virtually unlimited power to use a "military definition of reality" to pursue power, status, profit, and their vision of the US role in the world. Mills' argument that the US operated primarily at the relatively unified behest of a power elite of government, corporate and military elites, whose center was in military institutions, contrasts with a common pluralist notion of how things work. In that latter scheme, democratic checks and balances exist at many levels, protecting against the concentration of power in any segment of society, including the military. And it suggests how irrelevant formal civilian control of the military is.

Instead, Mills argued, a strong unanimity of thinking about war and foreign policy had emerged among civilian and military elites as a result of their shared identity as people different from, and in fact superior to, the average citizen. Their agreement on military matters comes from having walked in each others' shoes: large numbers of them regularly move between government, corporations, and the military. Former high ranking officers end up as well-paid employees of the companies they once bought weapons from, or they become members of Congress, granted special status as security policy experts or as appropriations committee members. And they share a metaphysic because institutional recruitment filters ensure new members enter only on accepting the military definition of reality, as evidenced by the progressive community organizer who ran for President in 2008 and came to argue for attacking Pakistan if necessary and increasing the size of forces deployed in various war zones.

The ascendance of the military came about only relatively recently in US history. While the US, as a state, was born through violence – Indian wars, the Revolution, and slave repression being the most important forms that violence took – it was founded on a suspicion of standing armies, and with civilian leadership ensured by Constitutional frameworks. Military leaders had relatively limited powers as a result; the public saw the military as a burden in peacetime and at best very occasionally necessary. Government-run armories and shipyards provided limited incentives for politicians and the business sector to argue for increased military spending. Middle-class families were reluctant to send their children into a military they saw as a virtual cesspool of vices.

The Second World War brought unprecedented levels of spending and coordination between private enterprise and the Federal government and massive conscription of young men into a 10-million person force. Money, story lines, and cultural capital were spread around for all to share. The war set in motion a process of militarization that has waxed and waned but never truly flagged in the seven decades since it began. The war gave the US a far-flung empire of bases, economic prerogatives, and cultural influence; yet militarization resulted not just from the attempt to sustain these, but from the incentives of all of the institutions and groups who benefited from a large military budget. Not only weapons-makers but companies like Procter & Gamble and the Disney Corporation came to enjoy and rely on immense military contracts. US universities were drawn up in a concerted government campaign to put much of the nation's scientific talent and university training at the disposal of the military, to the point where 45 percent of all computer science graduate students with federal support get it from the Pentagon, and 25 percent of all scientists and engineers work on its projects. The massive entangled system can go by the knotted moniker of the military-industrial-Congressional-media-entertainment-university complex.

The end of the Cold War resulted in a dip in military spending but it was no steeper than fluctuations in the past many decades. In that post-Cold War period as well the military normal began to cover an even more expansive swath of the national horizon, and by two routes. First, strategic planners argued that the US military, now absent any competitors, should aim to exert "full spectrum dominance" over untoward events anywhere, not just fight and win wars in which US national security would be deemed to be at risk. As a result, the number of US wars grew rapidly, with 33 open interventions in just the period from 1990 to 2008. Second, claims were made that the military was now better suited than any other institution to conduct all aspects of US foreign policy from war making to humanitarian rescue to development aid. The non-military components of the State Department and US aid budgets and functions shrank in direct result, with the regular Pentagon budget now thirty times their combined size. The Pentagon share of official development assistance rose from six percent of the whole in 2002 to 22 percent and rising in 2005. Foreign aid and diplomacy now often run, not ambassador to ambassador but military to military, strengthening those armies overseas as well.

The rapid growth of the Pentagon budget and functions, particularly in the post-9/11 period, has included takeover of other agencies' intelligence functions, even within the security sector. The Pentagon's intelligence budget is now $60 billion, dwarfing the CIA's $4 to 5 billion. The military normal suggests that this buying and spying, whoever does it, harvests security. The difficulty of even following the changes and scale of funding has also made it difficult to see how inconsequential are the merely million-dollar initiatives, like the Human Terrain Teams or Minerva, meant to ramp up the cultural intelligence used by the military.

Violence and the American Self-image

Despite the huge military budget, the frequent interventions overseas, and the morphing of foreign policy into military policy, Americans have been convinced that their nation is peace-loving (even when some relish the idea that no one trifles with the US without swift retribution). In its long-standing war narrative, the US fights reluctantly, rarely, and defensively, as Tom Engelhardt (1998) has so eloquently noted in his *The End of Victory Culture*. It is only when attacked that Americans rise to defend themselves. So it was a crucial and effective technique for the Bush administration to falsely link Iraq and the 9/11 attackers, to garner support for a war that was offensive in most senses of that term. Every invasion, in fact, has been portrayed this way – from the Dominican Republic in 1965, Vietnam in the 1960s, or Panama in 1989.

Remarkably, military and civilian leaders have even been successful in convincing people that the military rarely engages in killing. Military recruitment advertisements and official pronouncements from Pentagon, White House and Congress suggest as much. As Elaine Scarry (1985) has pointed out, these discussions disappear the broken bodies at war's center and replace them with war's supposed purpose, such as toppling a tyrant or freeing hostages. The preferential option for a view of the military as a defensive and innocent force for good in the world helps explain why US soldiers participating in invasions and armed attacks are most commonly described as "putting themselves in harm's way." Even images of troops being killed are now censored, with the *New York Times* counting just six realistic images of dead US soldiers over the entire war and across all media outlets. The work of moral hygiene that each day comes out of the mainstream media, and the Pentagon public relations and recruiting offices which feed them material, have made the war that most Americans know an almost non-physical imposition of will on others.

The military normal is sustained in part through this sense of innocence, a sense bestowed and maintained in two ways. The first involves the fictionalization of American war history via the ascendance of the Hollywood definition of reality, many of whose war films have had official Pentagon support. Besides the large new harvest of Iraq and Afghanistan veterans who know what combat looks like, most students I teach about war have learned what they already know about it through the gloss of film and television. They begin their questions and discussions with the military normal that those movies help reproduce, even if the message is sometimes the resigned notion that "war is hell."

The second involves the heavy censorship and cleaning up of actual wars' reality for public media consumption. CBS could receive a call from Dick Cheney in 2004 telling them not to publish the Abu Ghraib story, and the station would sit on the information for several weeks, emerging with it only after a leak of the official Taguba report to journalist Seymour Hersh made public knowledge inevitable. The embed system for reporters has successfully kept critical journalists from sources and outlets for their stories, and exerted great pressure on those who do embed to report warmly on the men and women in uniform, an additional incentive being provided by the fact that these people help keep the reporter alive. This was all further strengthened by a concerted campaign to portray the US military, as Andrew Bacevich (2005) has noted, as having invented a new, humane, highly targeted form of warfare. It was one based in smart weaponry and new strategy that decapitates demagogues rather than assaults a nation, one that sends bombs through the eye of a needle to wreak vengeance only on "the bad guys." This vision of a new, even more civilized American Way of War predated the recent celebration of the rise of General Petraeus's smarter, less kinetic brand of counterinsurgency warfare, but very much sets the context for the enthusiastic reception of Petraeus, the new *Counterinsurgency Field Manual*, and the idea of gathering academics to provide cultural knowledge to the military.

So the *Manual* was launched in 2007, a year when, by conservative estimates, the US military killed 713 Iraqi civilians, and was involved in firefights where 1,000 more were killed. The military normal is increasingly oriented around the idea of the exception – the civilian death as an exception, America as the exceptional nation, and the exception from rules called for by states of emergency, an emergency now decades long. It is guided by the spirit of a sign that Stan Goff, a Special Forces veteran, reports was hung in a Fort Bragg training area to encourage the sense of initiative desired in unconventional warriors: "Rule #1. There are no rules. Rule #2. Follow Rule #1." To be above the law is to be within the military normal.

This vision of the US military is also sustained by having two versions of every document that guide military activity – one more a document of civilization and the other of barbarism. So the *Counterinsurgency Field Manual* published by the University of Chicago Press (Sewall et al. 2007) has a doppelganger manual, the *Foreign Internal Defense Tactics Techniques and Procedures for Special Forces* (1994, 2004). The public-relations version of past US military action used by the Chicago version of the counterinsurgency manual sits in front of the well-recorded history of actually existing US counterinsurgencies in places like Vietnam and El Salvador, where the techniques of torture, assassination, and massive killing of civilians were in common and approved use.

The Counterinsurgency Campaign in the United States

It has often been said that modern warfare is centered in public relations more than weaponry, that the side which commands the story told about the fight – its rationale, justness, victims, and heroes – will win the war. Less often recognized is how much war and the military normal that makes it both possible and likely have depended on public relations campaigns at home, among the American public who must be convinced to continue to supply people to fight and money to buy weapons. From the Second World War's Office of War Information to the $20-million contract to monitor US and Middle Eastern media coverage of news from Iraq in order to "promote more positive coverage," reproducing support for war has required heavy lifting and significant investments.

The Pentagon has an annual budget of almost $3 billion for advertising and recruitment of new troops, a massive investment shaping domestic opinion. The GAO reported that, in the three years from 2003 to 2005, the Department of Defense spent $1.1 billion hiring advertising, public relations, and media firms to do the work of convincing the public that the war is important, going well, and requires new recruits and new dollars. The domestic propaganda is directed through the Pentagon's Soldiers News Service, Speakers Service, and other efforts to place news stories and advertising in US media. The military publishes hundreds of its own newspapers and magazines on bases around the world from the *Bavarian News* at US bases in Germany to the *Desert Voice Newspaper* in Kuwait to Fort Hood's *Sentinel* in Texas. It also has its own radio and television stations and a massive network of websites with "news," as one site puts it, on "the purpose and impact of Defense-wide programs," a number of which appear at first look to be civilian sites. The most effective part of the campaign focuses on soldier morale, recruitment, and public opinion simultaneously by encouraging civilians to respect and express gratitude to soldiers for what they do. This is affective labor many find easy to provide, especially when it is in exchange for not having to go to war or send one's children into the military.

This is itself a counterinsurgency campaign, ongoing since the Second World War, but especially intensified with the resistance that has emerged to the war and occupation of Iraq. The weapons of this campaign are the ideas articulated by powerful individuals in government and media, on the endless repeat that all marketers know is key to success. It centers on controlling what questions get asked – Is the surge working? Is the Army large enough? Are the Human Terrain Teams reducing casualties among civilians? Are our wounded veterans getting adequate care? – more than the answers. And the American public are more important long-term targets than "the Muslim world" or even the general population in Iraq and Afghanistan, because they theoretically control the purse strings and quite literally control whether they put their bodies or their sons' or daughters' bodies in uniform.

The military normal is constructed by a variety of factors, including the impact of years of advertising (only becoming ubiquitous in the media since the institution of the All Volunteer Force in 1973) at a level that not only brings in the requisite number of recruits each year, but convinces its other target audience, the American public in general, that the military is a reasonable and respectable institution, and that it makes our very way of life possible. In other words, without the military, we would not have the right to free speech or the other democratic freedoms we enjoy. That these freedoms were in fact ensured by legions of civilians campaigning against a state and a military that had come down on the side of their opposite, or that the military has frequently been used to deny those rights to others, as in Chile, Iran or Guatemala, gets scant attention. What also plays into the normalization and veneration of the military is the cumulative effect of the nation's 25 million veterans, many of whom are organized in powerful groups that act politically on military and foreign policy questions.

Threats to the Military Normal

The *Counterinsurgency Manual* is not just a cultural artifact of the exotic tribe at the Pentagon, or something created by a few individuals within the Pentagon or prompted by the Bush administration's particular failures and

challenges in Iraq and Afghanistan. It is, instead, an artifact of the American
whole. While its details might seem exotic, its foundational premises have
been these assumptions about the centrality and necessity of military force as
the core of US state functions. And its successful launch as a message about
what our military can accomplish – coercion without blood – depended on
this decades-long work to control the messages that the American people
receive and the beliefs they hold about the innocence and high civilizational
goals of the US military. It is the outcome of an entire political economy
centered on making war and preparing to make war.

How can counter-counterinsurgency hope to work in such a militarized
environment?

It can begin by identifying and challenging the pillars of belief and the
streams of profit that support business as usual within the military normal.
It would be twinned to campaigns for media democracy (given that the
military has been able to count on war cheerleading from the merged and
acquired corporate media) and for a university system unhooked from its
dependence on Pentagon research money and focused on researching how
the military-industrial-media-educational system actually works, what its
effects are domestically and overseas. It would take some heart from the fact
that so much work of public relations must go into trying to hide the war
system and its effects from people at home and around the world. Billion-
dollar campaigns of domestic counterinsurgency suggest that the hearts and
minds at stake are at home in the United States.

References

Bacevich, Andrew
    2005 *The New American Militarism: How Americans Are Seduced by War.* Oxford
        University Press, Oxford.
Engelhardt, Tom
    1998 *The End of Victory Culture: Cold War America and the Disillusioning of a Generation.*
        University of Massachusetts Press, Amherst, MA.
Mills, C. Wright
    1956 *The Power Elite.* Oxford University Press, New York.
Scarry, Elaine
    1985 *The Body in Pain: The Making and Unmaking of the World.* Oxford University Press,
        Oxford.
US Department of the Army
    2004 [1994] US Army Field Manual FM 31–20–3. *Foreign Internal Defense Tactics:*
        Techniques, and Procedures for Special Forces. Washington, DC.
    2007 *The US Army/Marine Corps Counterinsurgency Field Manual.* University of Chicago
        Press, Chicago.

Violence, "Terrorism", Otherness: Reshaping Enmity in Times of Terror*

Philippe Bonditti

Introduction

In recent years, the question of violence has mainly been brought to us by the grand narrative on "terrorism" and the necessity to eradicate what the administration of President George W. Bush, forty-fourth president of the United States of America, depicted as the "new political and strategic enemy" in the aftermath of the tragic events of September 11, 2001, an enemy against which this same administration decided to wage a "Global War on Terror" (GWOT). Whatever has been said about the latter, this war is not about the conflict between the Good and the Evil. Neither is it about a clash between civilizations – if indeed we could agree on what a civilization is supposed to be. Much more has been going on behind this war, and even more if we consider not just the GWOT, but the overall fight against "terrorism" that most governments have decided to engage in. What, if not the "fight against terrorism", seems more able to reconcile the United States, Iran, North Korea, China, France, Russia, Burma/Myanmar, Italy, Spain... Indeed, the different heads of state all seem of one mind about the necessity to fight "terrorism", except that they do not seem to agree on what this concept exactly is supposed to describe.

One thing among so many others that seems to be at stake in the contemporary fight against "terrorism" is nothing less than a deep mutation in the art of governing people (Bonditti 2008). This multifaceted transformation affects many different socio-political dimensions simultaneously: from the re-articulation of the modern state's security apparatuses (and the multiple power struggles it works with), to the reshaping of the systems of alliances at the international level, through the reformulation of the categories within which the mechanisms producing identity/difference have historically worked.

Even if there is no obvious clear-cut division between these dimensions, it is mainly this last aspect on which I will focus here, because it is precisely when considering the issue of the production of the collective-self identity and of radical otherness that the question of the multiple uses of the term "terrorism" appears to be the most crucial.

"Terrorism", "left-wing terrorism", "right-wing terrorism", "Islamist terrorism", "domestic terrorism", "international terrorism", "transnational terrorism", "technological/ catastrophic terrorism", "terrorist network", "terrorist attack", "war against terrorism": though nobody is fooled about the essentially contested nature of the term, it seems that "terrorism" has recently colonized the political rhetoric to the point that we have become comfortably numb to the "terrorist vocabulary". Rare are those who, among the professionals of politics, the professionals of security, and even worse among academics, explain what they are talking about when they refer to "terrorism". In this paper, I aim to engage directly and critically with the term "terrorism" in its multiple uses, to suggest eventually an alternative story about what this world's governments are doing when they say that they are fighting "terrorism".

In order to do this, I will here assume that "terrorism" does not exist as such or, to put it in a slightly less polemical way, that it is not a helpful analytical category to understand violence and its supposed transformations (Bigo 2005). On the contrary, *I consider "terrorism" through a series of discourses that together form a grand narrative about political violence – that is, a series of practices of violence that, as we shall see, are not just directed against established governments, but also disrupt the modern understanding of political spatiality by operating transnationally.* From this perspective, to analyze how the term "terrorism" is being used tells much more about those who speak about "terrorism" than about violence itself. I will hence argue that this grand narrative on "terrorism" has come to be the main *discursive locus* for the re-elaboration of the criteria through which political and radical otherness has historically been framed.[1] I will consider the official discourses on the part of the main US security agencies gradually equipped with antiterrorist prerogatives from the 1970s onward in order to establish a Foucauldian genealogy of the term "terrorism".[2] I believe such a perspective helps in exploring and making sense of the re-articulations that the narratives on "terrorism" have been making for almost half a century now, especially regarding the spatio-temporal distinctions along which we have come to understand and make sense of both violence and the political.

In the United States, before it became the main figure of the enemy we now all seem to be asked to share, the term "terrorism" was initially used by the military to describe the use made by insurgents and/or guerillas of bombings, sabotage, and kidnappings. According to the counterinsurgency doctrines of the 1960s, "terrorism" was a weapon, a tactic, and/or a strategy used by guerillas to maintain local populations in a climate of fear (US Department of the Army 1961, 1963, 1969; US Marines Corps 1967). Later on, in the 1970s and the 1980s, "terrorism" became mainly associated with "international terrorism" – that is, a series of acts of violence perceived as extraordinary and perpetrated outside US national territory and supported by foreign powers. The acts of violence identified at that time, in the database of the Rand Corporation Program on "terrorism" from 1968 and in the ITERATE 1 database initially created within the CIA Office of Political Research in 1972,[3] were the same as those described as "terrorist" by the military earlier in the 1960s: bombings, sabotage, and kidnappings.

There is, however, one crucial difference: during the 1970s and the 1980s, "terrorism" was not so much associated with guerilla activities, as with the USSR itself. Political violence was then analyzed in light of the ideological opposition of the bipolar era, and could only originate with the Soviet Union and its allies[4] – or so the argument went. Until the fall of the Berlin Wall, "terrorism" was then mainly presented as an illegitimate technique of foreign policy and even as a new form of warfare – notably according to some high-ranking military officers, who were arguing for the necessity to transform the armed forces (Jenkins 1970: 4, 6–7).[5] After the disappearance of the eastern bloc, the official narrative coming from the White House and the State Department then depicted "terrorism" as being supported by a set of states, the so-called *Rogue States*. Those states were not yet the official enemies of the United States in the post-Cold War world, but it was understood that they might become so, because of the support they were accused of providing to "terrorism". In other words, "terrorism" was not anymore perceived as being directly induced by states, but as an *autonomous* form of violence potentially supported by sovereign states. The designation of "terrorism" as the "new enemy" by the Bush administration is hence the last phase of a half-century-long shift by which what now seems to be elevated to the highest rank of political enmity is what had successively been presented as a tactic used by insurgents and guerillas in the 1960s, an illicit weapon of foreign policy/new form of warfare in the 1980s, and an autonomous phenomenon of violence in the 1990s.

To understand the very machinery of this shift and its implications better, one needs to plunge into the universe of US antiterrorism and take a closer look at the multiple definitions of "terrorism" that have been used by the US security agencies from the 1970s onwards.

Transnational Political Violence against Political Modernity

In the US, the "terrorist problematic" as a proper security issue progressively surfaced in the 1970s. By that time, a set of relatively well identified and self-proclaimed experts on terrorism started to publish prolifically on the subject matter: Brian Jenkins, Edward Mickolus, Yonah Alexander, Walter Laqueur, Paul Wilkinson, Bruce Hoffman, Alex Schmid, Neil C. Livingstone, Richard Clutterbuck, Charles A. Russell, just to mention a few of them. Some were former military officers (Brian Jenkins), others were close to the Intelligence apparatus (Edward Mickolus and Yonah Alexander), or to the military institutions (Neil C. Livingstone, Richard Clutterbuck, or Charles A. Russell). They had been on the staff of the same institutions (e.g., the Rand Corporation, the Center for Strategic and International Studies, and the Center for Security Studies), participated in the same seminars and conferences, and published in the same academic journals (*Terrorism and Political Violence*; *Studies in Conflict and Terrorism*) of which they were themselves the editors. By that time, their geographical, social, and institutional circulation, as well as the tightening of their intellectual trajectories, solidified a social space in the making within the academic world (and what eventually became the field of *Terrorism Studies*), while their publications were formalizing and homogenizing the mainly statistical knowledge on "terrorism" (Herman and O'Sullivan 1989; Reid and Chen 2007). During that period, the search for a definition of "terrorism" mobilized a large part of the efforts of these experts. In 1984, in their book *Political Terrorism*, Alex Schmid and Albert Jongman thus identified no less than 100 definitions of "terrorism" and 22 distinctive criteria.

Under all these definitions, "terrorism" was understood as the *use of violence* or *force*. The *physical* understanding of violence was mainly retained through the evocation of *acts of violence*. "Acts of violence" or "terrorist events" were thus compiled in the database of the Rand Corporation and the CIA Office of Political Research, as well as in those of the Terrorist Research and Analytical Center of the FBI later in the 1980s. But if "terrorism" was mainly defined in terms of *physical* violence, some definitions also retained a more symbolic aspect of "terrorism". Under this second set of definitions, "terrorism" was also about the fear/terror induced by the perpetrators within the population and reaching far beyond the mere act of violence and the immediate victims. Through "terrorism", political objectives were said to be pursued by means of the instrumental use of fear, by the inducement of a paralyzing and inhibitory terror which would make men more politically malleable. Directly deriving from the counterinsurgency discourse of the 1960s, the definitions later used by the CIA and the Department of Defense, identified fear, terror, and intimidation as three distinctive criteria of "terrorism".

Some experts focused on the criterion of publicity in order to insist on the fact that "terrorism" is not only an act of violence, but also and foremost an expressive act that is to be seen and that is to convey a message. It would hence open a temporality beyond the mere act of violence, a temporality during which fear would be the long-lasting outcome of the material act of violence. "Terrorism" was thus to create damage beyond the sole victims directly caused by the act. The potential impact of "terrorism" on the political course of events was seen as the ultimate goal. There is an implicit distinction here, to which I shall return, between violence as an act and its potential effects. But I will also try to show that it is the potential character of the act of violence, and not only its potential effects, which also came to structure the institutional definitions of "terrorism". Indeed these definitions insisted (and still insist) as much on the *use* of violence as on its *threat*.

Collectively these works constituted the framework from which the institutional definitions of "terrorism" emerged from the end of the 1970s onwards. Amongst the many definitions suggested by these experts, some proved more influential than others with anti-terrorist agencies over the long-run. This is the case for the definitions suggested by Brian Jenkins or David Milbank, an analyst at the CIA's Office of Political Research. Their definitions seem to caution the development of the ones eventually officially endorsed by the American anti-terrorist agencies. As we shall see, they established a double distinction: between "terrorism" and "international terrorism" and, more implicitly, between "international terrorism" and "domestic terrorism".

> Terrorism is the threat of violence. Individual acts of violence or a campaign of violence designed primarily to instill fear – to terrorize – may be called terrorism. Terrorism is violence for effect: not only, and sometimes not at all, for the effects on the actual victims of the terrorists. In fact, the victim may be totally unrelated to the terrorists' cause. Terrorism is violence aimed at the people watching. Fear is the intended effect, not the byproducts, of terrorism. That, at least, distinguishes terrorists' tactics from mugging and other forms of violent crime that may terrify but are not terrorism [Jenkins 1975].

This definition draws on ideas developed from counterinsurgency doctrines, according to which guerillas used fear to intimidate and silence local populations. This definition is hence also revealing of the personal experience of the author, a former member of the Special Forces in Vietnam. One year later, in 1976, David L. Milbank, author of the first CIA public report on *International and Transnational Terrorism* also proposed a definition:

> The threat or use of violence for political purposes when (1) such action is intended to influence the attitudes and behavior of a target group wider than its immediate victims, and (2) its ramifications transcend national boundaries (as a

result, for example, of the nationality or foreign ties of its perpetrators, its locale, the identity of its institutional or human victims, its declared objectives, or the mechanics of its resolution) [Milbank 1976].

As an analyst within the CIA Office of Political Research, Milbank insisted on the psychological dimension of "terrorism," in which the CIA had already shown an interest since the 1950s with its own psychological operations (PSYOPS). He also insisted on "terrorism's" reticular and transnational dimension ("*ramification*") – a dimension not unrelated to the agencies' own modalities of action outside of the United States.

Jenkins and Milbank also proposed a definition of "international terrorism":

> The most simple definition of international terrorism comprises acts of terrorism that have clear international consequences: incidents in which terrorists go abroad to strike their targets, select victims or targets because of their connections to a foreign state (diplomats, local executives or officers of foreign corporations), attack airliners in international flights or force airliners to fly to another country... International terrorism may also be defined as acts of violence or campaigns of violence waged outside the accepted rules and procedures of international diplomacy and war [Schmid and Jongman 1984: 58].

> *International Terrorism* [is terrorism] carried out by individuals or groups controlled by a sovereign state [Milbank 1976].

Under these definitions, "terrorism" is presented as "international" as soon as sovereign states retain control over it. Therefore, "terrorism" turns out to be an instrument of states which, in utilizing terrorism, take on the threatening attributes of (transnational) political violence.

According to Jenkins, Milbank and all the other experts on terrorism at the time, "terrorism" refers to the use of violence or the threat to use it. The term "terrorism" hence refers to a generic category of violence (or of potential violence). This (potential) use of violence emanates from groups of individuals trying to overthrow an established government (insurgency) through the techniques traditionally associated with guerrilla movements. It becomes "international" when these individuals are supported by a foreign organization or state. The international meaning of "terrorism" thus invites us to understand political violence as a new way of waging war without armies, by means of the taking of hostages, hijackings, assassinations, and bombings. These acts are perpetrated by "terrorist organizations," the interests of which are totally but erroneously conflated with the ones of the so-called sponsor-states. Nevertheless, this new form of "war" aims not at conquering new geographical spaces, but rather at the control over minds through the diffusion of fear. In sum, "international terrorism" would mark the return of age-old guerrilla techniques, the ones that had justified the 1960s counterinsurgency doctrine and the "winning hearts and minds" approach advocated by the US special forces.

The international form of "terrorism" made sense in the ideological context of the time in which there was, according to senior analysts, no doubt that the Soviet enemy supported the entrepreneurs of so-called "terrorist" violence. As an unambiguous expression of the Cold War, the definition of "international terrorism" was thus totally enmeshed in the opposition of the bipolar era that simultaneously justified the fight against "international terrorism". The aim was hence to wage war on those who were accused of conducting "a war against all civilized society" (President Ronald Reagan, *Statement Announcing Actions Against Terrorism*, June 20, 1985).[6]

More fundamentally, it is to be noticed that these definitions of "terrorism" – all based on (and thus extending) the founding division of political modernity between the "international" and the "domestic" – worked with the implicit distinction between "international" and "domestic terrorism". So that, in the 1970s and 1980s, what these definitions of "terrorism" were operating through was no less than the re-articulation of political violence along the spatial coordinates of political modernity, governed by the division of the internal/external (Walker 1993) and the geographical border, on both sides of which political violence was artificially redistributed. As we shall see, the international meaning of "terrorism" allowed for the reintegration of political violence into the order of state violence, while its domestic form limited it to the status of individual violence. In this way, the traditional categories of the political and the distinction between inter-state violence (war) on the one hand, and inter-personal violence (crime) on the other, was projected onto political violence in general. In this sense, the "international" and "domestic" qualifiers aimed at subsuming political violence under modernity's political economy of violence. Indeed, the reproduction of the categories of crime and war will allow, as we shall see, for the legal and/or legitimate intervention of governmental security agencies.

Nevertheless, in his analysis of "internationalized terror", David Milbank did not limit himself to definitions of "terrorism" and "international terrorism". He also established a definition of "transnational terrorism" that he distinguished from "international terrorism": "*Transnational Terrorism* [is terrorism] carried out by basically autonomous non-state actors, whether or not they enjoy some degree of support from sympathetic states" (Milbank 1976: 1). The focus was hence put on non-state actors and on the ramifications of their actions that might transcend national borders. During the same period, the first legal developments related to "terrorism" tried to account for this aspect, as shown in the definition advanced by the Foreign Intelligence Surveillance Act in 1978:

> (c) 'International terrorism' means activities that –
>   (1) involve violent acts or acts dangerous to human life that are a violation of the criminal laws of the United States or of any State, or that would be a criminal violation if committed within the jurisdiction of the United States or any State;
>   (2) appear to be intended –
>   (A) to intimidate or coerce a civilian population;
>   (B) to influence the policy of a government by intimidation or coercion; or
>   (C) to affect the conduct of a government by assassination or kidnapping; and
>   (3) occur totally outside the United States, or *transcend national boundaries* in terms of the means by which they are accomplished, the persons they appear intended to coerce or intimidate, or the locale in which their perpetrators operate or seek asylum [Title 50, Chapter 36, Sub-chapter 1: 1801].

Although the FISA accounts at the time for the transnational dimension of political violence and incorporates it into the legal order through the phrase "transcend national boundaries", the overall economy of the law does not depart from an understanding of this violence as violence of states. The FISA does in fact envision that "international terrorism" – understood as a form of violence supported by one or several foreign power(s) – might occur on domestic soil, in which case the FBI, in its function of counter-intelligence in the domestic sphere and under the control of the Foreign Intelligence Surveillance Court, might have to intervene. Although this definition accounts for the transnational dimension of political violence, political violence is here always implicitly perceived as instrumentalized by states. This narrative is partly tinged by an ideological reading of "terrorism" that sees it as the expression of the quest for world supremacy on the part of Moscow. But it is also, and perhaps even more so, linked to the territorial imaginary of political modernity through which social and political realities, whether conflictual or not, are interpreted through the demarcation between the internal and the external realms of the nation state. This is indeed implicit in Milbank's writing when he suggests that the interstate system is "ill-equipped to deal with the challenges of "internationalized terror" (Milbank 1976: 8).

By highlighting the fact that the international system did not have the appropriate attributes to regulate the violence of *autonomous* non-state actors, and by insisting on the latter features in terms of *mobility*, Milbank already sensed the arc of tension that would come to underlie the contemporary "global war against terrorism". Indeed, as early as the 1970s, the opposition between the fixed structures of a rigid interstate system (Ruggie 1993) and the growing mobility of non-state actors resorting to transnational political violence was in the making. In the 1970s and 1980s, the security architectures were still clearly determined by the modern national/domestic demarcations – some limited to internal security prerogatives, others by their external security prerogatives. This structural compartmentalization in turn determined the differentiated approach to political violence when it was actualized domestically or beyond national borders.

Thus despite the building tension between transnational realities and institutional limitations, the transnational dimensions of terrorism faded from the official definitions. Hence, from the beginning of the 1980s onwards, when the issue of "terrorism" is raised by the US administration, it exclusively referred to "international terrorism" – in other words, to a form of violence that mainly, if not exclusively, occurred outside the boundaries of the United States and was supported by foreign states. The antiterrorist apparatus that was then in the making was thus mainly devoted to the fight against "international terrorism". Nevertheless, a thorough analysis of the different definitions advanced by government agencies reveal that although all were agreed on the equation *political violence* = "*terrorism*", there was less unanimity that "*terrorism*" = "*international terrorism*". Naturalized and particularized by discourse, political violence has been treated differently when it occurs on the territory of the nation ("domestic terrorism") as opposed to beyond national borders ("international terrorism"). In the latter case, the government agencies that have progressively been mobilized since the 1970s were the State Department (in a preventive way, or in an attempt to solve conflict-situations related to "terrorism" in a peaceful way), the Department of Defense (in case of military reprisals), and the intelligence agencies (in order to prevent/ pre-empt the actualization of the threat). In the case of "domestic terrorism", this violence was to be dealt with by law enforcement agencies.

The Meaning and Significations of the Institutional Definitions of "Terrorism"

During the 1980s, the CIA[7], the Department of State,[8] the FBI,[9] the Department of Justice, the U.S. Army and the Department of Defense,[10] the Congress, as well as various states, came to develop their own definitions of "terrorism". How can this multiplicity of the definitions of "terrorism", as well as their coexistence, be interpreted? Which criteria have been retained by the agencies to define "terrorism" or, on the contrary, which criteria have been silenced by the texts? What were the underpinning reasons for which some criteria have been selected and not others?

The profusion of definitions of "terrorism" from the 1980s onwards does not in fact reveal a profound heterogeneity in the perception of political violence. All agencies, indeed, agree on the *political* character of "terrorism," as well as on the fact that it is resorted to by groups or individuals who may be supported by specific states ("international terrorism"). All these definitions, with no exception whatsoever, also insist on the criterion of intimidation, even if the notion of fear is not always used by all of the agencies. In other words, the different definitions of "terrorism" elaborated by the government agencies involved in anti-terrorism in the 1980s share a common base. There is thus no reason to highlight real divergences in the perception of political violence: at most, there are differences of appreciation. Indeed, at the same time, these definitions are not absolutely identical.

The Department of State for example highlights the *"non-combatant"* status (and not the civilian status) of the victims as a distinctive criterion of the targets of "terrorism" and hence of the "terrorist" nature of a specific act of violence. This definition allows for the State Department to label as "terrorist" any act committed against diplomats or against US civilians abroad, for whose protection it is responsible. Concomitantly, it allows for the justification of budgets related to the security of expatriate personnel and embassy security (Wieviorka 1990). More fundamentally, it allows for the dissociating of "terrorism" from a strictly military perspective. It actualizes the efforts deployed by US diplomacy in the 1970s to create a constraining legal antiterrorist regime at the international level. This regime was also to allow for the individualization and criminalization of transnational political violence.

The Department of Defense's definition, on the other hand, evokes motivations of a *religious* nature. It thus seems to respond to the attacks carried out against US interests at this time, first in Lebanon (against a Marine barracks), then in Kuwait, in a region that became at this very moment (1983–1986) a crucially important strategic area, as shown by the creation of the Central Command in charge of the Middle East. As with each of the other three regional commands, it is responsible for the protection of the US military personnel deployed in the area.

The US Army definition of terrorism insisted on *social* criteria as well as on *fear,* both of which are linked to the definition of guerrilla movements in the 1960s and which allowed the army to highlight and to actualize its well-routinized know-how developed in the context of counterinsurgency campaigns. The Army also did not put much focus on the illegal character of the acts of violence, preferring in this regard the more vague, "Terrorism *involves* a criminal act", to the less ambiguous phrase "Terrorism *is* the unlawful use of force or violence" of the FBI.

The case of the FBI is both more interesting and more complex. Its definition of "terrorism" also evokes the *social* dimension and not only the *political* dimension of such violence. It emphasizes damage done to property and goods, not just harm done to persons. This allows encompassing a vast range of violent political groups in the category of "terrorism". In the 1980s, the main targeted groups were the ones associated with, or invoking, an extreme-left ideology of Marxist-Leninist inspiration or the extreme-right and anti-Semitic groups aiming at "White Race" supremacy. Other targets included ethnically-based groups (African-Americans, Puerto Ricans, Jews, later on Armenians and Croats) and any other group that might pursue its objectives by violent means. It is the extensive character of this definition of "terrorism" established during the 1980s that explains how groups claiming to defend animal rights, to promote the civil rights of African Americans, or the rights of political refugees, were sometimes labeled as "terrorist" after the fall of the Berlin wall (Freeh 1997).

The FBI also insisted on the *illegal* character of "terrorist" acts, something totally neglected in the State Department's definition. Indeed, at this time, the State Department could not refer to any international legal (antiterrorist) norm, apart from a few international conventions signed in the 1970s that had a very limited reach (as highlighted by Milbank, above). Most importantly, the FBI was the only agency that suggested a definition of "domestic terrorism" along with one of "international terrorism". This fact is revealing of the FBI's dual institutional culture, with both law enforcement and counter-intelligence prerogatives. As with the other agencies, the FBI's definition of "international terrorism" highlights the idea of foreign state sponsorship. This allowed the federal agency to use, before the Foreign Intelligence Surveillance Court, the accusation of "conspiracy with a foreign power" to justify the use of wire-tapping against individuals in US territory and, from the 1990s, the interception of electronic messages. If its definition of "domestic terrorism" was not very useful from a legal point of view – as no specific legal provision was instated in matters of "domestic terrorism" – it was no less a (rhetorical) weapon allowing for the political disqualification of specific groups such as Puerto Ricans or extreme-right groups. The "terrorist" label casts a shadow of permanent suspicion on these groups and allowed the FBI to use its full arsenal of investigatory powers against them.

While this definition of "domestic terrorism" claimed by the FBI from 1987 onwards did not change the priority given by the US administration to the fight against "international terrorism", it did create an alternative perspective to the "terrorism" understood as an illegitimate weapon used by states in order to advance their strategic or foreign policy objectives. For the FBI at least, it opened the field of antiterrorism to its investigatory activities and crime-fighting prerogatives, as opposed to pertaining solely to the counterintelligence prerogatives of the agency. This definition of "domestic terrorism" was thus not so much underpinned by the idea of the instrumentalization of political violence by states in the context of a competitive international system, as by that of the necessary international cooperation between police agencies.[11] This cooperation would increase in the 1990s as a narrative on "transnational threats" emerged with the institutionalization of FBI liaison officers abroad (Nadelman 1993). Just as "domestic terrorism" changed the focus from a violence of states to a violence of individuals, it created the conditions of possibility for a way of dealing with the "terrorist" problem by means of police forces, rather than of intelligence-services and/ or the military.

The definitions of "terrorism" established by the different government agencies in the 1980s, then, did not as much reflect divergences in the perception of political violence, as divergences in interests and institutional cultures linked to the structuration of security prerogatives. The international/ domestic distinction established inside the definition of "terrorism" thus does not reflect a duality of widely different practices of violence occurring either on national territory or abroad. Above all, it mirrors spatial and functional divisions in the field of security (between internal and external security, between police and military, between external intelligence and internal counter-intelligence), along which the security apparatuses of modern states have historically been articulated. The instrumentalization of political violence is thus less the defining feature of "states sponsoring terrorism", as of the security agencies themselves. If not necessarily conscious, being more surely the result of complex processes of professional socializations than of any rational decision, the instrumental use of the "terrorist" label by government agencies nevertheless allowed them to justify their role in the antiterrorist architecture being created at that time.

These standpoints on political violence, which are all efforts to formalize the meaning of "terrorism", can be interpreted as an attempt to articulate political violence to spatial (and temporal, as we shall see) coordinates. From the 1980s on, they illustrate a dual movement of territorialization/ de-territorialization of political violence operated by complex discursive procedures. This dual movement corresponds to two distinct antiterrorist trends. The territorialization of "terrorism" can be observed through the elaboration of a definition of "international terrorism" emphasizing those states – as well as regions of the world – from which "terrorism" would originate. This move highlights an articulation of political violence on the territorial coordinates of sovereignty that are themselves linked to geographical boundaries. In this way, transnational political violence is brought back to the realm of the dark and cynical practices of certain states attempting to use it to advance their strategic and foreign policy interests.

This territorialization of terrorism was induced by and itself induced a trend in antiterrorist policies. It mobilized, against "terrorism", the techniques that the sovereign state had historically deployed when confronted by the hostile intent of like-units: the State Department's diplomacy in order to establish a regime of legal constraints at the international level, the paramilitary techniques of the CIA, or air raids to punish and retaliate against deviant governments. In the ideological context of bipolarity, these trends are illustrated by the activities of the CIA and the Department of State, before the Department of Defense tried to consolidate its low-intensity conflicts doctrine (LIC) in the 1980s, and subsequently by the approach in terms of "asymmetric warfare" that to a certain extent merely actualized the doctrine of non-conventional war of the 1950s and 1960s.

The de-territorialization of political violence also induced a second movement, one that removed it from the strict territorial/terrestrial order and reintegrated it into the social order. This move can be seen in the definition of "transnational terrorism" given by David L. Milbank, as well as in the FBI activities against "domestic terrorism" in the 1980s. The focus here is not put upon the cynical practices of states, but on groups and individuals. It is not the territory (in spite of what the term "domestic" seems to suggest), but rather the notion of network, that is the analytical frame through which individualized political violence is to be analyzed. It involved the identification of individuals as the perpetrators of violence and led to the designation of so-called "terrorist groups" – not just Rogue States – in the 1990s. Although this trend was not dominant in the 1980s, this reading of transnational political violence existed as a virtuality, similar to the virtuality of "transnational terrorism" in the definitions of the 1970s and 1980s, that would be actualized in the 1990s with the advent of "transnational threats" as the dominant narrative.

This dual movement of territoralization/deterritorialization shows a tension between two rationalities at play: on the one hand, a sovereign rationality or a rationality of sovereignty, underpinned by a spatial imaginary thought of in terms of geographical/terrestrial territories; and, on the other hand, a network-centric rationality underpinned by an imaginary in terms of networks and in which temporal necessities seem to be of crucial importance.

The Threat *of* the Enemy, and the Threat *as* the Enemy

There is another interesting distinction made by the experts on "terrorism" and the government agencies within the broader category of "terrorism". The issue in this case is not the spatialization of transnational political violence through its reintegration into the spatial categories of modernity, but rather the attempt to identify distinct temporalities. To the distinction between "international terrorism" and "domestic terrorism" another distinction is added: the one between *the use of violence* and *the threat of use of violence*. The definitions of "terrorism" are hence not only articulated around the distinctions between state/individual and war/crime, but also around the notion of "threat" on the one hand and of "event" or "act" on the other. In other words, in addition to the distinction between the international and the domestic, the internal and the external, there is the distinction between the actual and the potential.

The cross-analysis of the definitions of "terrorism" in relation to the prerogatives of agencies reveals a tension between the investigatory and law-enforcing activities of the FBI on the one hand, and the diplomatic prerogatives of the Department of State, the intelligence and external counter-intelligence prerogatives of the CIA and the internal counter-intelligence prerogatives of the FBI on the other. Until the attacks of the September 11, 2001, the FBI emphasized the act of violence itself in its definition of "terrorism", a distinction which was said to open up a temporality during which the agency could legally deploy its investigatory powers.[12] On the other hand, the CIA and the Departments of State and of Defense opted for a definition emphasizing both the *actual* use of violence as well as the *threat* of its use (CIA), or on the *premeditated* (Department of State) and *calculated* (Department of Defense) character of the use of violence. This option allowed for the deployment of an anticipative rationality and for intelligence activities (CIA) and diplomacy (Department of State) to following a preventive logic. It also allowed for the involvement of the US Army, very keen on reformulating the techniques and know-how of counterinsurgency in an actualized doctrine of low-intensity conflicts (LIC). One could also draw attention to the FBI's 1987 introduction of the category of *Suspected Terrorist Incidents*. It highlights the attempt to account for the potential occurrence of violence in a dynamic that would give rise, a few years later, to the narratives and practices of pro-active investigation focused on the identification of individual responsibilities for acts of violence that had not yet been committed.

The distinction between the potential order and the effective order of things is hence illustrated by the use of the notion of threat. Indeed, by encompassing in the "terrorist" terminology both *acts* of violence and the *threat of the use* of violence, a temporality is opened prior to the act of violence. It is not here the potentiality of the effects of violence that is stressed, but the potentiality of the act itself. Thus "terrorism" is no longer limited to a set of violent acts seen from the point of view of their factuality or of a temporality of effects in the aftermath of the act. Instead it came to embrace a temporality prior to the act itself, during which violence was anticipated and the potential erruption of violence itself was to be feared. The contemporary discourses on the "terrorist threat" emerge from this temporality. They reframe and recast political violence in the light of the threat, that which *could be* and not only what actually *is*. In other words, from the end of the 1980s onwards, one will no longer speak only of "terrorist violence," but also of "terrorist threats" when denouncing political violence. After the fall of the Berlin wall, this threat could no longer be conflated with the USSR. In the discourses of the government agencies, therefore, it progressively gained considerable autonomy from the structures of the modern international order to which Milbank had pointed. This movement (no longer speaking of "violence," so much as of "threats," when invoking "terrorism") was thus grafted upon the established distinction between potential and actual orders of violence. That which is threatening indeed never sorts under the order of the *effective*, of the *actual* (in the sense of what is in acts), of what happens, but always under the order of the *potential* in the sense of what exists virtually, of what is to come. It is in this attempt to account for the potential order of things that the elaboration of *worst-case scenarios* and discourses of fear, emergency, and necessity are anchored. So the discourses on *risk management* and *pro-active policing* that have become commonplace in the post-9/11 phase of antiterrorist policies originate in a process that has little to do with the actual attacks of September 11.

Since that date, official discourses on "terrorism" have clearly elevated transnational political violence to the status of the main political and strategic enemy, in other words, to the highest degree of political otherness – at least in the Schmittian categories in which these declarations unfold. This has two crucial implications. Firstly, when looking at the sets of legislation that have been passed in order to convict not only the "terrorists," but also those associated with them, it appears that to claim that "terrorism" is the enemy is potentially to declare that political opponents are enemies, the enemies of an established order that cannot be contested. This tendency might ultimately amount to the outlawing of political opposition, be it violent or not. This first aspect has already been widely explored in the existing literature and I will not expand on it here.

Secondly, the elevation of "terrorism" to the rank of a political and strategic enemy is not just about the outlawing of political opposition. It is also, and more fundamentally, about the reformulation of the traditional criteria that had historically prevailed in the apprehension of the political. Its main consequence is to make the *temporal division* between the actual and the potential prevail over *the spatial one* between the inside and the outside. In other words, if "terrorism" is not only the *use* of violence, but also the *threat* of violence, its potentiality, then the claim that "terrorism" is the enemy amounts to the elevation of the potential order of violence to the rank of enemy. This claim can at first glance appear to be devoid of any meaning; but that would to be missing a decisive historical turn. That is, radical otherness would no longer be embodied in territorial, terrestrial, effective, and material forms, through states and their agents as they had been seen until recently, but in the potential order of what is to come. Over the last 50 years, we have witnessed the shift from a discourse on the enemy in terms of a representation of radical political otherness embodied in the territorial form of a sovereign state or of a set of sovereign states (the USSR and its allies), to a discourse on the threat as the enemy, with the potentiality of violence (i.e., *terrorism*) becoming the major figure of radical political otherness.

Of course, one cannot limit oneself to the analysis of discourse when advancing such a conclusion. A thorough study of social, non-discursive practices is necessary in order to grasp the transformations to which this decisive turn in the order of discourses corresponds. I have written elsewhere on this issue (Bonditti 2008) and I will only mention a few crucial aspects here. Firstly, the temporal division between the actual and the potential that shaped narratives of the enemy and radical otherness was also the division along which the modern state's security apparatuses were urged to adapt. The shift in the narrative, from such notions as "enemy" and "power" to "threat" and "risk", corresponds to a shift from the investigatory logic of law enforcement to a more pro-active policing, and from conventional to network-centric warfare. This is, I suggest, how the primacy of "risk assessment" in security analysis, as well as the primacy of chronopolitics over traditional geopolitics in strategic analysis, can be understood (Virilio 1986; Der Derian 2009).

The study of the dynamics supporting the transformative process of the US security architecture reveals the primacy progressively given to the anticipatory rationality of intelligence over a more reactive posture that traditionally characterized the use of legitimate violence by sovereign states. The ever-growing use of computing tools and modeling since the mid-1970s is a crucial element in the restructuring of the US security architecture to conform with this anticipatory logic. To a certain extent, it represents a new phase in the attempt to coordinate agencies, or to make military forces inter-operable. Computing tools not only help in networking the different components of the US security architecture, they are also perceived as a way to integrate digitally, so as to incorporate those components into a single, high-tech, data-gathering apparatus of potential dangers and threats. Digital integration is thus a way to make sure that security agencies are provided with "the useful and necessary information" for the protection of the territory and the population in real time. At the heart of this dynamic is a quest for instantaneity in the anticipation of violence.

Hampered by institutional power struggles and bureaucratic inertia, this integration process actually revolves around the two main regulatory poles of antiterrorism in the United States, the military and the civilian. These two axes delineate two perspectives in the "fight against terrorism". The first offers us the world understood as a "global battlefield," in which the highly technological and non-linear armies of the twenty-first century are to face clandestine groups "lurking in the shadows"; this is the military perspective on the fight against terrorism, actualized in the GWOT in which network-centric warfare is the worthy technological heir of the unconventional warfare of the 1950s. The other tells us the story of a world society in the making, released from traditional territorial boundaries. It is a world society which should be technologically and permanently scrutinized from a multiplicity of different points (train stations, ports, airports, internet access) – in a word, the nodes of transnational mobility, both terrestrial and digital. In this perspective, the articulation of a punctual control in space and permanent surveillance in time through pro-active and intelligence-led policing practices should help identify potentially harmful elements and stop them before they enter national territories and/or harm populations. This second perspective is that of the law enforcement and civilian intelligence agencies. It is where a governmentality based on the digital trace (*traceability*) is being shaped: governing people by and through their mobility using the digital traces people leave behind them when moving.

These two perspectives differ both from the point of view of those who promote them and the instruments they mobilize; but they do have in common a crucial digital tool and a similar anticipatory rationality. Both the logic of military combat and law enforcement are now fully invested by the rationality of intelligence. From the strategic point of view, this gives rise to preventive wars and "defense-in-depth" strategies, which are seen protecting the territory and the population as far away as possible from national space, and thus as early as possible in time. From the law-enforcement perspective, this gives rise to pro-active policing, which, more than ever, works together with the disciplinary logic of the systematic census of individuals. From this same perspective, especially as regards the connections between law-enforcement services on the one hand, and border control and immigration services on the other, this leads to the implementation of "policing at a distance", allowing for the remote protection of populations against acts of violence carried out by unwanted individuals from abroad. But the discourse on shadowy terrorist networks, by reactivating the narrative of the enemy within, also leads to the implementation of such techniques now known as "intelligence-led policing," which aim at anticipating the violent acts of "terrorism" on the national territory, possibly perpetrated by citizens. These developments create the conditions of possibility for the de-compartmentalization of law enforcement and intelligence apparatuses, of foreign and domestic intelligence, as shown by the creation of a new category of information – "terrorism information" (Intelligence Reform and Terrorism Prevention Act 2004) – which consists of information gathered on people abroad as well as within the nation. In short, what can be observed is a complete reorientation of the US security architecture, the entities of which are to be organized along the temporal division between the actual and the potential, after having been organized along the spatial distinctions between the inside and the outside.

Conclusion

The efforts made to formalize "terrorism" in the 1970s and 1980s are part of the broader historical process of the *de-legitimization of violence* that is inseparable from the formation of the modern state. They naturalize protean forms of violence involving a heterogeneous set of practices and actors into the category of "terrorism". They institute a whole that, by means of the criterion of the *political*, gathers diverse acts ranging from the taking of hostages and hijackings, to bomb-attacks committed in different places and contexts. This whole is then deemed to reveal the overall coherence through which the specific order of "terrorism" is founded. Hence two orders of violence are distinguished: *a first order of "normal or tolerated violence"* (which does not make it legitimate, however) and *a second order of "terrorist" violence*. The first one is normal or tolerated, in the sense that it is inseparable from the historical coordinates of sovereignty: the criminal type of violence (against which the modern state develops police techniques in the realm of the internal and forges mechanisms of cooperation when it transcends the national borders) and the military type (armed forces, alliances).

The order of "terrorist" violence, neither really criminal, nor really military, is thus differentiated from the two main orders of violence that the Western world had known until then. This particularization of a form of violence, by means of the criterion of the political, frees this violence from the coordinates of sovereignty. It has, since September 11, 2001, bred a discourse on the new "terrorist era" that has replaced the "bipolar" era. From the 1990s onwards, this autonomy from the coordinates of sovereignty fostered the idea of the necessity of renewed techniques and know-how that are neither to be exclusively police-related, nor exclusively strategic or military in nature, and that progressively came to be structured around the anticipatory rationality of intelligence.

Indeed, both the policing and military perspectives highlighted above share the anticipatory rationality that establishes the primacy of the temporal dimension over the strictly spatial one. In each of these two perspectives, territory becomes secondary, basically reduced to ground – or support, in Deleuzian terms – and not the place of origin of the use of violence, as in the Weberian understanding of state sovereignty. So what the fight against terrorism reveals, I suggest, is the opposition between two alternative modalities through which space can be occupied with the crucial importance of speed, as Paul Virilio (1986) suggested years ago. When the heads of the modern states argue for the necessity to "fight terrorism", describing the latter in terms of "shadowy networks that are adaptive, flexible, and arguably more agile than we are [i.e. the modern states]" (Jacoby 2003: 3) and that are "exploiting ungoverned or under-governed areas as safe havens" (The White House 2006: 16), not only are they talking about the outside of the interstate system – as could be argued following Deleuze and Guattari (1986) – but also about a renewed radical otherness. Against the latter, they are thus urging the necessity of preserving the interstate system as the main modality through which human populations should be organized. At the same time they are arguing for the necessity of de-territorializing not only the means of legitimate violence, or the control of legitimate circulation (Torpey 1999), but also the digital means through which they will legitimately control temporality, gaining absolute speed (instantaneous information sharing) so as to anticipate the potential emergence of violence.

Notes

*   I am grateful to Christian Olsson who translated this paper. The editor would also like to note that this paper was written in 2009 – a fact that is reflected in the references.
1.   On the spatio-temporal criteria through which the political (and radical otherness) have historically been framed, as well as on the conditions of possibility that prevail in understanding contemporary world realities, see Walker (2006); and, for a more detailed argument, Walker (1993, 2009).
2.   On the utility of a genealogical perspective, see Ashley (1987).
3.   In the late 1960s and early 1970s, the Rand Corporation program on terrorism and political violence (which basically consisted in establishing a chronology of the "so-called terrorist events" identified throughout the world), and the program of the Office of Political Research within the CIA, were the two programs with the main databases developed by that time on the issue of "terrorism". The Rand Corporation program was led by Brian Jenkins, a now well-known expert on "terrorism" and former member of the Army Special Operations in Vietnam.
4.   The most popular version is Claire Sterling's *Terror Network* (1981).
5.   See also Neil C. Livingstone, *Discourse at the National Defense University* (1983), quoted in Klare and Kornbluh (1988: 4).
6.   See also Jeane Kirkpatrick, US ambassador at the UN: "I would like to suggest this morning one conclusion from my reflection on this subject and reading and experience

with it and with policies dealing with it inside the United Nations, and my fundamental conclusion, gentlemen, is that terrorism is a contemporary form of war" (Kirkpatrick 1986).

7. "Terrorism: The threat or use of violence for political purposes by individuals or groups, whether acting for, or in opposition to, established governmental authority, when such actions are intended to shock or intimidate a target group wider than the immediate victims; International Terrorism: Terrorism conducted with the support of a foreign government or organization and/or directed against foreign nationals, institutions, or governments. Terrorism has involved groups seeking to overthrow specific regimes (for example, Yugoslavia and El Salvador), to rectify national or group grievances (for example, the Palestinians), or to undermine international order as an end in itself (for example, the Japanese Red Army)" [National Foreign Assessment Center, CIA 1978: 1]

8. "Terrorism is premeditated, politically motivated violence perpetrated against non-combatant targets by sub-national groups or clandestine state agents; International terrorism is terrorism involving citizens or territory of more than one country. International terrorism is terrorism involving citizens or territory of more than one country." [US Department of State 1984: 1]

9. "Terrorism is the unlawful use of force or violence against persons or property to intimidate or coerce a government, the civilian population, or any segment thereof, in furtherance of political or social objectives.

    The FBI categorizes 2 types of terrorism in the United-states: *international terrorism* which involves groups or individuals who are foreign based and/or directed by countries or groups outside the United States or whose activities transcend national boundaries; and *domestic terrorism* which involves groups or individuals who are based and operate entirely within the United States and are directed at elements of our government or population without foreign direction.

    Domestic Terrorist groups are composed of both *left-wing and right-wing interests*. They seek to change the existing American social and political environment through violent means. Left-wing terrorist groups are generally Marxist-Leninist in ideology and strive to bring about revolution in the United States. Right-wing terrorist groups are influenced by racist, anti-Semitic philosophy, which advocates the supremacy of the white race. Also included in the domestic category are Puerto Ricans terrorist groups, Jewish terrorist elements, and other organizations which may resort to violent means to achieve their goals.

    International terrorist groups are further divided into two areas: *state sponsored or subnational*. State-sponsored groups represent governments or governmental factions which support terrorism as an instrument of foreign policy. Subnational terrorist groups seek political change. These are anti-regime elements which operate with the goal of creating their own independent state within an existing governmental boundary, or seek to overthrow present governments.

    Terrorist incident: A terrorist incident is a violent act, or an act dangerous to human life, in violation of the criminal laws of the United States or any state, to intimidate or coerce a government, the civilian population, or any segment thereof, in furtherance of political or social objectives" [US Department of Justice 1987: 34]

10. "The unlawful use or threatened use of force or violence by a revolutionary organization against individuals or property with the intention of coercing or intimidating governments or societies, often for political or ideological purposes" [Schmid and Jongman 1984: 352]. From 1990 onward, the Department of Defense would use the definition developed by the US Army in 1983 (US Departments of the Army and the Air Force 1990: 1–3).

11. For a similar argument on the dynamics at play in Europe, see Bigo (1996).

12. One may find an expression of this idea of an *opening* of a specific temporality in the
title of *National Security Decision Directive* 30 (1982): *Managing Terrorist Incidents*. Also
worth mentioning is the creation at about this time of the *Federal Emergency Management
Agency,* one part of whose mission was to develop civil defense programs adapted to
the aftermath of a nuclear attack carried out by the USSR. The NSDD 30 concedes
antiterrorist prerogatives to FEMA, giving it responsibility for the management of the
consequences of "terrorism".

References

Ashley R.
  1987 The Geopolitics of Geopolitical Space: Toward a Critical Social Theory of
        International Politics. *Alternatives* 12(4): 403–434.

Bigo, Didier
  1996 *Police en réseaux*. Presses de Sciences Po, Paris.
  2005 L'impossible cartographie du terrorisme. *Cultures & Conflits* 25 February 2005
        (http://conflits.revues.org/1149).

Bonditti, Philippe
  2008 Antiterrorism in the United States: A Foucauldian Analysis of the Transformation of
        the Exercise of Sovereign Power and of the Art of Governing. Unpublished Ph.D.
        Dissertation, Sciences Po, Paris.

Deleuze, Gilles, and Félix Guattari
  1986 *Nomadology: The War Machine*. MIT Press/ Semiotext(e), Cambridge,
        Massachusetts.

Der Derian, James
  2009 *Virtuous War*. Routledge, New York.

Freeh, Louis J.
  1997 *Counterterrorism*. Statement before the Senate Appropriations Committee, Hearing
        on Counterterrorism, United States Senate, Washington, 13 May 1997.

Herman, Edward, and Gerry O'Sullivan
  1989 *The 'Terrorism' Industry: The Experts and Institutions that Shape our View of Terror*.
        Pantheon Books, New York.

Intelligence Reform and Terrorism Prevention Act
  2004 *Public Law* 108–458, December 17, 2004, Section 1016 (a) 2, 2004, pp. 118 STAT.
        3665.

Jacoby, Vice Admiral Lowell E.
  2003 *Current and Projected National Security Threats to the United-States*. Statement for
        the Record for the Senate Select Committee on Intelligence, February 11, 2003.

Jenkins, Brian
  1970 *Unchangeable War*. Prepared for the Advanced Research Project Agency, ARPA
        Order no. 189–1, RM-6278–2–ARPA. Rand Corporation.
  1975 *International Terrorism: A New Mode of Conflicts*. California Seminar on Arms
        Control and Foreign Policy, Research Paper No. 48: 1.

Kirkpatrick, Jeane

1986   *States-sponsored Terrorism.* Hearing before the Committee on Armed Services, United States Senate, 99th Congress, Second Session, January 28, 1986. US Government Printing Office, Washington, D.C.

Klare, Michael, and Peter Kornbluh
1988   *Low Intensity Warfare: Counterinsurgency, Pro-insurgency and Antiterrorism in the Eighties*: Pantheon Books, New York.

Milbank, David L.
1976   *International and Transnational Terrorism: Diagnosis and Prognosis.* Research Study, Central Intelligence Agency. Central Intelligence Agency, Washington, D.C. (Available from Document Expediting (DOCEX) Project, Exchange and Gift Division, Library of Congress.)

Nadelmann, Ethan
1993   *Cops Across: The Internationalization of U.S. Criminal Law Enforcement.* Pennsylvania State University Press, University Park.

National Foreign Assessment Center, CIA
1978   *International Terrorism: 1977* (August 1978).

Reid, Edna, and Hsinchun Chen,
2007   Mapping the Contemporary Terrorism Research Domain. *International Journal of Human-Computer Studies* 65: 42–56.

Ruggie, John
1993   Territoriality and Beyond: Problematizing Modernity in International Relations. *International Organization* 47(1): 139–174.

Schmid, Alex, and Albert Jongman
1984   *Political Terrorism: A Research Guide to Concepts, Theories, Databases and Literature.* Transaction Books, New Brunswick.

Sterling, Claire
1981   *The Terror Network: The Secret War of International Terrorism.* Holt, Rinehart, and Winston, New York.

The White House
2006   *National Strategy for Combating Terrorism* (September 2006).

Torpey, John
1999   *The Invention of the Passport: Surveillance, Citizenship and the State.* Cambridge University Press, Cambridge.

Walker, Rob B.J.
1993   *Inside/Outside: International Relations as Political Theory.* Cambridge University Press, Cambridge.
2006   The Double Outside of the Modern International. *Ephemera* 6(1): 56–69.
2009   *After the Globe, Before the World.* Routledge, New York.

US Department of Justice
1987   *Terrorism in the United States: 1987.* Terrorist Research and Analytical Center, Counter-terrorism Section, Criminal Investigative Division, FBI, December 31, 1987.

US Department of State

1984   *Patterns of Global Terrorism: 1983* (September 1984).

US Department of the Army

1961   *FM 31–15: Operations Against Irregular Forces.*

1963   *FM 31–22: US Army Counterinsurgency Forces.*

1969   *FM 41–10: Civil Affairs Operations.*

US Departments of the Army and the Air Force

1990   *Military Operations in Low Intensity Conflict, Field Manual 100–20/Air Force Pamphlet 3–20.* Departments of the Army and the Air Force, Washington, DC.

US Marines Corps

1967   *FM 8–2: Counterinsurgency Operations.*

Virilio, Paul

1986   *Speed and Politics: An Essay on Dromology.* Trans. Mark Polizzotti. Semiotext(e) Foreign Agents Series. Columbia University, New York.

Wieviorka, Michel

1990   Defining and Implementing Foreign Policy: The US Experience in Anti-Terrorism. In *The 1988–1989 Annual on Terrorism*, edited by Yonah Alexander and Abraham Foxman, pp. 71–201. Nijhoff, Dordrecht.

Index